Paul Scott is a bestselling author and journalist who has written biographies of Robbie Williams and Gary Barlow. He has contributed to several national newspapers including the *Daily Mail*. He is a life-long fan of F [illegible] of Eric Clapton.

# MOTHERLESS CHILD

*The Definitive Biography of Eric Clapton*

PAUL SCOTT

headline

First published in 2015 by
HEADLINE PUBLISHING GROUP

First published in paperback in 2016 by
HEADLINE PUBLISHING GROUP

1



Cataloguing in Publication Data is available from the British Library

Paperback ISBN 978 1 4722 1273 3

Typeset in Berkeley by Avon DataSet Ltd, Bidford-on-Avon, Warwickshire

Printed and bound in Great Britain by Clays Ltd St Ives plc

MIX
Paper from responsible sources
FSC® C104740

Headline's policy is to use papers that are natural, renewable and recyclable products and made from wood grown in well-managed forests and other controlled sources. The logging and manufacturing processes are expected to conform to the environmental regulations of the country of origin.

HEADLINE PUBLISHING GROUP
An Hachette UK Company
Carmelite House
50 Victoria Embankment
London EC4Y 0DZ

www.headline.co.uk
www.hachette.co.uk

# Contents

# ONE

# God

Standing alone in the centre of the stage at London's Hammersmith Odeon just before Christmas 1974, Eric Clapton blinked, bleary-eyed, into the lights and stood there wondering if the incessant thudding in his ears was the sound of the 3500 fans in the audience, stomping their feet as one in wild appreciation, or the familiar banging headache brought on by the bottle of Courvoisier brandy that was his preferred aperitif before stepping out to face his adoring public. Now, at last, the clamour was subsiding and people were beginning to sit back down in their seats as they waited for the show to continue. Then, from somewhere at the back, came the strangulated sound of somebody shouting, indistinct at first, but now louder, bolder. 'Clapton is God,' the voice was now booming, 'Clapton is God'. In an instant, the crowd was up on its feet again, cheering, stamping, applauding. Silently Clapton surveyed the scene, then lifted his guitar strap over his head, took the instrument in both hands and slowly laid it flat on the stage in front of him, as though making a peace offering to an invading horde. Now he moved forward to the microphone, his arms outstretched in supplication. 'I'm not God,' he said, almost despairingly. 'I'm just a guitarist.'

*

In recent years, it had become a ritual. Every New Year's Eve, Clapton and a few musician pals play a gig for family, friends and local recovering alcoholics and addicts in the municipal surroundings of the Woking Leisure Centre, not far from his Surrey home. It's a private event, strictly invitation only – and strictly booze-free. The wooden-floored sports hall is cleared of the usual badminton nets and five-a-side posts, and Clapton and his friends get up on a spartan and hastily erected stage to belt out ragged versions of a few blues standards: Robert Johnson's 'Sweet Home Chicago' and the T-Bone Walker tune 'Stormy Monday' placed incongruously alongside that most perennial of football anthems 'You'll Never Walk Alone'. The whole evening has the feeling of an end-of-term school disco or an on-the-cheap wedding. The air is filled with the scent of chlorine from the swimming pool next door combined, unmistakably and unpleasantly, with Jeyes Fluid and gym shoes. There's a definite karaoke flavour to the proceedings, even when the band plays one of Clapton's own numbers. The screw-ups, the forgotten lyrics and duff chords, are part of the deal too. Around midnight, and before a communal version of 'Auld Lang Syne', Eric himself leads the group in the first lines of the Serenity Prayer, the Alcoholics Anonymous mantra and the basis of the twelve-step recovery programme: 'God, grant me the serenity to accept the things I cannot change, the courage to change the things I can, and the wisdom to know the difference.'

Clapton has always imagined himself as the lone blues singer; one man and his guitar against the world. In his mind, he is no different from his heroes, Mississippi Delta men like

Robert Johnson and Son House – rootless figures, nomadic and solitary. He schooled himself in the romantic notion of the bluesman playing for dimes on street corners, or drinks in bars and juke joints, heated by simple kerosene burners. It's why he loves the end-of-year shindig in Woking. For once there is no computer-driven lighting rig, no PRs, no corporate glad-handing, no meeting the sponsors. It takes him back to his days hustling for tips in the pubs of Richmond, singing the Jesse Fuller tune 'San Francisco Bay Blues' and the Jimmy Cox-penned 'Nobody Knows You When You're Down And Out' for the drinkers. His love affair with the blues has been the most profound relationship in his life. In the music of Mississippi and Chicago, Clapton found expression for the longing, the deep-seated sense of isolation, the rage and despair that have characterised large swathes of his seven decades. In a life often littered with fractured and dysfunctional personal relationships, the blues has been a constant. It has given Clapton an outlet and a purpose. On another continent, in the music of men and women, living and dead, he found a heritage, a way of surviving and a way of understanding and communicating his sense of disenfranchisement. In this music, as in no other, Clapton, the outsider, the illegitimate child, the rejected son, found the sense of belonging that had eluded him, and the chance of ultimate redemption through it.

No examination of Eric Clapton's life can ever fully explain how and why this music came to impact so forcefully and completely on him. But it came when he needed it most, when he was open to it, when he was searching for something to hold on to as a lifeline and an anchor. He has, of course, in the intervening years, flirted with other musical genres, but the blues is the foundation on which he has built. It is, perhaps, hardly surprising that his association with a music that is so primal, so spiritual and powerful as to inspire almost religious fervour, should have led him – as its first superstar proponent – to be saddled with the 'Clapton is God' graffiti that first sprung up in 1965 London. Clapton became the poster boy for the legions of white British kids who were discovering, and breathing life into, an art form that was being read the last rites in the country of its birth. As a consequence of his high profile, it was Clapton, like Elvis Presley before him, who was to bear the brunt of the backlash when it came to accusations of cultural theft. But Clapton no more stole the music of Robert Johnson and Big Bill Broonzy than Presley did that of Arthur 'Big Boy' Crudup. If he was to be prohibited from singing and playing the music of African-Americans, how far would this musical colour bar go? Would conservatoire students in Lagos be discouraged from playing Bach? It is impossible for the listener to ascribe music on racial, political and cultural grounds before allowing it into the consciousness. Surely that would be the real crime.

For Clapton, music has never been about colour. Unlike his fellow white blues disciple Stevie Ray Vaughan, Eric never wanted to be black. He is not motivated by a strong social or political conscience. The social history that shaped the music he loves has not touched him anywhere near as deeply as the raw human emotion it speaks of. Clapton has never seen his blues mission in terms of the people who first played it; only what they played was important. The shared experience of love, loss, jealousy and desire has always been what has fundamentally bound him to his blues forefathers. The reality is that Clapton is as important to the blues tradition as the men he is alleged to have robbed. There are other Britons, like Alexis Korner and John Mayall, whose contribution to the blues cause is inestimable, but it was Clapton who was the primary mover in shipping it back to a nation which had all but forgotten one of its most precious creations. If Clapton achieved only one thing – to help wake up America to its forgotten heritage – his place at the centre of the history of popular music should be assured. In doing so, he gave a platform, long denied, to men like Muddy Waters, B.B. King, Otis Rush and Buddy Guy. His impact will surely be felt for generations to come.

# TWO

# Pat

One image stands out, pin-sharp and Technicolor, amid the muddy monochrome of the dingy post-war years. It is of a woman, hard and beautiful, emerging as if spotlit by a Hollywood cinematographer from a throng of passengers disembarking down the gangplank of an ocean liner at Southampton in 1954. Among the milling and mayhem, the sea of blurred faces and the bric-a-brac of snatched conversations and shouted welcomes, she holds the eye, serene and aloof, her auburn hair swept up fashionably high on her head, one small child clutching her hand, another in her arms. It is a picture of cold glamour, of latent power and unattainable longing.

Clapton was nine the first time he remembers setting eyes on his mother Pat. She had spent the previous seven years in Canada, where she was married to a Canadian called Frank McDonald. They had made a family of their own in the intervening years, Eric's half-brother Brian, who was six, and a half-sister Cheryl, one. Now Pat and the children were arriving out of the blue, and Eric and his grandmother Rose were waiting to meet them at the dockside.

He had been told by Rose and her husband Jack that he was

meeting his sister. But despite his tender years, Eric was already wise to the deception. From as far back as he could remember, he was used to picking up fragments of conversations when relatives met for gossipy get-togethers at the family home at 1 The Green, Ripley, Surrey, or on Sundays, when he was taken for a weekly bath at the nearby flat of his Auntie Audrey, his grandfather's sister. He would sit on the floor, as if invisible, as some aunt or other would ask Rose, 'Have you heard from his mother?' The rationale seems to have been that the young Rick, as he was known to everyone, would find out soon enough. After all, the fact that Pat, who was Rose's youngest child, had got herself 'in trouble' by a Canadian soldier during the dog days of the war was pretty much an open secret, traded with increasing carelessness behind the lace curtains by Ripley's closely knit, insular housewives who practised a narrow-mindedness neither more nor less typical of the times. At home, his big brother Adrian, who was actually his uncle, used to call him 'Little Bastard'. Rick may have had a New World bloodline, but Old World prejudices die hard.

His illegitimacy made him stand out, but he was not alone. Some 30,000 children were estimated to have been born to unmarried British women and Canadian servicemen during and immediately after the war. Between 1939 and 1945, nearly half a million Canadian soldiers poured into Britain, with most stationed in southern England. Upwards of 330,000 passed through training in Aldershot, twenty minutes away from Ripley, and were given the task of defending England from invasion, with so many of the country's own soldiers fighting abroad. And in the cramped south-east, that meant young men, often away from home for the first time, were looking to pass the time by going to dances and meeting local girls.

One of those girls was fifteen-year-old Pat Clapton. She was born the daughter of Rose Mitchell, from Rose's first marriage to Rex Clapton, an Oxford-educated son of an Indian army officer. By all accounts, his courtship of the working-class Rose had caused ructions with Rex's well-off parents, who did their best to persuade their son against marrying her. Even so, they did get married in 1927, but not – scandalously for the time – until several weeks after the birth of their first child, Adrian. Two years later came a second child, Patricia. But in 1932 Rex died of TB, and Rose and the children returned from Woking to the village of Ripley, five miles away, where she met her second husband Jack Clapp. They married in 1942.

When the teenage Pat's son, christened Eric Patrick, was born on 30 March 1945, he was officially given his mother's surname of Clapton. But in reality, the deception had begun before Pat went into labour. Her baby would be born secretly in the upstairs bedroom of Rose and Jack's tiny house. Eric's newborn cries were for a mother who would, because of Dickensian convention, be forced to disown him the moment he took his first breath. The plan was simple and age old: Pat, little more than a schoolgirl herself, would cast herself in the role of the new baby's elder sister and her mother Rose, Eric's grandmother, would assume the part of his natural mother. From now on, the baby would be known to everyone locally as little Eric Clapp, Rose and Jack's boy.

Nor would the charade be complicated by the need to explain away the presence of the baby's father. He was long gone. He had been a married Canadian airman called Edward

Fryer, whom Pat met at a dance, where he was playing piano in the band. Eric would not even learn the name of his natural father for another fifty-three years. Even then, his mother was non-committal about whether Fryer was actually his father. There may have been other boyfriends, he wondered. Either way, Clapton never felt able to pin Pat down on anything but the bare facts of his birth and she would, eventually, take the secrets of the past to her grave.

But charade it was. Even from the outset, the conspiracy was only partially successful. Indeed, the fact that Pat had been 'going with' a foreign serviceman was pretty widely known in Ripley. Now the village is part of the commuter belt; at the end of the war, and for some time after, it was a country community of poorly paid agricultural workers whose lifestyle had not changed greatly in a century. With not much else to do, people liked to gossip, and the topic of much of that gossip was Pat. She was subjected to a vicious campaign of hatred by the locals. Kids spat at her in the street, malicious graffiti appeared on walls around the village. Pat, a feisty figure not prone to letting bygones be bygones, understandably bore a grudge about her treatment until the end of her life. She once said: 'It was a hard time, but I've got a long memory for the people who blacklisted me then. There's people in Ripley who wouldn't walk on the same side of the street as me in those days. Now, because of Eric, they cross the road wanting to talk to me.'

Pat stayed on only until Eric was two, and left for Canada after meeting and falling in love with Frank McDonald who, like Fryer, had been stationed nearby. Now she was back, striding off the ship after her transatlantic voyage, ready to torpedo Eric's apparently idyllic world.

She arrived bearing gifts: brightly coloured silk jackets with dragons on, pretty lacquered boxes that Frank had sent over from Korea during the war. Eric remembers his mother as good-looking, but with a 'coldness to her looks, a sharpness'. For the next twelve months, she, Brian and Cheryl moved back into the family home in Ripley and the whole can of worms was re-opened. Little, if any, thought appears to have been given to how this would affect the nine-year-old Eric. But at some point in the weeks after she arrived, it became clear to him that the woman he was supposed to think was his long-lost big sister was in fact his natural mother, back home, apparently for good. For a time, the unspoken truth remained firmly off the agenda, though Eric's grandparents, Rose and Jack, were certainly aware that he knew Pat was his real mother.

Finally, imagining that the pretence was all but dropped, Eric blurted out one evening to Pat: 'Can I call you Mummy now?' There followed a moment of excruciating and embarrassed silence. Finally, Pat spoke, her voice soft and kindly. But her rejection of him had already passed between them in the preceding long moments of cruel quietness. 'I think it's best,' she began at last, 'after all they've done for you, that you go on calling your grandparents Mum and Dad.'

'I had expected she would sweep me up into her arms and take me to wherever she had come from,' Clapton would recall later.

On such moments do lives turn. It was as though a switch had been flicked. Almost immediately, feelings of resentment and rejection turned to visceral hatred and bitterness. The once well-adjusted schoolboy, who had passed his early life in trouble-free good humour, became overnight a surly, withdrawn and sour-tempered spectre in the house. All attempts at affection were rebuffed. Brian, his younger half-brother, who instantly looked up to Eric on his arrival, was given the cold shoulder, particularly because he and his younger sister were given star treatment by the kids in the village, thanks to their North American accents.

Eric got his attention fix by throwing high-decibel tantrums. One day, in a temper, he stormed out of the house and made his way to the green, the piece of communal grass in front of the house. Pat, seeking to placate him, followed him out. 'I wish you'd never come! I wish you'd go away!' he shouted at her.

The upsetting incident only served, in his mind, to underline just how charmed his rural existence had been up until his mother's unwelcome return from foreign shores. Until then, his world had revolved around Rose, Jack and his uncle, Adrian. Rose, gentle-natured, kind and indulgent, had a deep scar under her cheek from when, aged thirty, she was in the middle of having an operation performed on her palate and a power cut meant the surgery had to be abandoned. It left her with what looked like a deep depression on the left-hand side of her face. To make extra money for the family, she would sometimes go out to clean the bigger houses on the edge of the village. Jack, well-built and ruggedly handsome, with the centre-parting of a pre-war footballer, smoked roll-ups and, for the most, lived according to the accepted version of maleness passed down through the Clapp/Mitchell clan. A benevolent authoritarian, he avoided any show of affection like the plague, on the assumption, apparently, that human warmth in a man denotes inherent weakness of character.

However, he attended to his working life with care and devotion and Jack was a master plasterer, master carpenter and master bricklayer. Rose and Jack's home, like the rest of the houses in the same row, had formerly been an alms-house. It consisted of four simple rooms, two bedrooms upstairs and a small front room and kitchen downstairs. It wasn't exactly a case of all mod cons. There was no bathroom, just an outside loo, no electricity and gas lamps to light it. Rose and Jack had one bedroom and Uncle Adrian the other. The young Eric slept on a camp bed, either in his grandparents' room or, later, downstairs.

The summer months were spent outside, on the green on to which the front door of the house opened. The fields that surrounded Ripley became his playground, as did the banks of the River Wey and the 'Fuzzies', as the woods beyond the green were known to the local kids. Throughout, the young Eric's capacity for mischief went no further than stealing sweets from the village sweetshop, owned by the Farr sisters, where rationing was still the order of the day.

The change in his character due to the painful episode after his mother's arrival was marked. Where once he had been an attentive and interested pupil at Ripley Church of England Primary School, now he became insolent, resistant to authority and self-contained. Not surprisingly, his work suffered. The safety he felt as part of a family evaporated. He imagined people were talking about him, whispering behind hands. 'I wanted the ground to open up and swallow me,' he remembered. 'I thought I was obviously a piece of shit and that was why I had been treated in the way I had been.'

It also coincided with him developing the first of many addictions – in this case a serious dependence on sugar, which he ate in bread and butter sandwiches. Nor was the rejection by his mother the only thing he was struggling with. By chance, at around the same time he discovered his illegitimacy, he caught himself in profile in the mirror and noticed, to his horror, that he had a weak chin. 'I was playing around with my grandma's compact, with a little mirror you know, and I saw myself in two mirrors for the first time . . . I was so upset. I saw a receding chin and I thought my life is over,' he said later. As soon as he was old enough, he would begin the process of camouflaging this apparently grave anatomical defect with beards of various lengths, something which lasted for most of his adult life.

To make up for these early disappointments, he retreated into a world of make-believe, occupied by larger-than-life characters. Principal to this parallel existence was the young Clapton's alter ego, the dashing Johnny Malingo, a suave man/boy who meted out brutal force to anyone daring to get in his way. Crucially, his creation, Malingo, sought no friendships other than the family's black Labrador, Prince. Instead, he demanded respect through sheer force of will. Johnny would sometimes become a cowboy and ride on another of his creations in this fantasyland, Bushbranch, the pony who went with him everywhere.

Eric would also sit downstairs in the kitchen drawing obsessively. Bizarrely, an early fascination was for sketching pies. Perhaps because he was the baby of the family, perhaps because his grandparents felt guilty about his predicament, he was spoilt by them. Rose would go out and buy him the latest comics, from which he would copy the characters, and Jack spent his free time making him toys to play with. Later, Rose kitted him out with a bamboo fishing rod, reel and tackle, bought 'on tick' in weekly instalments from a catalogue.

Such indulgence didn't stop him getting into trouble. Not long after Pat's arrival, the nine-year-old Eric was playing out on the green when he discovered a rather rudimentary home-made version of *Penthouse* magazine, featuring various pages stapled together on which were hand-drawn pictures of genitalia. Fascinated and shocked by the crudely sketched images, it gave him the courage to ask the new girl in his class: 'Do you fancy a shag?' Of course, all hell broke loose and he found himself paraded before the ginger-haired Scots headmaster, Mr Dickson, who insisted an apology was forthcoming to the girl and administered 'six of the best' for his troubles. For a naïve schoolboy, unsure of what exactly he had asked his classmate to do in the first place, it must have been a deeply affecting experience. From then on sex might well have become associated with shame and punishment, a source of sullied fascination, but fraught with the risk of humiliation and retribution. That bitter legacy would be the cause of much more angst to come. Moreover, his fractured relationship with his mother would only serve to crystallise further his sense of anger towards all women. 'She abandoned me and I blamed her,' he has said of her rejection of him. 'That is where it all began. Then I realised I was capable of doing exactly the same to the opposite sex – and worse than she ever did to me.'

Having wreaked havoc with her homecoming, less than a year after showing up, Pat suddenly disappeared back to

Canada with Eric's half-siblings, leaving him to deal with yet another abandonment. Because of his lack of effort in the classroom, it was no surprise to Rose and Jack when Eric failed his eleven-plus examination, which would have ensured him a place at Guildford or Woking grammar schools. Instead, he was dispatched to St Bede's Secondary Modern in nearby Send. If failing to get into grammar school was a disappointment, it was more than made up for by the fact that virtually all his friends from the village were also making their way to St Bede's, in likely preparation for eventually being taken on as apprentice tradesmen or by the nearby Stansfield fizzy-drink factory, where Eric got a mind-numbingly dull holiday job sticking labels on bottles of lemonade.

While he may have been happy to be at school with all the familiar faces from Ripley, the sense that he was – and would remain – an outsider was already imprinting itself. He had no interest in football or cricket, unlike the rest of the boys in his year – though he would develop belated fascinations with both sports. Instead, he acquired parallel nascent obsessions, with clothes and buying records. These passions he shared with his only real friend, John Constantine.

John's well-off parents had a radiogram – part wireless, part record player – which was out of the reach of most families in the village, Clapton's included. Together, John and Eric would listen to 78s of Elvis Presley's 'Hound Dog'. John's family also had a TV, a rarity in 1956 Britain, which gave the awestruck Clapton his first glimpse of a Fender Stratocaster guitar, which looked like a cross between an American car and a rocket ship, as played by Buddy Holly on *Sunday Night at the London Palladium*. Constantine was the embodiment of the lifestyle to which Clapton aspired, where money and possessions bought the respect and status he craved. But there was something else too, an assuredness and certainty the Constantine family had about their position that seemed to come naturally to the higher social orders and which the adolescent Eric found magnetic. It would become a feature of numerous of his significant relationships in the years to come; he was drawn to those possessing not just money and status, but the unwavering certitude of where they fitted in to things. That assuredness didn't reach as far as their schoolmates – to them, Eric and John did not fit in at all. He and the 'posh' Constantine were dismissed sneeringly as 'the Loonies' and subjected to the sort of low-level abuse that leaves scars nonetheless.

In 1957 Rose bought Eric his own record player, a Dansette, on which he played Buddy Holly and the Crickets, Elvis and Little Richard. They became his crutches and they helped him forget. Music became a refuge for the young Clapton.

And music was in his blood. Rose's father, Granddad Mitchell, played the accordion and violin and, as a girl, Rose had learnt to play the piano. She kept a harmonium in the front room in Ripley, later replaced by a small upright piano, at which she would croon popular Gracie Fields and Josef Locke tunes of the 40s. And Eric's Uncle Adrian could play the mouth organ and fancied himself as a dancer. When Adrian wasn't Brylcreeming his hair or tarting up a succession of Ford Cortinas with fake-fur interiors, he was listening to his beloved jazz – Benny Goodman and the likes of the Dorsey Brothers. Eric was bought an old violin by his grandparents and for a while tried to emulate what he heard his Granddad Mitchell playing on the instrument, but he quickly gave up, put off by the discordant screeching of bow on strings whenever he picked it up. There would be a few more false starts to come before he could begin making music himself.

# THREE

# Music

In the summer of 1958 Eric passed the thirteen-plus examination, which was designed as a safety net for those children who had failed the eleven-plus but had shown signs in the intervening period that they deserved, after all, the chance of a more academic education. His success was down in no small part to the interest shown in him by a certain Mr Swan, the art teacher at St Bede's, who had recognised a nascent talent for the subject in the young Clapton which he nurtured by helping him improve his drawing and giving him lessons in handwriting.

So it was that Eric found himself being transferred from St Bede's to Hollyfield Road School, which meant embarking on a half-hour bus ride from Ripley every morning. Although also technically a secondary school, it operated an experimental specialist three-year art course for talented children from the age of thirteen, with the separate art school located half a mile away from the main complex. There, students would spend two days a week drawing and clay-modelling. In order to get there, the art students, who made sure they stood out by their taste for trendy clothes and haircuts, had to walk past Surbiton's musical Mecca, Bell's. While 1950s Surbiton, that unrivalled bastion of comfortable middle-class conformity, still had some way to go to rival Greenwich Village, New York, as the spiritual home of budding beatniks everywhere, it did have Bell's music shop. And Bell's held almost religious significance for every adolescent boy south of the Thames who had ever heard skiffle, or had a vague plan that one day he might grow a beard. It also had a multi-coloured display of the latest guitars in the window. And like the rest of the art-school boys, Eric would stop en route and salivate.

Having succeeded in upgrading schools, however, Eric was happy to coast. The minimum effort was put in, though he won plaudits for his poetry, which appeared in the school magazine and was, according to one contemporary at Hollyfield Road, Anthony 'Top' Topham – who would go on to be a founding member of the Yardbirds – 'surprisingly good'. Otherwise, Clapton fell into a fairly regular habit of bunking off lessons to go shopping at Bentalls department store in Kingston to buy New Orleans jazz and folk records. But the dream was to own a guitar of his own and after much pleading and cajoling, his grandparents joined him on the bus to Bell's, where a deposit was placed on a German-made Hoyer which cost £2 and was designed on the lines of a Spanish, classical-style acoustic, but with the addition of steel strings.

The combination of a wide neck and strings set high over the fretboard made it very hard to play, and Eric found it a feat of contortion even to get his left hand around the neck, let alone 'fret' – hold down – the metal strings that cut into the fingers like cheese wire. Yet there was, in his own words, something 'virginal' about it. Over the weeks to come, however, the Hoyer would be abandoned on a regular basis in frustration at his inability to get even a half-decent sound out of the instrument. He found the whole process mundane and boring, and matters were complicated by the fact that he had no idea how to tune it. But, bit by bit, his fumbling attempts began to make slow progress. He spent hours in his bedroom learning note for note the folk song 'Scarlet Ribbons' by Harry Belafonte. And as he mastered another section of the tune, he would record his efforts on a Grundig reel-to-reel portable tape recorder that had been a birthday present from Rose and Jack. When a string broke, he would make do with five or fewer. Indeed, it was not unknown for Clapton to be seen out and about wearing a hat with, oddly, the name of British trad jazz clarinettist Acker Bilk written on it and carrying an acoustic guitar that somehow never seemed to possess more than two strings. Before too long, string-breaking would become something of a trademark.

At the same time he was developing his rudimentary guitar chops, Eric was also discovering a lifelong love of clothes. His taste for expensively cut tailoring, which in future decades would see him blow fortunes in the gilded ateliers of Giorgio Armani and Gianni Versace, could be traced back to a trip to the British Museum while at school. A bowler-hatted dandy walked by wearing a slim-fitting pinstripe suit. It was, even to Clapton's untrained eye, a serious piece of tailoring, with narrow-legged trousers and deep vents in the jacket. One day, Eric promised himself, he would own a suit just like it. In the meantime, a more humble approach was called for and he began cajoling Rose to buy him Italian-style suits with fashionably short jackets from the Littlewoods catalogue and, later, skinny jeans. At home, he posed in front of the mirror with his guitar, on which he had written 'Lord Eric' in ballpoint pen, as he mimed to his heroes, American rockers like Jerry Lee Lewis, Gene Vincent and Little Richard.

He was also discovering, to his delight, that a combat jacket, bought from Millets, and a guitar slung casually over one shoulder was catnip to a particular variety of teenage female, and he began dating a pretty local girl called Diane Coleman. After school, they would moon over each other as they listened to records in her mum's front room.

Before long, the Hoyer was upgraded to a thin-bodied acoustic, which had a painting of a naked woman stuck on the back, and which Eric found at a flea market in Kingston. As with some of the other essentials of teenage life, the second-hand guitar – which was made by the Washburn company of Chicago and was much easier to play than the more basic model it replaced – was bought in part by 'borrowing' cash from Rose's handbag. With a more professional instrument in his hands, he began to make steady improvement. The turning point came when one day he figured out the motif from 'Honey Bee', the song by Mississippi-born bluesman Muddy Waters. At that moment, Clapton says, it 'felt like I'd mastered the entire vocabulary of the guitar. You just get one thing right and it makes it feel like it's serious and it's real.'

Crucially, too, he had discovered a genre of music that spoke directly to his sense of isolation and the rage at his mother's abandonment of him. Interviewed by Melvyn Bragg in 1987, on an edition of ITV's *South Bank Show* devoted to his career, he said: 'I felt through most of my youth that my back was against the wall and that the only way to survive was with dignity and pride and courage. I heard that in certain forms of music and I heard it in the blues, because it was always an individual. It was one man and his guitar versus the world. It wasn't a company, or a band, or a group; when it came down to it, it was one guy who was completely alone and had no options, no alternatives other than to sing and play to ease his pain. And that echoed what I felt in many aspects of my own life.'

Eric fell in with a group of budding guitar players from Hollyfield Road School, including 'Top' Topham and Chris Dreja. Topham's father was an artist and Kingston's principal, and probably only, genuine bohemian. Long before the blues had become the buzzword for the kids of south-west London and Surrey, Topham Sr had been a devotee and walking encyclopaedia. He had passed on his love of the music to his son Anthony, a talented fifteen-year-old guitar player and already recognised among his peers as a fine artist in the making. Understandably, then, the Topham residence at 52 Clifton Road, Kingston, was the place to be on a Saturday morning for the blues aficionados of the art school. There, they would sit in the living room of the Victorian semi and gorge themselves on rare imports by the greats of the genre, Lead Belly, Big Bill Broonzy and Josh White. An added bonus was that Top's mum fed everyone, the teenage Clapton included.

'What you have to remember is that you could only buy between about twelve and eighteen blues records in those days,' says Topham. 'It was terribly limited. Until a few compilations started to come out and then very quickly things began to change. We were all learning to play songs and it started off very much with country blues. Eric would play a song, someone else would play one, and we'd learn like that.

Jesse Fuller was very popular and we all ended up playing his song "San Francisco Bay Blues". I remember playing that with Eric. Songs like that were part of our foundation and origin in the blues.'

To his fellow wannabe guitar-slingers, Clapton did not exactly stand out from the pack as having more or less talent than the rest. But what was to become clear to the gaggle of music-lovers was a quiet determination and patience when it came to his attempts to master the instrument. 'Eric had an aspect of discipline about himself which I don't think we really realised at the time,' says Topham. 'He used to spend hour on hour practising and copying everybody's licks that he could get his hands on, but he always shared his discoveries. One day, he would say he'd learnt a Chuck Berry song and would show you how to play the sliding solo.'

And with his love of the blues igniting, Clapton voraciously sought out the records of more and more artists, the more obscure, the better. 'One Saturday morning, Eric came up to the house in a terrible state,' remembers Topham. 'He'd bought his first Robert Johnson album and he was standing waiting for a bus in Kingston and put it down, leaning against the bus stop. He got on the bus and realised he'd left the album behind, and by the time he had jumped off at the next stop and headed back, it was gone. He was in a hell of a state because you were talking about thirty bob, which was a lot of money in those days.'

He was introduced to Johnson by another Hollyfield pupil, Clive Blewchamp, and for Clapton, Johnson's mesmeric appeal went beyond music. As well as his searing, haunting singing and guitar-playing, the mythology surrounding Johnson's brief life and career has been woven deep into the fabric of the blues legend. A Faustian parable had emerged about Johnson that went to the heart of the conviction for some that the blues was truly the 'Devil's music'. It was said that Johnson was a merely average talent who had been so driven by his obsessive desire to become a great musician that he submitted to a pact with Beelzebub himself. The legend goes that as a young man in rural Mississippi, Johnson found himself at a lonely crossroads at midnight, near Dockery Plantation, between the Delta towns of Ruleville and Cleveland. There, he was met by the Devil, in the guise of a large black man who took Johnson's guitar from him, tuned the instrument and played blues music of dark and terrifying intensity. When he gave the guitar back to Johnson, he too played, and where previously he had been merely proficient, now his skills rivalled those of the Dark Lord himself. The deal struck between them, however, was that in return for having this otherworldly talent bestowed on him, Johnson would have to sell his soul to the Devil. Added weight was given to the legend by the fact that Johnson's existence remained – and remains – an enigma. Few details of his life are known and only three verified photographs exist of him; the most striking image shows him in close-up, insolently eyeing the camera, an unlit cigarette drooping lazily from his mouth, spidery fingers holding down a chord. Most potent of all, however, is the manner of his death at the age of twenty-seven in 1938. He is said to have been poisoned by a jealous husband and spent his dying moments on all fours, howling like a banshee.

In keeping with the Johnson myth, even the exact circumstances of his birth are sketchy. He is believed to have been born on 8 May 1911, in Hazlehurst, Mississippi, though no one is precisely sure. Like Clapton, he was an 'outside child', born illegitimate, the eleventh child of Julia Major Dobbs, a married woman, during an affair with a plantation worker called Noah Johnson. The affair broke up her marriage to her husband Charles Dobbs, and Robert began a nomadic life with his mother in the Deep South as they moved from plantation to plantation and labour camps before he was sent back to live with Julia's resentful ex-husband. From the age of two or three, he would, like Clapton, be separated from his mother for the next several years until she remarried and he, his mother and stepfather moved to the town of Robinsonville. By 1930, Johnson was married, but his sixteen-year-old wife died in childbirth. After learning the harmonica and 'Jew's harp', he took up guitar in the Delta blues style that had originated in and around the Mississippi town of Drew, in the very heart of the Delta, at around the time that Johnson was born. The genre's primary exponent was a singer called Charley Patton, who was born in the late 1880s and lived on the vast Will Dockery's Plantation. Patton sang church songs, so-called 'knife tunes' – because the guitar was played with a penknife raked across the strings – old-time dance numbers and the popular tunes of the day with a rasping, impassioned delivery.

Johnson began playing Patton's songs, earning money by busking or playing in the rowdy 'juke joints', ramshackle drinking dens, gambling halls and music venues dotted all over the south-east. After marrying for a second time, he disappeared deep into the Delta for a year or so. When he returned to his hometown of Robinsonville, his contemporaries, like the bluesmen Son House and Willie Brown, were shocked by how quickly his musicianship had advanced. Before long, the tales that Johnson had sold his soul to the Devil in exchange for his prodigious talents were doing the rounds. Such rumours were given extra credence by his self-penned songs, like 'Cross Road Blues', which while never explicitly mentioning his so-called pact with Lucifer, conjured up chilling images of a lost soul in torment and ended with the line: 'I'm standing at the crossroads, I believe I'm sinking down.' Other tunes included the bleakly unnerving 'Hell Hound on My Trail'.

As his reputation for virtuoso playing and singing grew, Johnson travelled further afield to St Louis, Detroit, Chicago and New York. But despite his phenomenal skills as a singer and guitar player, he remained almost unknown to white audiences in the South and beyond. Consequently, only two separate sessions of his recordings were made, featuring twenty-nine songs. The first took place on 23 November 1936, in room 414 of the Gunter Hotel in San Antonio, Texas, which had been set up as a temporary studio to record sessions for the ARC record label. When the 25-year-old was asked to play in front of some Mexican musicians in the studio, Johnson, who jealously guarded his guitar technique, turned his back to them before starting to play, all of which only added to the Devil theory and the rumour that he was hiding something dark. He recorded sixteen songs in three days of sessions, which were broken up, so the story goes, by him being jailed on vagrancy charges and later released. The songs, like 'Cross Road Blues', 'Kind Hearted Woman Blues', 'Sweet Home Chicago' and 'I Believe I'll Dust My Broom', would go on to become blues standards.

The following year, on the weekend of 19 and 20 June

1937, Johnson recorded again, this time in Dallas, in another makeshift studio at 508 Park Avenue, which was then the Vitagraph/Warner Brothers Exchange Building. Here, he made thirteen recordings, including 'I'm a Steady Rollin' Man', 'Malted Milk', 'From Four Until Late' and the sexually suggestive 'Traveling Riverside Blues', which included the risqué line: 'You can squeeze my lemon till the juice run down my leg.' And as if to address the Faustian rumours, he also made 'Me and the Devil Blues', which includes the lines: 'Early this morning, when you knocked upon my door. And I said, "Hello, Satan, I believe it's time to go."'

Both recording sessions were made on rudimentary equipment and behind closed windows and curtains, to drown out the traffic noise outside. Yet Johnson's voice, by turns an otherworldly high falsetto, sinister, desperate, tormented and pleading, had the power to evoke scimitars and holocausts. But neither recording session would turn Johnson into a star in his lifetime. He earned between $75 and $100 from the first and no more from the second.

By the time his big break was on the horizon, Johnson was already dead. On 23 December 1938 the white American record producer and civil rights activist John Hammond, who discovered or encouraged the likes of Billie Holiday and Count Basie, staged a concert in the prestigious surroundings of Carnegie Hall in New York. Entitled 'From Spirituals to Swing', it was a showcase of black music. Hammond sent scouts from the Vocalion record label down south to track Johnson down and give him the news that he was to perform at the event. They returned with the news that he had died in strange circumstances. As with almost everything to do with Johnson, his death remains shrouded in mystery. Evidently, Johnson performed at a dance in a one-horse town called Three Forks, about fifteen miles from Greenwood, Mississippi. According to those who were there, Johnson had been flirting with the wife of another man. As revenge, the man gave Johnson a bottle of whisky laced with poison. It took three days of agony and convulsions before he eventually died on 16 August 1938. No doctor was called for him and he was buried in a makeshift coffin provided by the county. The show in New York went ahead without him, with fellow bluesman Big Bill Broonzy hired to take his place, though Hammond insisted that two of Johnson's records were played.

For the best part of a quarter of a century, Johnson's legacy to the world of music would remain as though in a time capsule, until the release of *Robert Johnson: King of the Delta Blues Singers* in 1961 on the Columbia Records label. With very little information available about Johnson and his music, many of those who heard him for the first time, including Clapton and another devotee, Keith Richards, assumed that the distinctive guitar sound on the records – which consisted of a relentless 'walking' bass line, while simultaneously a melody was picked out on the higher strings – was so complex and involved that it was actually the result of two people playing. It was also almost impossible to copy.

Even so, Clapton was hooked. He would later say he'd heard Johnson was shy and identified with him. 'At first the music almost repelled me, it was so intense,' Eric observed. 'I realised that, on some level, I had found the master, and that following this man's example would be my life's work. It is the finest music I have ever heard. I have always trusted its purity, and I always will. Up until I heard his music, everything I had ever heard seemed as if it was dressed up for a shop window somewhere, so that when I heard him for the first time, it was like he was singing only for himself, and now and then, maybe God. At first, it scared me in its intensity, and I could only take it in small doses. Then, I would build up strength and take a little more, but I could never really get away from it, and in the end it spoiled me for everything else.'

At sixteen, Eric moved to Kingston School of Art, on a year's probation, to take his A level in art. But, increasingly, his studies were playing second fiddle to his education in music. Weekends were devoted exclusively to the pursuit of music and revolved around meeting like-minded individuals to play and listen to records with. Saturday afternoons were invariably spent at a coffee bar in Richmond called L'Auberge, where aspiring musicians like Clapton and Long John Baldry, so called because he was 6ft 7in tall, would meet up to play guitar, or sit outside drinking coffee in the summer. And just around the corner was Potter's music shop, which sold blues records.

In the evening, there would be an exodus over to Eel Pie Island, which is situated in the middle of the Thames and on which had been erected a huge old timber-built dance hall and gin palace in the nineteenth century. Once popular with ballroom dancers in the 20s and 30s, by the early 60s, it had long since seen its best days. When it was packed with punters, the vast, creaky wooden floor would literally bounce and flex as they danced. It was reached by a footbridge on which was stationed a 'crone' at a turnstile who charged the penny admission. 'There was an old hag there and out would come this hand with fingerless gloves on and you'd put your penny on there,' remembers Top Topham. 'Sometimes we'd try and crawl under to get out of paying and she'd let out a howl.'

At Eel Pie, Eric met Dave Brock, who for a while acted as his unofficial guitar teacher, showing him the basics of finger-picking technique. Brock, who would go on to be a founding member of 'space rock' band Hawkwind, was nearly four years Clapton's senior and had developed almost superstar-like status locally because he was the proud owner of a small collection of resonator guitars, so called because of a metal cone at their centre which made them louder. Another regular was Rod Stewart, who spent evenings standing around posing.

Eel Pie had primarily been known for hosting trad jazz bands, but in the early 60s it hosted rhythm and blues outfits like the hugely influential Cyril Davies All-Stars and Alexis Korner's Blues Incorporated. Davies would later give the Yardbirds their first gig at Eel Pie, during the interval in his own set.

Sundays invariably found the same crowd squeezing into the Station Hotel, opposite the train station in Richmond, where the Rolling Stones, who had been formed in the middle of 1962, played. The band had a residency in a room at the back, which was christened the Crawdaddy Club, after the Bo Diddley song 'Doing the Craw-Daddy', a version of which the Stones regularly played during their set.

For his part, Eric was now firmly established among a crowd of full-on beatniks, which involved him frequently getting the train to London to hang out at the happening Soho pubs the Marquis of Granby and the Duke of York. He would watch any guitar players he could, pushing himself to the front to get a closer view, before taking the train home again and sitting up practising for hours at a stretch. For the first time, drink began to play a part in his world. Socially inept and intimidated around girls, the teenage Clapton began getting wasted on Mackeson Stout, rum and black, and gin and tonic, in the vain hope that his drinking prowess would attract girls. Invariably, however, it just led to him making a fool of himself and becoming very sick. In his 2007 autobiography, Clapton describes a particularly embarrassing incident at Beaulieu Jazz Festival, where he got stupendously drunk and was abandoned by the so-called friends with whom he had pitched camp. The following morning, he woke up not knowing where he was. He had been sick over himself and worse, much worse. Suffice to say, the trip back to Ripley in that state was not pleasant.

His fear of rejection, the legacy of his fractured relationship with his mother, made making proper friendships tough. Matters were not helped by having a chip on his shoulder about his working-class background, particularly when hanging out with a new well-off set of acquaintances who frequented the Crown pub in Kingston. Forever the outsider, he used playing music as a way of being accepted. Frequently, this sense of being set apart from others manifested itself as a chippiness which, according to one at least, often made him a pain to be around.

'Eric actually wasn't a very nice person,' says Top Topham. 'He was really quite unpleasant, just nasty and unnecessarily snidey. He used to say things about me to his friends. Or he'd go on about how the guitar his grandmother had given him was absolutely crap and unplayable. He wasn't popular. There were always girls involved, of course, and one girl that he went out with – who I think was the first girl he slept with – latched on to me, which didn't go down well. But I think he was really resentful of the fact that I had a mother and father. Emotionally, he had been very messed up from his early days. And yet he was terribly spoilt by his grandmother. His first electric guitar his grandparents bought him was a Kay, which looked amazing and cost a fortune by the standard of the day. Nobody we knew had anything like that.'

Topham adds: 'Over the years, I have never found him an easy guy for some reason. I could meet him and he would be very cold and not very nice and on another day you could see him and he was like your lost brother. He was always like that. One day he was on, the next day he was completely off.'

Clapton's awkwardness extended to the subject of girls and sex. He lost his virginity to an older girl called Lucy at a house party, when they turned the lights out. He would later describe being 'terrified and fumbly'. Nor did things on that front get better fast. On his second time, with a different girl, the condom split and the girl rang him a few weeks later to say she thought she was pregnant and that he had to get some money for her to have an abortion. Unsurprisingly, from then, sex was for Clapton viewed with equal parts excitement and terror.

Given the many obvious distractions at play, it was no surprise when, at the end of his first year, he was told he was not going to be kept on by Kingston School of Art. His grandparents, who were naturally deeply upset by the turn of events – not least because an ashamed Eric had kept the bad news secret from them before finally coming clean – decided to practise some tough love. Jack told him in no uncertain terms that he would have to get a job or leave home. So it was that Eric, who only had vague thoughts about a professional career in music, found himself reluctantly taking on the role of his grandfather's 'mate' at £15 a week. This involved carrying hods of plaster and mortar up a ladder and on to a scaffold, where Jack was laying bricks. But for all that Eric knew a career in the building game would not be for him, it also taught him a valuable lesson. Watching his granddad's pride in laying a true line of bricks or expertly plastering a wall in graceful sweeps made him realise that only by fervent application was he ever going to achieve what he wanted in music.

Evenings, when he wasn't out listening to bands, were spent practising incessantly, until poor Rose and Jack were driven half demented as their grandson began an obsession with the electric blues of Muddy Waters and B.B. King, as well as the blues/hillbilly melding of Chuck Berry. Understandably, Eric was desperate to go electric too, but there was an even more pressing need to trade up from the Washburn acoustic he'd been learning on. Just before being kicked out of art school, Rose had taken the decision that the Clapp/Clapton clan should stage a reunion in Germany, where Pat and her husband Frank, who was known by the nickname Mac, were stationed at an air force base near Bremen. It would be a chance for the family to catch up, particularly because four years earlier, in 1958, Pat had given birth to a second daughter, Heather.

Predictably, the trip was not a success. First, Eric was told, to his horror, that he would not be allowed into the mess to eat unless he got his hair cut. He was adamant that his hair, which was hardly what you would call long, though it did cover the tops of his ears, would go unmolested. But his attempts to gain support for his cause were rebuffed by his siblings and finally, crushingly, even Rose joined the ranks of those demanding a dramatic rug re-think. Realising the game was up, an angry and humiliated Eric submitted to a crew cut. Nor was his simmering mood of discontent eased by an act of unintentional destruction by his half-brother Brian. One day, while Eric was moping in his room, Brian came gaily in and plonked himself down on the bed, right on Eric's beloved Washburn. There was a strangulated twang of strings and an ominous cracking of wood, and when Eric examined the damage he was horrified to find the neck had broken clean off. He was fuming, not just with the hapless Brian, who had hitherto displayed only mild hero-worship towards his older half-brother, but the whole of his mother's family. In all his unreasoned fury, here was Pat on another of her wrecking sprees. His guitar was part of his identity; now, thanks to her offspring, it was destroyed. As far as he was concerned, wherever Pat went, misery, humiliation and mayhem were sure to follow. From now on, he vowed, she and her family could stick it. He made the conscious decision to retreat even further from her and them.

The upside, however, was that on their return to Ripley, and with Eric in a foul mood, Rose had no option but to take the bus back to Bell's in Surbiton and put down a deposit on a Kay electric costing £10. A 'sunburst' model, it was to all intents and purposes a copy of a Gibson ES335 semi-acoustic, which meant that instead of having a solid body, it was hollow and could be played like an acoustic, but also had electric pickups. From the beginning, it was the cause of much irritation because of its high 'action' – the height of the strings above the neck – which made it hard to play, and the neck started to bow worryingly almost immediately. But if it was not exactly the real thing, the American-built Kay was still a step up from most of the instruments his contemporaries were playing. It would also be the guitar that would see him through the transition from keen amateur to budding professional musician.

# FOUR

# Yardbirds

If the Prince of Wales pub in New Malden had operated a stricter dress-code policy, Eric's, admittedly short-lived, stint with his first professional band, the Roosters, might have been even more fleeting. Thankfully, in January 1963, the Prince of Wales was a boozer with few pretensions. So it was that Clapton, dressed in work overalls and his hair dusted in the dry gypsum plaster he had been mixing all day on the building site, arrived for rehearsals with a bunch of fellow budding musos, all with high hopes of making it big. The band was formed when Eric was introduced to another local blues aficionado called Tom McGuinness. McGuinness, who would go on to join Manfred Mann, was a studious and rather geeky lover of the blues with thick-rimmed glasses (McGuinness had previously been in a band with keyboard player Paul Jones, who would also later find fame in Manfred Mann, and guitarist Brian Jones, later of the Rolling Stones).

The Roosters' line-up was McGuinness and Clapton on guitar, Robin Benwell Palmer on keyboards, Robin Mason on drums and an elaborately bequiffed schoolfriend of McGuinness called Terry Brennan on vocals. Nobody had apparently thought they might need a bass player, so they managed without, and with the whole band's output going through one undersized amplifier. Of the dozen or so gigs the Roosters would play, most were reached by cramming themselves and their equipment in the Morris Oxford convertible owned by Benwell Palmer, or Ben as he was known to his friends. As well as practising at the Prince of Wales, they also rehearsed above a pub in Surbiton, learning Chuck Berry licks and Muddy Waters songs.

In fact, the Roosters were as much a talking shop as a proper gigging group, with rehearsal time set aside for band members to sit around discussing the latest obscure black artist from America they had discovered. One such bluesman was Freddie King, a Texan guitarist whose playing style would become the single biggest influence on Clapton and whose phrasing can be heard in his soloing to this day. At one session, McGuinness introduced Eric to 'Hideaway', an instrumental recorded by King in 1960 on the Cincinnati-based Federal record label.

In his autobiography, Clapton described hearing King for the first time as feeling like he'd met 'an alien from outer space'. 'It simply blew my mind,' he wrote. As impressive as the track was, however, it was the B-side, a slow blues number called 'I Love the Woman', that hit him like a sledgehammer. For the first time, Clapton was struck by the power and poignancy that could be achieved by a guitar solo. King played with not only flawless technical skill, but also a restraint and sparseness that only upped the emotional intensity. Until then, Eric had seen the guitar purely as an accompaniment to a singer, not the star in its own right. But here, King's soloing was the standout feature and 'I Love the Woman' opened up spine-tingling new possibilities. Eric instantly set about mimicking King's distinctive sound, his aggressive vibrato and use of string-bending to add more fire and feeling to his own playing.

Soon, he was putting the word out about his discovery. 'What Eric used to do was find someone we'd never heard of, like Freddie King, and then start telling us that everything we were listening to was crap and Freddie was God,' remembers fellow guitarist Top Topham. 'Everything was polarised with Eric and as he discovered someone new they became the biggest thing ever. And Freddie King was his biggest influence in those days. If you listen to the early Freddie King albums, they are absolutely wonderful and you can hear all the licks that Eric uses, they're all there. That's where he picked it all up.'

But while the idea of being in a band was undoubtedly exciting, the prospect of becoming a pop star was anathema. As the Roosters applied their scholarly approach to unearthing music, often by people who were already dead, or possibly driving a truck in some part of the southern United States to earn a dollar, they firmly considered themselves to be at the vanguard of the anti-pop movement. Clapton particularly detested Beatlemania, a term first coined in 1963. For him, their fans were sheep, dressing like each other and listening to a bunch of blokes from Liverpool when they could have been searching out the real thing. Worse, other groups were getting on the bandwagon as quickly as they could, copying the Fab Four's sound, style and clothes. As far as Clapton was concerned, these people were 'despicable'. Nor was he impressed when he met the Beatles themselves for the first time when they came to see the Stones at the Crawdaddy Club, all wearing their stage clothes. Clapton's first impression was that the four Scousers were a 'bunch of wankers'.

Instead, he was adamant that the Roosters would countenance no such selling out, which may have explained why they practised far more than they actually played to paying audiences. The few gigs they did secure were mainly on what was known as the Ricky Tick club circuit, a series of small venues close to London. They also supported Manfred Mann, who were on the cusp of making it big, at the Marquee Club in London's West End. The Roosters played together for six months before calling it a day, but rather than the usual fall-outs over 'artistic differences' that cause so many bands to break up, they rather amiably drifted off in their own directions. All of which came as a huge relief to Benwell Palmer, who suffered terrifying stage fright, even in front of the thirty or so audience members they were used to playing to. The band played a final gig at the Marquee on 25 July.

The Marquee operated a specialist blues night every Thursday, and Eric was a regular, taking the train up from Ripley. Invariably, with nowhere to stay in town and with the last train already gone, he would then wander around the empty London streets until dawn, when he could catch the first train home from Waterloo Station.

Ex-Rooster Tom McGuinness was also responsible for recruiting Clapton to his next band, the rather inauspiciously named Casey Jones and the Engineers. The band had been founded by Brian Casser, a singer nine years older than Eric from the north-east who had spent time living in Liverpool. Casser ran a Soho nightclub called the Blue Gardenia and his previous band, Cass and the Casanovas, played clubs in the north-west, in and around Manchester. By way of branding, he insisted that all members of his new outfit would have to wear all-black outfits and Confederate army caps made of cardboard on stage, where they trotted out dull pop covers from the charts and a few Little Richard songs. Suffice to say, they weren't great and only played a handful of gigs, not least because Eric hated it and after six weeks he and Tom left.

A succession of blues and R&B clubs were beginning to spring up in London. A Jewish émigré, Alexis Korner, had opened one, the Ealing Club, in west London in March 1962, which hosted Rod Stewart and an early incarnation of the Who. Meanwhile, an entrepreneur and music manager called Giorgio Gomelsky had opened the Crawdaddy Club in the Station Hotel, Richmond, where the band he championed, the Rolling Stones, played a residency on Sunday nights and where teenagers high on nothing more than hormones and hairspray hung from the ceiling on steel joists to get a better view. Clapton had already got to know three of the Stones, Mick Jagger, Keith Richards and Brian Jones, at the Marquee and he and Mick had become quite friendly because of their shared love of the blues. Once or twice, when the Stones were just getting started, Eric even stood in as a replacement for Mick when he went down with tonsillitis while playing ad hoc gigs at the Ealing Club.

Gomelsky was a larger-than-life 29-year-old who had been born in the Soviet republic of Georgia and had arrived in England via Switzerland, France and Italy. Boisterous and bearded, he had a colourful, heavily accented turn of phrase in the manner of a continental version of Austin Powers. Everyone was referred to as 'Baby' and bands were 'happening'. After effectively discovering the Rolling Stones and nurturing Mick, Keith and co., Gomelsky had the rug pulled from under him when they decided to sign with a rival manager, Andrew Loog Oldham, who had formerly worked for Brian Epstein, the Beatles' manager. Gomelsky was understandably shattered by the experience of losing out on the Stones and the golden ticket that managing them would have meant. Now he was on the lookout for the next big thing. Enter the Yardbirds.

The Yardbirds had emerged out of two bands playing the pubs and clubs in the Kingston area. Rhythm guitarist Chris Dreja had been at school with lead guitar player Anthony 'Top' Topham, and bassist Paul Samwell-Smith and drummer Jim McCarty were old friends, while singer Keith Relf and Samwell-Smith had played in a short-lived band called the Metropolitan Blues Quartet. The Yardbirds' early repertoire had consisted of various well-known blues numbers like Sonny Boy Williamson's 'Good Morning, Little School Girl' and 'Smokestack Lightning' by Howlin' Wolf. Now, with the Stones off on tour, they could take over the residency at the Crawdaddy.

They made an immediate impact and in the spring of 1963, in Keith Relf's family home in suburban Ham on the fringes of south-west London, the group was snapped up by Gomelsky, all signing contracts in the presence of their parents.

The only problem was that Topham was only fifteen, and a prodigiously talented artist. His mother and father were keen he should continue his path to art school and refused point blank to let him go professional. Meanwhile, Clapton met singer Relf at a party in Kingston and was invited to hear the band play at the Crawdaddy. Relf told him that the odds were that Topham would have to quit sooner rather than later and when Topham went on holiday with his parents to Spain, Eric sat in as his replacement. By the autumn, as Relf had predicted, Topham had quit, and the eighteen-year-old Clapton was in.

Topham was devastated at having to give up his hopes of a music career to concentrate on his school work. What made matters worse for him was that the band's new guitarist had, apparently, unwittingly carried on using the Gibson amplifier that Topham's father had bought on hire purchase for nearly £100 – a fortune at the time – and it was not returned until a solicitor's letter was sent. 'I felt very upset to have missed out,' says Topham. 'I put the guitar under the bed and I didn't touch it for months and months. I thought I would just give it up because I wasn't interested anymore.'

Topham's misfortune was Clapton's big chance. In October, Gomelsky, keen not to miss out again, put the band under a proper watertight contract which Rose and Jack had to countersign. 'We all looked at each other, wondering what we were signing,' remembered Rose. Best of all, Gomelsky began paying them weekly wages and, finally, it meant Eric could give up working for his grandfather and concentrate on music full time. Their new manager also rented the band a flat in an old house just off the South Circular in Kew, and Eric, who had previously been schlepping up to town from Ripley, was able to leave home at last.

He and Chris Dreja, with whom he shared a room, became firm friends and the Yardbirds began a three-month period during which they would play thirty-three gigs, doing purely blues covers, at the Crawdaddy, the Ricky Tick in Windsor and the Star Club, Croydon. The Yardbirds were on their way.

At the same time, British promoters realised that the blues

explosion at home meant there was an audience for the original stars of the genre from America. In 1963, blues festivals began cropping up in the UK featuring legends from the States, some of whom had not worked in years. Luckily, British audiences, unlike their American counterparts, could not get enough of the blues, and early tours featured the likes of Muddy Waters, Willie Dixon, Big Joe Williams, New Orleans guitarist Lonnie Johnson and singer Victoria Spivey.

Another blues legend who found himself in England on one of those early festival tours was Sonny Boy Williamson. Like Robert Johnson, of whom he was a contemporary in the Mississippi Delta, Williamson was an enigmatic figure whose life story was a little hazy. No one was quite sure when he was born and he had appropriated (stolen) the name Sonny Boy Williamson from another influential bluesman, John Lee 'Sonny Boy' Williamson, the Tennessee-born singer and harmonica player who settled in Chicago. The original Sonny Boy had a series of hits, including 'Good Morning, School Girl' – later universally re-titled 'Good Morning, Little School Girl' – before his death in 1948 at the age of thirty-four, when he was the victim of a Chicago street robbery.

Sonny Boy Williamson II, as he became known, was actually born Aleck 'Rice' Miller on a plantation in Tallahatchie County, Mississippi. In the early 40s, the sponsor of a radio show Miller appeared on began billing Miller as Sonny Boy Williamson in a bid to cash in on the fame of the real Sonny Boy. Naturally enough, having his personality acquired by another musician didn't go down too well with the original Sonny Boy during his lifetime, but no legal action was ever taken. And while getting murdered was a drag for Sonny Boy I, it was a tremendous career fillip for the brazen imposter Miller, who from then on began describing himself as 'the one and only Sonny Boy Williamson'. That said, Miller, an accomplished singer and harmonica player, was, in blues terms at least, the real thing. He had recorded in his own right on the legendary Chess Records label in Chicago and played with a list of notables which included Howlin' Wolf, Elmore James and Arthur 'Big Boy' Crudup, who wrote 'That's All Right' and 'My Baby Left Me', which were later recorded by Elvis Presley.

Gomelsky sensed that a tie-up between Sonny Boy II, who was already in his late fifties or early sixties, and the young upstarts would be good business, and he arranged for the Yardbirds to join the bluesman on a tour of England. A gig they played together at the Crawdaddy in December 1963 was recorded and released two years later, under the title *Sonny Boy Williamson and the Yardbirds*.

However, things did not get off to a good start when Clapton and Williamson were introduced one night at the Crawdaddy. Keen to display his encyclopaedic knowledge of the blues and its history, Eric began the conversation by asking him innocently: 'Isn't your name Rice Miller?' Bad move. Having the evidence of his decades of deception thrown in his face did not leave Miller in the best of tempers. With one slow, deliberate motion, he fished out a penknife from his pocket and bared the blade at Clapton menacingly. Even so, that was still probably the high point of Williamson's relationship with his teenage backing band. In a nutshell, he thought they were crap. Nor was he the type to sugar-coat it. Asked about what it was like to be playing with the Yardbirds at the time, the straight-talking old rogue replied: 'Those English kids want to play the blues so bad, and they play the blues so bad.' By way of putting them in their place on stage, he would make them kneel while he did a rather creakily shambolic early version of the Michael Jackson moonwalk around them.

Still, Sonny Boy was a link back to the bluesmen, like Johnson, whom Clapton revered. But if he was in genuine awe of Williamson, Eric was not exactly showing it. Topham, having recently quit the Yardbirds, was keeping close tabs on what was happening through his friends in the band. The word was that Clapton was not exactly genuflecting at the mere presence of a bona fide alumni of the Delta. 'He was so rude to Sonny Boy,' says Top Topham. 'As far as Eric was concerned, he was second rate, which was surprising because at least Sonny Boy was the real deal. But I think the big problem was that Sonny Boy was pissed out of his brain most of the time.'

Drunk or not, Williamson was not alone in thinking that the Yardbirds' lead guitarist was not exactly pulling up any trees in those early days. 'To be absolutely honest, Eric wasn't a particularly good lead guitarist at that time,' adds Topham. 'His rhythm playing was very good and he knew all the numbers, but he wasn't that far ahead of the rest of us.'

Still, the Yardbirds were good enough to secure a record deal with Columbia Records in February 1964. Immediately, they went into a studio the size of a box bedroom in New Malden called RG Jones and recorded their first single, a cover of 'I Wish You Would', the 1955 song by Chicago bluesman Billy Boy Arnold. And while it was a catchy enough affair, with Keith Relf's harmonica rather than Clapton's guitar out front, it failed to chart in Britain or America. For Eric, the choice of song very much fitted into the 'pure' bracket of music he was determined that the band should be playing. But even then, he was ambivalent about the whole process of being a recording artist. For him, just going into the studio smacked of the commercialism that, publicly at least, he claimed to abhor. It was not exactly the most thought through of positions to take, given that most of the unknown Delta blues players he admired would have happily given up working like dogs on the share-cropping plantations of the Deep South if they'd had the chance to make a few more records. Likewise, if it hadn't been for the early record producers trying to make a buck, or talent scouts like Jackson-based record-shop owner H. C. Speir, who auditioned Robert Johnson and Skip James, these phenomenal talents would never have been able to leave their legacy of recorded music for future generations to discover. Part of Eric's reticence when it came to the subject of recording was also rooted, however, in feelings of inadequacy – understandably, given his tender years and limited experience. Of the first Yardbirds demo recording session, Clapton would later say: 'It was the first time I ever heard myself played back and that was a shock. You realise how clumsy you sound. What feels so sophisticated and smooth as you're doing it sounds so rough on playback. We were very, very nervous.'

Nor was he overly impressed by their second single, a rocked-up version of 'Good Morning, Little School Girl', which got to number forty-four in Britain and included a short Clapton guitar solo in the middle. As far as Eric was concerned, when put up alongside the true originals, his band sounded 'white' and 'lame'. When the Yardbirds played live, however, it was something of a different matter. The rawness and passion which was the defining quality of the artists he loved was able to shine through on occasion, and he was more comfortable with the band's live debut album, *Five Live Yardbirds*, which included versions of Howlin' Wolf's 'Smokestack Lightning', the John Lee Hooker song 'Louise' and Chuck Berry's 'Too Much Monkey Business'. The live shows also gave the band an option to employ the so-called 'rave up', an extended instrumental interlude that made heavy use of dynamics – variations in volume and intensity – building inexorably to an exultant crescendo.

Egged on by the band's bass player, Paul Samwell-Smith, they began improvising at length, stretching songs that originally lasted no more than two and a half minutes into five- or six-minute affairs. The downside of playing these extended solos was the effect they had on the strings of Clapton's guitar. At the time, he was going through a brief period of playing an American-made Fender Telecaster – a genuine Titan in the world of serious guitars, but never an instrument particularly associated with him. In order to be able to bend the strings of the instrument, a must for any self-respecting blues guitarist, Eric fitted his instrument with a light gauge of strings, meaning that if he got too carried away, it invariably meant breaking the thinnest one, the high E. Soon it became an almost nightly occurrence for the audience at live gigs to break out in a good-natured slow handclap as he hurriedly changed strings on stage. As a result, Gomelsky coined the nickname 'Slowhand Clapton', later shortened to 'Slowhand' – a moniker that would stay with him for the rest of his career.

He was certainly getting through the strings, because by the summer of 1964, the band had already done 140 gigs as Gomelsky sought to make up for where he had lost out financially when the Stones slipped from his grasp. As their popularity increased, he even signed the Yardbirds up to promote non-iron shirts made by a firm called Rael-Brook Toplin.

Clapton and the rest of his bandmates were earning £20 a week, a not inconsiderable sum at the time, given their age, and Clapton proceeded to lavish the lot on himself. Jolly jaunts were made from Kew to the West End, on record-buying sprees or in search of the latest 'threads' at Austin's in Shaftesbury Avenue, where he'd happily blow a week's money on a Madras check jacket or imported denims from America. These extravagances didn't leave much left for the bills at the band's rented lodgings, much to the chagrin of the others. Once, when he got into a row with another musician about money, the angry chap picked up Clapton's red Telecaster and hit him over the head with it in exasperation. The other Yardbirds were not exactly sympathetic, noting wryly that such were the Tele's impeccably workmanlike credentials that it didn't even go out of tune.

Happily, being in a band with a growing appeal meant that other joyous by-product of musical success – girls – began to appear on the scene in large enough numbers to ensure that Clapton's obsession with music was at least occasionally put to one side in favour of more carnal pastimes. Indeed, his smooth-talking success with the gangs of girls who began attaching themselves to the band was somewhat at odds with his otherwise diffident and introverted persona. He became adept at talking women – some of whom, let's face it, did not need too much persuading – into sharing his bed at the band's flat. On at least one occasion, Dreja, who bunked down in the same room, was awoken in the middle of the night by Eric, already between the sheets with a fairly willing female, giving her a car salesman-style pitch about why going all the way wouldn't be a bad thing for either of them. In a later interview with *Rolling Stone* magazine, Clapton recalled trying to sleep with as many women as possible during his days in the Yardbirds. 'It was an obviously novel thing to try and do,' he reasoned. 'You come out of school, you get into a group and you've got thousands of chicks there. I mean, you were at school and you were pimply and no one wanted to know you. And then there you are – on stage, with thousands of girls screaming their heads off. Power!'

For the most part, girls he would earnestly profess undying love for were pretty soon given the brush-off once he had tired of them. He developed a temporary infatuation with Ronnie Ronette (real name Veronica Bennett), who he would later say made a move on him when she and her band, the Ronettes, were sharing the bill with the Yardbirds in late 1964 – though at the time his bandmates were convinced the flirtation had remained unconsummated. At the end of the tour, a smitten Eric, who was in the grip of love and lust, hung around like a puppy at the London hotel where Ronnie was staying with her band. But he was devastated when he caught sight of Ronnie and one of her fellow members of the all-female trio emerging on the arms of Mick Jagger and Keith Richards. Instinctively, of course, he knew a Stone trumped a Yardbird and slunk off home, dejected. To add insult to injury, some years later, Ronnie had the nerve to tell Clapton he reminded her of her ex-husband, legendary record producer Phil Spector. Given that Spector was an elaborately bewigged, off-his-rocker borderline psychopath who regularly pulled guns on his girlfriends – and John Lennon, whom he chased around the studio while screaming threats when the ex-Beatle hired him to co-produce his 1975 album *Rock 'n' Roll* – it was not much of a compliment.

All the time Clapton's playing was moving up through the gears. By the time the Yardbirds recorded 'I Ain't Got You', which was released in October 1964, his confidence was growing. 'I remember time passing and doing some more sessions and thinking, "Well, this is just like falling off a log,"' he recalls. 'In the short amount of time that passed between those sessions, we really got polished very quick.'

Clapton and Lennon's paths would cross when the Yardbirds were hired to support the Beatles during their series of Christmas shows at the Hammersmith Odeon in London at the end of 1964, during which the Fab Four featured in a comedy sketch with the DJ Jimmy Savile, who would later be posthumously exposed as a serial pervert and sexual abuser. From the outset, Eric did not warm to John, though he struck up an instant rapport with George, who showed him his collection of Gretsch guitars from America, while Clapton gave him advice on choosing a lighter gauge of strings to ease playing solos. By comparison, Lennon came across as loutish and uncouth. In his 2007 autobiography, Clapton recalls travelling to Hammersmith one night, ready to perform on the same bill as the Beatles, when he met an elderly American woman who was lost and asking for directions. They got chatting and when he said he was appearing with the Fab Four, she asked if she could tag along. Once there, Eric took her backstage to meet the Liverpudlian superstars, who were all polite and friendly, except John. When Clapton introduced the lady to Lennon, he made a face of mock boredom and started making wanking motions underneath his coat. Eric wrote of the encounter: 'I was really shocked and quite offended, because I felt responsible for this harmless little old lady, and in a sense, of course, he was insulting me. I got to know John quite well in our later lives, and we were friends, I suppose, but I was always aware that he was capable of doing pretty weird stuff.'

As their success grew, so the money began to come in, and Eric splashed out on the guitar of his dreams, a cherry-red Gibson ES335, like the one Freddie King played. Like the now abandoned Kay, it was a semi-acoustic with a warm, rich tone unlike the twangy, thinner sound of the Fender Telecaster. But the more he began to emulate his hero sonically, the more he distanced himself from the other members of the Yardbirds. They, like their manager, Giorgio Gomelsky, were keen on the idea of emulating the success and fame of the Beatles. Clapton clung to his idea of musical authenticity, rejecting what he saw as commercialism. Tensions, already bubbling under the surface, began to emerge inevitably into the open. Clapton would alternately bemoan the fact that they were not rehearsing enough and then not turn up to practice sessions. He would also constantly badger Gomelsky to allow him time off for 'family reasons'. Relations with Keith Relf, the group's frontman, were often chilly at best, the others having to act as intermediaries, as they each refused to speak to the other. (As has become something of an unfortunate trend with a number of ex-bandmates of Clapton, Relf was to come to an untimely end, dying at the age of thirty-three in 1976, when he was electrocuted while playing the guitar at home.) Clapton was also adept at mimicking the quirks, facial tics and patterns of speech of the others and, though clever, it was not always done with humorous intent and could very easily veer towards the malicious when the mood took him.

Elsewhere, there was mounting evidence of his rampant pomposity. As well as denouncing anyone who wasn't playing pure blues, he took up residence in Pseuds Corner, developing a taste for Ginsberg, Kerouac and translations of Baudelaire's French verse, plus a liking for incomprehensible Gallic and Japanese cinema. All in all, then, he was getting to be a pain. To make matters worse, his bandmates were becoming increasingly aware that Clapton, though still far from the finished article, was eclipsing them on stage – and not just musically; his morose demeanour at shows had made him something of a cult figure among the similarly miserable masses of glum youths they invariably encountered at their shows.

Eric, however, was not overly impressed by the acclaim he was receiving as the standout member of the Yardbirds. As far as he was concerned, you could count the number of white blues guitar players at the time on the fingers of one hand, and the big names, Keith Richards and Brian Jones, were more influenced by Chuck Berry and Bo Diddley. 'I wanted to be more like Freddie King and B.B. King. So I had no competition,' Clapton later remarked. In his own view, at least, he was top dog in a field of one.

Later, he was more than willing to admit how insufferable he had become. Speaking to music writer Ray Coleman twenty years later, he observed: 'I took it all far too seriously. Perhaps if I'd been able to temper it, I might not have been so frustrated.

I have regrets about my seriousness throughout my career. I still take it too seriously, in terms of relationships and being able to get on with other musicians. I'm far too judgemental, and in those days I was a complete purist. If it wasn't black music, it was rubbish.'

While their popularity was building steadily, the Yardbirds were still lacking an all-important hit single. Gomelsky told them to go out and find one, and Paul Samwell-Smith came back with the unashamedly poppy 'For Your Love', which had been written by Graham Gouldman, who would later go on to be a founding member of 10cc. Clapton instantly knew two things: 1) that the song would be a big hit, and 2) that it was the beginning of the end for him in the band. What made it so much worse was that the others clearly loved everything about the song, including the fact that it was going to make them big stars at last. For Clapton, ever the purist, it was a complete sell-out. Nonetheless, he reluctantly went through with playing on the song, providing a blink-and-you'd-miss-it bluesy riff in the middle eight section. The single, which was released in March 1965, sold more than a million copies, becoming a number three hit in Britain and getting to number six in the States. While the others celebrated, Eric was distraught.

His mood only became bleaker when Giorgio summarily promoted Samwell-Smith to the role of the group's official leader without consulting the others. On 3 March 1965, Gomelsky issued a memo the morning before a gig at the Corn Exchange in Bristol to all band members, warning them about slipping standards when it came to discipline. 'Time is money,' he wrote. 'If you're late for rehearsals, you will be fined . . . and if you have any queries about this, report to Paul Samwell-

Smith or come to my office immediately.' This was a red rag to Clapton, who had always considered the middle-class Samwell-Smith 'precious' anyway. Worse still, Paul liked the Shadows and their naff, regimented dance moves. The next day, Eric marched into his manager's office and explained that he could not put up with the current situation and had decided to leave. He did not receive the response he had bargained for. 'Good,' replied Gomelsky, unperturbed. 'Okay, well, we're not really surprised. I can't say I'm happy about you going, but we wish you well.'

Clapton would insist that while he wasn't exactly fired, Gomelsky 'invited me to resign'. There were few tears shed by the remaining members of the group over his departure. 'There wasn't a great deal of sadness that Eric was leaving,' says fellow ex-Yardbird Top Topham. 'The truth is he was a difficult person and a nightmare to work with.'

The official announcement of his decision to go came in an article in *Melody Maker*, which announced that Jeff Beck would replace Clapton and blamed the parting of the ways on the band being 'too commercial'. Keith Relf was quoted as saying: 'It's very sad because we're all friends. There was no bad feeling at all, but Eric does not get on well with the business. He does not like commercialisation. He loves the blues so much I suppose he did not like it being played badly by a white shower like us.'

While Eric left with the publicly stated best wishes of his manager and bandmates, the feeling was most certainly not reciprocated. For Clapton, it was far from a case of 'goodbye and good luck'. 'When I left the Yardbirds, I thought, "That's the end of them,"' he recalled. '"They don't try to whip *me* into shape. I'll leave them and we'll see who wins." And they then found Jeff Beck and I thought, "Now they've found someone better than me!" That was an early nudge to say, "Hang on, you're not the only one in the garden.'"

Suddenly without a band, a record contract or a job, Eric thought seriously about quitting music for good. In reality, he wouldn't be out of work for long.

# FIVE

# Bluesbreakers

In his middle years, John Mayall, having gone vegetarian and moved to Los Angeles, adopted a gym-honed Muscle Beach physique that he liked to show off by wearing a sleeveless gilet of the type favoured by Aussie Rules footballers. In the spring of 1965, however, Mayall was rocking an altogether different look: a bowl haircut and chin-beard combo that made him look like a cross between a Benedictine abbot and an extra from *A Man for All Seasons*. But he obviously thought he looked pretty cool, and as dubious hairstyles of the day went, his was no worse than most.

Mayall's grounding in music had started in his native Macclesfield, Cheshire, where his father was an aficionado of Django Reinhardt, Duke Ellington, Louis Armstrong, Eddie Lang, Joe Venuti, Dick McDonough and Charlie Christian. Massively inspired by Alexis Korner's band, Blues Incorporated, whose fluid membership included future members of the Rolling Stones, Led Zeppelin, Cream and Manfred Mann, John gave up his job in graphic design and moved permanently to London in 1963, at the relatively advanced age of thirty. The following year, he and his band, the Bluesbreakers, recorded their first single on Decca, called 'Crawling up a Hill'. And in

1965, a second single, 'Crocodile Walk', followed.

Eric Clapton had heard both records and couldn't stand either of them. So his decision to join Mayall's group just a few months after leaving the Yardbirds seems slightly perplexing. He had first met Mayall at the Marquee in Oxford Street a couple of years earlier, while he was still in the Roosters. More likely, it was the fact that Mayall and his cohorts in the Bluesbreakers looked nothing like pop stars that made the idea a little more appealing. The offer to join the band also came at a very good time.

After leaving the Yardbirds, Eric briefly went home to Ripley to mope, then moved to Oxford to stay with his old Roosters bandmate Ben Palmer. At the time, Palmer, whose purist love of the blues rivalled Eric's own, was living above a stable block in the Parktown area of the city, where he kept a huge collection of records by the likes of Little Walter, Big Bill Broonzy and Muddy Waters. With nothing else to do, Eric hung out and practised the guitar morning, noon and night, fortified by a diet of beans and Algerian red wine. This sabbatical, which lasted no more than a month or so, would take on almost mythical meaning to some of his fans, who likened it to how his hero Robert Johnson had disappeared into the Delta a merely competent player, and come back months later displaying a genius-like mastery of his instrument, his deal with the Devil having been struck. Likewise, when Clapton emerged from his period hidden away in Oxford with a new fire and intensity to his playing, some speculated that Clapton may have come to a similar accommodation with the Prince of Darkness at a deserted crossroads just off the A40. The reality was rather more prosaic and was the result of simple hard work and dedication to playing. Even so, the implication that something metaphysical had been going on would crop up again and again in the years to come.

In the meantime, four months after leaving the Yardbirds, Clapton was facing an all too terrestrial problem: he was broke. Attempts to get more royalties out of Gomelsky were largely fruitless and when he wasn't living free at the expense of Ben Palmer, he was popping back to Ripley to cadge money off his grandmother, or falling on the mercy of various girls he met about the place. So Mayall's phone call to Clapton on 11 April 1965 with a job offer could not have come at a better time. A friend, June Child, later the wife of Marc Bolan, had passed on Ben's number to John and he rang to ask Eric if he wanted to join the band.

Despite the promising clue in the band's title, Clapton and Mayall's Bluesbreakers were not an obvious fit. Hitherto, the group's music had verged more towards R&B than straight-ahead blues. Then there was Mayall himself. Not only was his voice rather thin, but his stage antics – stripping to the waist and leaping around like a deranged Morris dancer – were a bit out there. But, if nothing else, Mayall did at least have a 'credible' reputation as a blues musician. And what he lacked as a frontman, he made up for with a genuine love of the blues and an instinct for spotting nascent talent. In many ways, he was a bandleader in the jazz-age sense, a nurturer and musical father figure who ran operations in an almost military fashion.

Clapton had an unbending approach to what he would and would not play, and was convinced early on that, despite Mayall's discipline, he could re-mould Mayall's musical outlook when it came to the band and impose his own ideas. Clapton also knew that, to some extent at least, he was holding the upper hand. Despite his inexperience and his bruising time with the Yardbirds, his reputation was growing rapidly, and this gave him an advantage in his dealings with Mayall. And Mayall did, in fact, quickly acquiesce to Clapton over what material they should be doing, though it would be too simplistic to paint Mayall as either grudging or vanquished. The reality was far more that as well as understanding the leverage Clapton had because of his impending fame, John also intuitively trusted the younger man's ideas when it came to the way he wanted the band to take the blues forward.

The Bluesbreakers gig also came with another advantage. Mayall, as well as offering £35 a week in wages, agreed to open up his home to the band's latest arrival. Eric, still a month off his twentieth birthday, was allocated an attic room in the house in Lee Green, in suburban south-east London, that Mayall shared with his schoolteacher wife Pamela and four children. He was also afforded free access to his host's extensive record collection. For the best part of the next year, Clapton would sit, locked away upstairs, letting the music of Buddy Guy, Elmore James, Otis Rush, Hubert Sumlin and Robert Lockwood Jr. seep into him. He also practised with a fervour and discipline that reached near-religious levels, focused on what he described as his 'microscopic vision' of improving his playing. 'I did nothing but play,' he recalls. 'Girls and friends meant nothing to me for that year.'

The band was a tight musical unit, with Hughie Flint, who like Mayall was an exile from the north-west, on drums, John McVie, later of Fleetwood Mac, on bass and Mayall taking over the singing and keyboard duties. McVie was a brilliant player with a finely tuned sense of humour and a liking for booze that infuriated the health-conscious Mayall. Soon he and Clapton had formed a partnership that relied to a large extent on taking the piss out of the band's frontman whenever possible, giggling behind his back and telling him openly that he couldn't sing. Frequently, a riled Mayall would refuse to allow McVie into the van after gigs and once threw him out on to the side of the road on the way back from a show up north. Consequently, a 'him and us' situation developed between Mayall on one side and Clapton and McVie on the other.

Despite McVie and Eric's antics, and Eric's growing influence on the band's musical direction, Mayall was still the boss. He didn't give any quarter when it came to working them as hard as possible. They kept up a gruelling schedule, appearing all over the country, but never staying in a hotel and always returning in Mayall's Ford Transit van to London, where they would then regularly go on to an all-nighter. Life became a long round of such venues as the Club a Go-Go in Newcastle and Twisted Wheel in Manchester. The mood was only lifted for Eric by the chance of groping some willing girl at as many gigs as possible.

Almost immediately, Eric was restless. Partly consumed by what he saw as the musical limitations of the Bluesbreakers, he was also still seething about his virtual ejection from the Yardbirds, whom he wasted no opportunity to denigrate in front of his new band members. The effect this inner angst and frustration had on his playing was marked; suddenly he was playing with a new intensity and passion.

It also coincided with him discovering the perfect combination of guitar and amplifier that would give him his trademark sound. While he had kept his semi-acoustic Gibson ES335, he now also invested in a solid-bodied Gibson Les Paul Standard, which he bought in London. At the time, the Les Paul was considered an obsolete instrument, and the guitar's American makers had decided, in their wisdom, to withdraw it from production in 1961. Clapton bought the guitar, which had a 'sunburst' finish, after hearing Freddie King play a 'Gold Top' version of the same instrument. Eric played it through an amp made by the British maker Jim Marshall. Fellow guitarist Top Topham remembers being invited into the dressing room at the Crawdaddy Club in Richmond shortly after he bought the guitar. 'Eric said, "You've got to look at this guitar." It was a Les Paul,' says Topham. 'I'd never seen one before and I said that was the guitar Freddie King plays, and Eric just replied proudly, "Yeah". That's when his playing and his sound really came together.'

And Eric's 'sound' was working. Crowds began turning up to Bluesbreakers shows purely to see Clapton play. Suddenly, he was in demand from elsewhere too. Shortly after joining the band, Eric was invited by Mayall to play on some tracks he was collaborating on with Bob Dylan, who was recording in London. Later, record producer Mike Vernon, who owned Blue Horizon Records, asked Eric to play a session with Muddy Waters and the Chicago blues pianist Otis Spann. It was the first time he had met any of his genuine heroes. They recorded a song called 'Pretty Girls Everywhere I Go', on which Clapton played lead guitar. His reputation was building.

It was around the same time that he heard whispers that someone had written 'Clapton is God' on the wall of Islington tube station. Next, people began shouting it out at gigs.

Clapton's reaction to this level of adulation was one of ambivalence. On the one hand, which guitarist – who had faith in their own abilities – wouldn't find being feted as some sort of genius of the instrument appealing? Particularly as he still bore a grudge about being deemed surplus to requirements by his last band (the fact that the Yardbirds had garnered a string of hits with his replacement, Jeff Beck, in the line-up didn't help). On the other hand, Eric also felt a fraud, as if he was being given credit for inventing the blues. 'I was a bit mystified and part of me ran a mile from it,' he would say later. 'I didn't really want that kind of notoriety. I knew it would bring some kind of trouble. Another part of me really liked the idea that what I had been fostering all these years was finally getting some recognition.'

With the benefit of the passing decades, he would attest that he also found the accolade embarrassing because he was aware that there were 'hundreds' of guitar players who were better than him – even white Brits like Albert Lee and Bernie Watson, as well as Memphis session man Reggie Young. At the time, however, he was more gung-ho about his position in the pecking order of guitar slingers. 'I didn't think there was anyone around at that time doing what I was doing, playing the blues as straight as me,' he told Ray Coleman in 1985. 'I was trying to do it absolutely according to the rules. Oh yeah, I was very confident. I didn't think there was anybody as good. The only person I ever met who was trying to be as good as me was Mike Bloomfield [the Chicago-born Jewish-American guitarist] and when he came to England he bowed down to me straight away. So I thought, well, that's that.'

But ultimately for Clapton, the whole 'Clapton is God' thing was just a little too close to pop stardom for comfort. Which may explain what happened next. In the summer of 1965, he began hanging around at the Covent Garden flat of an avant-garde poet and musician called Ted Milton. Clapton himself describes Milton's work, which involved dressing up in a 'Biggles' flying hat and putting on puppet shows featuring a dead weight being hoisted up into the air and dropped over and over again, as 'visionary'. Others might call him 'weird'.

He, Milton, Milton's girlfriend Clarissa and a ragtag bunch of their friends would sit around drinking Mateus rosé wine with Eric getting off his head smoking dope. It was during one of these sessions that it was decided on the spot that a group of them should up sticks, form a band and take their travelling road show on a tour around the world – funded by playing gigs wherever they stopped. The group would be called the Glands and featured John Bailey, an anthropology student, on vocals, Bernie Greenwood, a Notting Hill doctor, on sax, Ted Milton's brother Jake on drums, a chap called Bob Rae on bass and Eric's old friend Ben Palmer on the piano. Eric would, of course, play lead guitar. Greenwood traded his MGA sports car for an American Ford Galaxy station wagon and, in August 1965, they set off on their exciting journey of discovery, driving through France and Belgium. The only problem was that, in the excitement, Eric failed to mention the trip to John Mayall, who was forced to scrabble around trying to find a replacement to fill the void. It would not be a successful trip.

In his memoirs, Clapton describes them all having a fight after a big fall-out at a beer festival in Munich. Then, on a cobbled road between Zagreb and Belgrade, the car shook so much it came apart and the chassis had to be tied back on with rope. In Greece, they were so hungry they ate raw meat in a butcher's shop, but in Athens they finally got hired to play in a club called the Igloo by the venue's owner, a flamboyant Greek who wore his hair lacquered back and carried a cane for effect. They played three sets a night, alongside a house band called the Juniors, who did pop tunes and Beatles stuff. The Glands would be expected to play Elvis and Chuck Berry numbers, plus, bizarrely, on the instructions of the owner, show tunes from *South Pacific*. Aside from the issue of their material, they were rubbish, and became used to getting heckled by the audience.

Then a car carrying the Juniors crashed, killing two of their members, and Eric was roped in by the club owner, who had developed something of a shine for him, to play sets for both bands, meaning he was on stage for six hours at a stretch. When he and the Glands announced they were moving on, the manager, who also had a taste for smashing the club up, threatened to cut off Clapton's hands if he quit. So a plan was formulated for them to do a flit. Train tickets were bought and, during a rehearsal with the Juniors, Eric said he was going to the toilet and instead legged it to a waiting car, which took him and Ben Palmer straight to the station and a train to London. In the dash to freedom, however, he left behind his Marshall amp and Les Paul, though the guitar was later reunited with him. The rest of the Glands carried on around Europe, minus guitar player and pianist.

If the whole imbroglio was a subconscious attempt to derail his apparently inexorable ascent to stardom, it came perilously close to working. By the time Eric got back to England in October 1965, he was out of a job. Mayall, angry at being left in the lurch, had given his berth in the Bluesbreakers to Peter Green, then a nineteen-year-old wunderkind who would go on to establish a reputation as one of the finest blues guitarists of his generation in his own band, Fleetwood Mac. But after some humming and hawing, Mayall dropped Green in favour of Clapton. While Eric had been away, he had also fired the troublesome John McVie and a Scots bass player called Jack Bruce was hired in his place. However, Bruce would move on himself within a few weeks to join Manfred Mann, allowing McVie to get his job back.

At the end of March 1966, John Mayall threw a fancy-dress party to celebrate Eric's twenty-first birthday at his house in Lee Green. The young guitarist, who came dressed as a gorilla, smoked his first cigarette, a habit he wouldn't be able to shake off for another thirty years. But the festivities were the prelude to some hard work. The following month, the band went into the studio to record the album that would make Clapton's name. Officially titled *Bluesbreakers: John Mayall with Eric Clapton*, it would forever be known simply as 'the Beano album' because Eric, reluctant to pose for the record's cover shot with the rest of the band, sat taciturnly reading the children's comic and refusing pointedly to look at the camera.

The recording took place over three days at the Decca studios in West Hampstead. But essentially the record was cut in little more than a weekend and consisted of the band simply recording their live club set, with most songs needing only one take. The track list featured a combination of blues standards: the Otis Rush song 'All Your Love', on which Eric played a fairly faithful version of the original's arpeggio-based solo, the Freddie King instrumental 'Hideaway' and the Robert Johnson tune 'Ramblin' On My Mind', on which Mayall persuaded a reluctant Clapton to sing the lead vocal (though Eric thought his voice sounded like a 'high-pitched whine').

The idea was that the record should be as near to their live sound as possible. That presented a problem for the technicians recording the sessions because the nature of studio recording called for lower volume if the overall effort was not going to be a muddy mess, with the individual instruments bleeding into each other in the final mix. But Clapton, driven by dogma and his own inalienable conviction that he was right, insisted that his guitar must be recorded at the ear-splitting volumes he employed on stage.

He decreed, much to the chagrin of producer Mike Vernon and engineer Gus Dudgeon, that his Marshall would be cranked up, with a microphone positioned just the right distance from the amp to replicate his live club sound. He used the bridge pickup of his 1960 Gibson Les Paul with the bass turned up, creating a very thick sound that flirted with out-and-out distortion. With amps and guitar volume maxed out, he was able to sustain notes, controlling the distortion and feedback from the amp. It was a sound that came about initially by accident, as he tried to recreate the trebly attack of Freddie King's signature sound and came up with a much fatter, warmer sound. But Eric's insistence on playing flat out at such high volume also caused grumbles among McVie and drummer Flint, who complained that their instruments were being drowned out by his guitar. In the end, it fell to Mayall to instruct the engineer to follow Clapton's wishes.

Mike Vernon remembers: 'Clapton had said, "This is going to be your biggest challenge, recording my sound!" We didn't realise how big a challenge it was going to be but, thank God, we had a young engineer who became a very famous producer, Gus Dudgeon, who was ready for any challenge whatsoever. Sadly, he's no longer with us [Dudgeon died in a road accident in 2002], but I can remember seeing his face the very first time Clapton plugged into the Marshall stack and turned it up and started playing at the sort of volume he was going to play. You could almost see Gus's eyes meet over the middle of his nose, and it was almost like he was just going to fall over from the sheer power of it all. But after an enormous amount of fiddling around and moving amps around, we got a sound that worked. I think all the solos, with the possible exception of "Steppin' Out", were done live. You can actually tell they were because the drums suffer as a result of it. There was an enormous amount of guitar on the drums. The studio wasn't very big – it was big enough, but nobody had had to deal with a band making that kind of noise.'

Eric's determination not to budge an inch was to prove well placed. The album, which spent seventeen weeks in the UK charts and garnered rave reviews, almost all feting Clapton, signalled the birth of the first bona fide guitar hero. Not only that, it also dramatically lifted the fortunes of Gibson. As the Les Paul went on to become the axe of choice for a new generation of budding guitar gods, the company reintroduced production, which had been replaced by the aesthetically less pleasing SG model in 1961. Over the years, the value of the rare Les Paul models from the same era as Clapton's 1960 model has skyrocketed, and by 2014 had reached between £110,000 and £250,000, depending on condition and provenance. Sadly, Clapton's Beano guitar, which with his connection would make it worth multiples of those figures in the current market, was stolen later that same year, during rehearsal for his first tour with Cream, and was never recovered.

When the record that cemented his status as a proto-rock star and unrivalled virtuoso talent was eventually released at the end of July, there was no time to indulge in celebrations – Clapton had already left the band.

# SIX

# Cream

In hindsight, Eric should have known what sort of hair-raising ride he was letting himself in for with Cream as he sat in the passenger seat of Ginger Baker's brand-new Rover 3000, his blood-drained fingers welded rigidly to the dashboard, as Ginger hurtled at breakneck speed down the A40 from Oxford to London one evening in the spring of 1966. Ginger drove like he played the drums, manically. Nor was his adherence to the Highway Code helped by the fact that he was at the time an alcoholic and registered heroin addict. Suffice to say, in Baker's hands, the high-powered Rover was one and a half tonnes of not-so-guided missile. So it was not a particularly smart move on Eric's part to throw a hand grenade into the proceedings.

Ginger, then the drummer with the Graham Bond Organisation, a jazz and R&B outfit founded by Essex-born Barnado's boy Bond, came to see Eric at a Bluesbreakers gig in the university city with a proposal that they should form a band together. Eric had met Baker a few times, mainly at the Marquee. He didn't know him well, but he certainly knew of his reputation as a top drummer. He also knew that Ginger was famous for having a hair-trigger temper and a propensity for spontaneous acts of violence. Like a lot of people at the time, Clapton was a bit scared of Ginger – with good reason. Which made his ultimatum that he would only think about joining a band with Baker on condition that Jack Bruce be recruited as the bass player an act of wilful self-endangerment – Ginger nearly crashed the car.

Everyone knew that Ginger and Jack couldn't stand each other. They had played together in the Graham Bond Organisation and their relationship had been one of visceral antipathy and loathing from minute one. During the period they shared as the rhythm section, their burning dislike had regularly turned violent. Ginger had all but run Bond's band and after one bad-tempered gig had sacked Bruce, saying he didn't fit in. The stubborn and pugnacious Jack simply refused to be fired and continued turning up at shows and playing as usual. Then, one night when they were on stage in Golders Green, north London, Jack, who was annoyed that Ginger's drums were too loud, turned to him and mouthed 'Shhhhhhh'. Ginger went ballistic and started throwing drumsticks at him, which were bouncing off his head. In retaliation, Bruce hoisted up his double bass to shoulder height and chucked it at the drummer sitting behind his kit. Within seconds, they were rolling around on the stage, punching the living daylights out of each other as the audience bayed for more.

Those who knew Ginger well reckoned his acts of fearsomeness were just a cover for someone who was by nature a shy soul, tender, with a largely hidden capacity for great compassion. Those who didn't, assumed he was a raving nutter and kept a safe distance. One thing everyone was agreed on, however, was that Ginger could play.

Born in London two weeks before the outbreak of the Second World War, Baker had taken rather too literally a letter left for him by his late father, Frederick, who was killed in action in Greece in 1943, which advised sagely: 'Use your fists; they are your best pals.' When his lifelong stroppiness was not getting him into punch-ups, he was taking out his seething anger and aggression on his drum kit. In an era of pretty boys like Davy Jones of the Monkees and Cliff Richard, the wild-eyed and even wilder-haired Baker was something of an oddity. Even though he was still only twenty-six when Cream was formed, Ginger looked prematurely ancient, an unlovely cross between Wilfrid Brambell and Catweazle's ginger brother.

Nor did he exactly buy into the prevailing cult of flower power and the 'love is all you need' mantra. He denounced Mick Jagger as 'effeminate'. Indeed, generally speaking, Jagger made him seethe. He thought the flamboyant Stones frontman was a 'stupid little cunt' whom he took great pleasure in 'terrifying the shit out of'.

But his enmity towards Jagger was a tea party compared to Baker's frothy-mouthed loathing of Jack Bruce. Now, as Ginger gave Clapton a lift home from the gig in Oxford, the sought-after guitarist was suggesting that it would be a deal-breaker if Jack wasn't in the proposed new band. Eric had played with the talented bassist during a short spell when Jack joined the Bluesbreakers for a tour of southern England the previous autumn and his opinion of him was that here was the most forceful bass player he had worked with, a man who was so confident in his own talent that he believed his instrument should be the focal point of any band he played in. Eric had also heard Jack play with Ginger and was struck by the musical understanding between them on stage.

Even so, Ginger was loath to renew his acquaintance with his old sparring partner and told Eric he needed time to consider. Finally, he called him to say that if the only way the group could get off the ground was with Jack as a member, then, reluctantly, he was in.

Given the success that was to follow, the new band's first coming together was an inauspicious affair, convened in the front room of Ginger's house in Birchen Grove, Neasden, north London. It was March 1966, a month before Clapton recorded his Bluesbreakers album. Thankfully for Ginger's neighbours, however, they played through some songs acoustically rather than plugging in microphones and amps. True to form, Bruce and Baker started things off by having a row, and both clearly had gone into the project thinking they would be the leader of the group. But before long, all three were smiling at the musical chemistry that seemed to happen naturally between them. For his part, Clapton had for some time been envisaging himself as the frontman of a three-piece band because he was a huge fan of the exceptionally talented Chicago blues guitarist Buddy Guy, whose trio was tight and raw. It was only when they played electrically for the first time that Eric began to have his first doubts that he didn't have Guy's capacity to fill in the gaps in what he thought was a sound that was too sparse, too empty. Subconsciously, perhaps, he also knew that if he was not able to plug the holes in their sound, then inevitably the self-regarding Jack and Ginger would. Tentatively, he suggested they recruit a keyboard player. Having seen the precociously talented Steve Winwood, who was eighteen at

Stigwood, who had negotiated an impressive £400 fee, bought them a black Austin Westminster car to travel in, and Eric's friend, and ex-member of the Roosters, Ben Palmer was roped in at the last minute to act as their roadie. They weren't greeted with the fanfare they might have expected. In fact, the club was half-empty because Cream, or 'the Cream', as they insisted on calling themselves, were only a late addition to the bill. They played a few souped-up covers: 'Cross Road Blues', now known simply as 'Crossroads', the Willie Dixon-penned 'Spoonful', and 'I'm So Glad', the blues tune recorded by Skip James in 1931. They also performed the instrumental 'Toad' and 'Traintime', a song written by Jack Bruce.

Two nights later, they played the sixth National Jazz and Blues Festival at Windsor Racecourse, where they topped the bill in front of 15,000 people. The new band hardly went down a storm, perhaps because it was a rain-soaked affair. Instead, the crowd gave them a warm, if not exactly rapturous, ovation at the end of their performance. In truth, this may have had something to do with the fact that the band's preparation was woefully inept. They were so short of songs they all could play, they ended up having to play their set twice and were forced to improvise for long periods over twelve-bar blues progressions to pad out the show. An embarrassed Ginger apologised to the crowd for having so little material.

That performance was symptomatic of the ad hoc nature of the band in those early days, which Ben Palmer described as 'shambolic'. For his part, Clapton's fears that, as a live unit, Cream were going to be limited by being a trio really started to hit home. His assessment was shared by another former

Yardbirds guitarist, Top Topham, who was in the audience that night. 'I got to like Cream very much later, particularly on record, but on that day I was disappointed,' he says. 'They seemed to be playing too much, like they were overplaying to fill the gaps because there was just the three of them. There was just too much going on. They sounded like they needed another person.'

Even so, reviews of the Windsor gig christened them as the first 'supergroup'. But the big breakthrough that they and Stigwood were envisaging would take longer to come, and they reverted to the small club circuit.

Ginger Baker was another who found the live sound of the band too busy and it soon became a source of bitter contention between him and Jack, whom he constantly accused of overplaying. Jack's reaction was that without a keyboard player to hold down the music harmonically and melodically, it was down to him to step into the breach with his complicated, jazzy bass lines.

Undoubtedly, Bruce had a high opinion of himself – with obvious justification. Born in Bishopbriggs, ten or so miles from Glasgow, he was encouraged by his musical parents to play piano and won a scholarship to study cello and composition at the Royal Scottish Academy of Music and Drama. He also played in the Glasgow Schools Orchestra before forming a skiffle group, and in his teens, got his first gigs on upright bass with a local dance band. Later, he fell in love with the playing of Charles Mingus, the double bass-playing American jazz man, and after Bruce arrived in London in the early 1960s, he joined British blues godfather Alexis Korner's band Blues Incorporated with, among others, future Rolling Stone Charlie

Watts and, later, Baker. Evidence of the full extent of Bruce's self-regard was on show when he released a forty-year retrospective of his career in 2008 called *Can You Follow?* – and it stretched to six coma-inducing CDs. Likewise, when he was once asked who he considered to be the best bass players in pop and rock history, he answered at once: 'If you're talking electric bass, it's very, very simple: James Jamerson [the Motown session man], Paul McCartney, Jaco Pastorius, me.'

With two cocksure characters like Bruce and Baker in the band, it was, invariably, Clapton who found himself caught in the crossfire. Once, when they were en route to a gig in Copenhagen, Eric burst into tears during one snarling argument between his drummer and bassist. Later, on a tour of the States, Jack downed tools and ran away after yet another row with Ginger over their sound. He was discovered by the band's roadies at the airport, holding a ticket he had bought to fly home, and had to be physically dragged back.

Clapton, in his naïvety, had envisioned himself as the leader of Cream. But the reality was very different. Later, he would say of the band's power base: 'I did not have, nor do I have now, the amount of personal power or aggression to keep the other two guys in place. And I wouldn't want to.' Perhaps what he really meant was 'in *their* place'. The one thing Jack and Ginger seemed incapable of knowing was 'their place'.

'It wouldn't have been right to try to exercise authority over them,' Clapton went on. 'Jack is a far superior musical brain than I am, and he could argue his way out of anything I could insist on. Ginger would not accept it. It would be too much of a battle for me to take it on.'

Publicly, at least, Clapton was keeping up the pretence that all was sweetness and light. However, one thing that was undeniably true was that playing with his warring compatriots had opened up his mind to what could be achieved by abandoning his formerly rigid approach to the blues format and embracing the jazzier sensibilities that Jack and Ginger brought to the table. Immediately after joining Cream, which he insisted on calling 'the Cream', Clapton said: 'I was out on my own mentally. Now I'm with a band I really dig . . . My whole musical outlook has changed. I listen to the same sounds and records, but with a different ear. I'm no longer trying to play anything other than like a white man. This is overdue: people should play like what they are and what colour they are. I don't believe I've ever played so well in my life. More is expected of me in the Cream. I have to play rhythm guitar as well.'

For all Eric's talk of bright new musical horizons, the paradox was that having quit the Yardbirds over 'For Your Love', the first Cream single, the Jack Bruce/Pete Brown-penned ditty 'Wrapping Paper', was a throwaway piece of flaccid pop bubblegum. The argument put forward by Bruce at the time was that the song was so avant-garde, so not what the critics and music-buying public were expecting, that it would cock a huge snook at the musical establishment. If the world was expecting some heavy rock anthem, he reasoned, then Cream would give them something completely different. Hardly surprisingly, given what self-indulgent clever clogs they were trying to be, 'Wrapping Paper' flopped dismally, only getting to number thirty-four in the UK charts. Ginger was later quoted as saying that the song was 'the most appalling piece of shit I've ever heard in my life' and that he and Clapton were against it from the outset.

Clapton still felt the urge to come out into the open to defend the direction the band was taking. 'A lot of biased listeners say that all we are playing is pop numbers,' he countered. 'In actual fact, closer listening reveals that none of us are playing anything that vaguely resembles pop, although it might sound deceptively like that. "Wrapping Paper" is an excuse for a twelve-bar blues. That's all it is – a good tune, very commercial, with the sort of feel that represents *us*. We do exploit this kind of feeling, but we retain the beauty as well, all the time we play. Although we might play a number very loudly, and it might appear violent, in fact the tune and lyrics are very sweet.'

Indeed, far from being a cop-out to commercialism, his move into other forms of music was, as far as Clapton was concerned, a simple case of logic. To his mind, for all the adulation he was receiving, he was still merely an 'imitator' when it came to the blues. Robert Johnson and Muddy Waters were the 'real thing' in Clapton's book. 'That's what made me give up trying to be a 100 per cent bluesman,' he reasoned, 'because I realised I would always be that far behind my ideal.'

The release of the disappointing 'Wrapping Paper' in October 1966 coincided with a far more seismic event in Clapton's career. It would be too simplistic to argue that the death knell for Cream was sounded when an unknown American called Jimi Hendrix joined them on stage to jam on 1 October at the Central London Polytechnic in New Cavendish Street, but Clapton was under no illusion that his crown had been well and truly ripped from him. Hendrix's manager, Chas Chandler, who was the bass player in the Animals, arrived with his protégé and asked if Jimi could sit in. Ginger was not keen, but Eric and Jack agreed quite happily. They did not know what they were letting themselves in for, as Hendrix tore up the stage with a turbo-charged interpretation of the Howlin' Wolf song 'Killing Floor'.

'He got up and played two songs with us and I knew it was all over in terms of guitar heroes,' Clapton remembers. 'Jimi had everything. He'd got all the tricks, he played like a genius, but he could also play it with his teeth, or behind his head, or on the ground. Jack and Ginger did not like it at all. They probably saw the end of their careers looming. He was going to get a trio and tour, just like us. I didn't see Hendrix in terms of competition. I just thought: a kindred spirit. Someone I can talk to about the music I love. We just fell in love with one another. But everyone else was very: "Who's this? Can't have this around."'

Could Clapton really have been so sanguine about being relegated down the guitarist pecking order so brutally and summarily? *New Musical Express* journalist Keith Altham remembered events slightly differently. According to him, he went into the dressing room after Clapton left the stage in the middle of 'Killing Floor'. Clapton was furiously puffing on a cigarette and telling Chandler: 'You never told me he was *that* fucking good.'

Eric would say later: 'I knew what the guy was capable of from the minute I met him. It was the complete embodiment of the different aspects of rock 'n' roll guitar rolled into one. I could sense it coming off the guy. The audience were completely gobsmacked by what they saw and heard. They loved it and I loved it too, but I remember thinking that here was a force to be reckoned with. It scared me, because he was clearly going to be a huge star and just as we were finding our speed, here was the real thing.'

While Clapton was just beginning to see the nascent possibilities of combining the genres of blues, rock, pop, jazz and soul into one cohesive blend, Hendrix's amalgam of these previously distinct musical spheres came fully formed. His combination of powerhouse playing and subtle and beautiful lyricism – often using outrageous distortion, feedback, wah-wah pedals and fuzz boxes – took the instrument somewhere that Clapton may well have been heading himself in time. Now, though, Eric had had the rug pulled; Hendrix had beaten him to the punch. And when it came to authenticity, without wanting to state the obvious, Hendrix was also what Clapton could never be: black and American.

Hendrix, like Buddy Guy, was also patently more than capable of carrying a trio with his guitar. Clapton's own sense of falling short on this front was not an issue when Cream were in the studio. There, they could overdub with rhythm guitar, while Jack played keyboards as well as bass. Indeed, they hardly ever recorded as a basic three-piece. Live was a different matter, and it meant Eric adapting his style to fill the space. He experimented with barre chords and so-called drone notes – hitting an open bass string and allowing it to ring out while playing a solo higher up the register. But for the most part, Clapton was prepared to allow Bruce and Baker to determine the band's musical direction, primarily because they were the ones writing the songs.

Jack had formed a writing partnership with a Surrey-born poet called Pete Brown, who would later go on to join a little-known band called the Battered Ornaments. Brown wrote the lyrics for Cream's second single, the psychedelic 'I Feel Free', recorded in September at Ryemuse Studios in South Molton Street in London's West End, and released in December. In Britain, at least, it scored a marked improvement on 'Wrapping Paper', getting to number eleven in the charts, though in the US it only got as far as 116. Both songs were left off the group's debut album, *Fresh Cream*, which was released just prior to Christmas, though 'I Feel Free' did appear on the American version of the LP. Elsewhere on the album, Clapton took over lead vocal duties on a cover of Robert Johnson's 'From Four Until Late', but for the most part Jack Bruce earmarked the role of singer for himself.

This most certainly was not what Eric had been envisaging when he first latched on to the concept of having his own blues trio during the dog days of his stint in the Bluesbreakers. Nor was the idea of Jack being front and centre exactly what the shrewd Stigwood had been planning when he took on the management of Cream. Stigwood may have had the hots for Clapton, but he also knew that with Eric as a frontman and a strong rhythm section behind him, they would be on to a winner. Stigwood was joined in his assessment that it was Clapton, and not Bruce, who should be fronting the band by Ahmet Ertegun, who ran the US label Atco, a subsidiary of Atlantic Records, who had signed Cream in America. And Ertegun, a well-bred Turkish immigrant who'd moved to America at the age of twelve, had impeccable taste: he had recorded, among others, Ray Charles, Aretha Franklin and the Drifters.

Ertegun had actually met Eric earlier in 1966, when he threw a party in London at the Scotch of St James club where

Clapton played. He signed Cream and told Stigwood they needed to go to the US to promote *Fresh Cream*. However, Ertegun, with his sharp eye for star quality, was convinced that Cream should be first and foremost Clapton's band and Eric's noisy compatriots should be relegated down the group's pecking order. Ertegun later said of his first impressions of Cream: 'When I first heard them, I already knew what I had – and what I had was Eric Clapton. The trio was a great trio, but the soul part was Eric Clapton.'

With his innate capacity for freeloading, Eric had, for several months, been bunking down on sofas and floors with friends, ever since leaving the sanctuary of John Mayall's spare room, but now he needed a place of his own. He moved in with three American girls in Ladbroke Square, Notting Hill. After his teen romance with Diane Coleman, he had moved on to a brief affair with a West Indian girl called Maggie who was a dancer on *Top of the Pops*, but the set-up at his new flat with the Americans was a platonic affair. By way of celebrating his newfound freedom, new home and having a bit of money in his pocket, Clapton bought his first car, a right-hand-drive Cadillac Fleetwood, a boat of a thing, for £750. The only problem was that as he had not learnt to drive, the huge white elephant sat parked outside the flat, gradually rotting away.

There would be no time to drive it anyway. At the end of March 1967, the three members of Cream stepped off a flight in New York to begin an exhausting assault on America. The preceding months had seen something of a dramatic change in their appearances. A couple of months earlier, Clapton had been to see Jimi Hendrix play at the Bag O'Nails club in Soho. The American guitarist was already a big draw among the rock cognoscenti, and Paul McCartney, John Lennon, Pete Townshend, Mick Jagger and a host of other musicians were present to see him perform. Jimi, as usual, was rocking a look that involved tie-dye, all manner of semi-precious rings, gold chains and general metal wear. Mesmerised not only by Hendrix's playing, but also his stage persona, Eric went back to Ginger and Jack and announced that they all needed a makeover. Out went the rather austere military look of *Fresh Cream* and in came a psychedelic smorgasbord of loon pants, kaftans, kimonos and bracelets, and Eric went out and got a curly perm (in fact, he could only have gone further in his emulation of Hendrix if he'd actually blacked-up).

In New York, Stigwood checked the band into the grotty – and cheap – Gorham Hotel on West 55th Street and booked them to perform daily on Murray the K's radio show. The elaborately bewigged Murray, whose real name was Murray Kaufman, was the biggest DJ in New York and he affected a zany, fast-talking persona that disguised the fact that behind the scenes he was a tough taskmaster. His shows went out from the RKO Theater on 58th Street and Third Avenue.

Without a hit in America, Cream were by no means top of a bill which included the Who, Wilson Pickett, Mitch Ryder and the Detroit Wheels and Simon and Garfunkel. It was a gruelling schedule. For ten days, they did five shows a day, in five-minute slots, starting from 10.30 a.m. until 8.30 p.m., performing 'I Feel Free' over and over again. It was an ad hoc affair, with interludes featuring dancing girls and performing midgets, often playing to school kids in the morning, empty houses in the afternoon and unimpressed adults in the evening. Cream had to borrow the Who's equipment, and matters were not helped by the fact that Murray was less than complimentary about Britain's first supergroup, no-so-privately calling Cream 'this piece of shit'. Meanwhile, he announced he could not pay them because he had lost the equivalent of £27,000 on the whole messy carnival.

Still, as far as Clapton was concerned, he had reached the promised land of hamburgers, milkshakes, clothes, music – and women. On the first day, a beautiful seventeen-year-old blonde called Catherine James and her friend Emeretta managed to con their way into rehearsals via a rear stage door and were sitting in the back row watching the Who singing 'My Generation' when Clapton sidled up and presumptuously settled down in the next seat to them. He was wearing purple velvet trousers and snakeskin boots. Californian Catherine, who remembers Clapton as being 'mysterious and beyond cool', had just returned from England herself, where she had been involved in an on-off affair with Denny Laine, who had been in the Moody Blues and would go on to join Paul McCartney in Wings. Catherine took Eric to buy cowboy boots and to the legendary Manny's musical instrument shop on 48th Street, where he later bought her a Guild guitar for her eighteenth birthday. As this was the mid-60s and free love was in the air, she immediately invited him to move into the apartment she was sharing with her friend Eileen Rubinstein.

With his new girlfriend as his guide, Eric set off on a journey of exploration around the trendier bits of New York, such as the Café au Go Go on Bleecker Street in Greenwich Village, where one night he met and jammed with B.B. King. He also got friendly with another of those on the Murray the K bill, Al Kooper, the Brooklyn-born multi-instrumentalist from the

Blues Project who had played on a lot of Bob Dylan tracks. On the last day of their short residency on 58th Street, Eric, Ginger and Jack sneaked out to join the city's first Be-In which, though technically a protest against the Vietnam War, was basically a chance for 10,000 hippies to descend on the Sheep Meadow in Central Park and get off their faces on drugs while sprinkling daffodil petals on police cars. Someone spiked Jack's popcorn with acid and when they returned to give their final Murray the K performance, they were stoned and troublesome. By way of revenge on the DJ for not paying them, they dumped the contents of fourteen bags of flour and a few dozen eggs in their dressing room.

With a couple of days left in America before their visas ran out, Ahmet Ertegun turned up at their hotel and invited them to Atlantic Studios. Here, his brother and fellow producer Nesuhi oversaw the recording of one track, a version of the song 'Hey Lawdy Mama', a 1930s number recorded by, among others, Georgia bluesman Buddy Moss and also by Junior Wells and Buddy Guy, on their collaborative album *Hoodoo Man Blues*. Plans were made for Cream to return to the States the following month.

Back in swinging 1967 London, the Speakeasy was *the* place for the see-and-be-seen brigade. On any given evening in 'the Speak', as it was known to the in-crowd, you could spot a couple of Beatles, a Rolling Stone or two and a succession of blondes and brunettes, high on hormones and on the lookout for a pop-star boyfriend. Situated on Margaret Street, just at the back of Oxford Street, it was reached by a flight of red-carpeted stairs that opened on to a large room with elevated sections and cloistered private booths. There was a stage and, off to the right, a raised restaurant, sectioned off by a glass screen, which sold filet mignon sandwiches and creamed petits pois. The Italian maître d' made a point of knowing everyone.

Eric was a regular and, like most of the musicians who frequented the place, would regularly get up for a spontaneous jamming session with whichever house band was playing that night. The Speakeasy was run by Laurie O'Leary and his brother Alphi, who were friends of the notorious London gangsters the Kray twins and had managed clubs for them, including Esmeralda's Barn, the twins' gambling joint in Wilton Place, Knightsbridge. Alphi would later go on to be Clapton's personal assistant and bodyguard for more than twenty years.

It was in the Speakeasy that Eric met Charlotte Martin, a leggy French model with huge eyes and the sort of gamine figure that was a prerequisite of being a flower-power beauty. Together they moved into a flat in Regent's Park that was owned by Stigwood's business partner David Shaw. Later, at the same club, Charlotte introduced her new boyfriend to a friend called Martin Sharp, an Australian who wrote poetry and drew cartoons and who was one of the founders of the satirical magazine *Oz*, which scandalised 60s society and faced obscenity charges in Sydney and London. Sharp had no idea who Clapton was and when he found out he was a musician, he told him he'd written the lyrics to a song. Clapton told him he had a tune, but no words. With that, Sharp grabbed a paper napkin and jotted down the lyrics to 'Tales of Brave Ulysses', as well as his address on the King's Road. He had originally written the verses to the tune of Leonard Cohen's 'Suzanne' and was inspired to write about 'laughing purple fishes' by his holidays to Ibiza and Formentera in the Balearics. A few months later, Clapton arrived at Sharp's studio with a copy of the Cream single 'Strange Brew', with 'Tales of Brave Ulysses' on the flipside. 'I was disappointed it was only on the B-side,' remembered Sharp.

It was also in the Speak that Eric took his first acid trip. As the likes of the Monkees and Lulu partied, the Beatles arrived with an acetate, or early test copy, of 'Sgt. Pepper's Lonely Hearts Club Band' and George Harrison handed it to the DJ to play. Someone was giving out pills called STPs, a potent acid whose effect was reputed to last for days. Clapton and some of the others took it. Immediately, he began seeing strange hieroglyphics and mathematical equations and, once back home, he could not sleep and thought he was going mad. Thankfully, Charlotte Martin had not taken the LSD herself and was able to look after him until he came back from his trip.

Drugs weren't the only things Clapton borrowed from the Beatles; he also followed their lead in hiring two London-based Dutch artists called Simon Posthuma and Marijke Koger, known collectively as 'The Fool'. They had created a giant mural for the Beatles at their Apple Boutique on Baker Street, and Eric commissioned them to paint his 1964 Gibson SG guitar in garish Day-Glo, with a cherub holding a triangle.

A month after their first trip to New York, Eric, Jack and Ginger were back to record the follow-up to *Fresh Cream*. This time, Stigwood checked them into the far more salubrious Drake Hotel on Park Avenue, where they quickly made the most of things by ordering vast quantities of food from room service, smashing up the TV in Clapton's room, chasing each other down the corridors in the dead of night and hiding in laundry trolleys.

The new album, *Disraeli Gears*, named after a slip of the tongue by one of the band's roadies while discussing the derailleur gears on a racing bicycle, would ultimately cement Cream's reputation as a supergroup on both sides of the Atlantic and see Clapton step out of Jack Bruce's shadow once and for all.

With Cream in New York, Ahmet Ertegun was able to call the shots and he instructed the new record's up-and-coming producer, a 28-year-old New Yorker called Felix Pappalardi, and his engineer, Tom Dowd, to give Clapton the prominence his talents deserved. Dowd would go on to become a pivotal figure in Clapton's career and twiddled the knobs on recordings by everyone who was anybody in blues, jazz and Motown, including Ray Charles, Charlie Parker, John Coltrane, the Modern Jazz Quartet, Booker T and the MG's, the Drifters, the Coasters, the Allman Brothers, Otis Redding and Aretha Franklin.

Ertegun's plan, however, would not go down well with either Bruce or Baker, who saw quickly that the writing was on the wall as far as Atlantic's opinion about the future of the band was concerned. Certainly, this came as unwelcome news to Jack Bruce, who had elected himself the spiritual leader and vocalist of Cream. 'I was kind of gutted really,' he admitted later. 'I'd done a lot of work and I was the lead singer and it was working pretty well the way that it was. I had to get over the slight of my material not being taken seriously because I really believed in it, I knew this stuff was happening.' Likewise, Ginger was less than thrilled that the powers-that-be at their US label wanted to move Clapton to his rightful place as the new frontman. 'Ahmet saw it as the guitar player, much like Chuck Berry, and the rhythm section was there, but not featured,' Baker says of the recording of the album.

Understandably, then, there was tension from the outset, given how peeved Jack and Ginger were at having their noses put out of joint. But Ertegun did have a valid point: in the best part of a year since the band had been in existence, they had had precisely zero top thirty hits in America. Something needed to change. It was the classically trained Pappalardi who was charged with putting the plan into action. Indeed, to a large extent, over the seven days it took to make the album, the vision of where Cream should be heading came to revolve as much around Pappalardi as the band's members themselves.

His first move was to take the tape of bluesy 'Hey Lawdy Mama', recorded on their previous trip, and dump the original lyrics, sung by Clapton, before replacing them with new ones he hoped would more catch the zeitgeist. The result, 'Strange Brew', was an unashamed psychedelic pop song and in order to placate the anti-pop Clapton – and to persuade him to sing the new lyrics – an unspoken agreement was made between them. It was decided that Clapton would give the track a more rootsy feel by playing a hard-edged, staccato Albert King-inspired guitar solo. Even so, Clapton never warmed to the song.

The mood continued with the incomprehensible 'SWLABR', which included the unforgettably daft line 'the rainbow has a beard' and was a drug-inspired tune which, according to the song's lyricist, Pete Brown, who was trying to kick his own habit at the time, was about a man who compares his girlfriend to the *Mona Lisa* then goes around defacing her image when she dumps him. Meanwhile, in more familiar territory, Clapton sang lead vocals on 'Outside Woman Blues', which was originally recorded by Blind Joe Reynolds in 1929. 'Take It Back' was a fairly uninspiring protest against the Vietnam War written by Jack Bruce, but the bassist saved his best work for 'Sunshine of Your Love', whose riff has become an all-time rock classic.

Jack had written the song as a tribute to Jimi Hendrix after he and Clapton had been to see him play at the Saville Theatre in London's West End. Bruce, who had previously been somewhat immune to the buzz surrounding Hendrix, was instantly converted. He went home after the gig and came up with the song's iconic riff. Clapton added the turnaround in the chorus and some of the lyrics. For the slightly discordant guitar solo, Eric employed his so-called 'woman tone', achieved by turning the tone controls on his Gibson's pickup right down and cranking the guitar's volume knobs up to full, producing a rich, warm sound. Clapton's guitar work on 'Tales of Brave Ulysses', the structure of which is straight out of the Lovin' Spoonful's 1966 hit 'Summer In The City', was also notable for his subtle use of the wah-wah pedal, which Felix Pappalardi took him to buy at Manny's music store.

Despite the tension engendered by Clapton's move to the front and centre of the band, all three of them knew they had just made something special. They arrived back in London full of themselves, thinking, with some justification, they had just produced a groundbreaking, technically advanced hybrid of rock, blues and pop which would change the musical landscape in an instant. In Clapton's words: 'We had found ourselves. We had found our promise as individuals in the different areas we were in.' The only problem was that Jimi Hendrix had stolen their thunder with his just-released album *Are You*

*Experienced*, which would go on to be one of the most influential debut albums ever made. On the record, Hendrix seamlessly combined psychedelia with blues, funk and pop in tracks like 'Foxy Lady', 'Manic Depression' and 'Red House', the latter of which was a slow blues that had an opening right out of Robert Johnson's repertoire and was a tour-de-force, updating the blues with Hendrix's incendiary playing.

It was a particular kick in the teeth to Clapton, who thought they had made a 'definitive' album. Now no one cared about it. All everyone wanted to talk about was Hendrix. Later, Clapton would contend that this was the beginning of his disenchantment with Britain. This was not quite true. In fact, during the latter months of his time in the Bluesbreakers, he had been complaining that only in America would he be taken seriously as a blues disciple and purist. But now things were different. With Hendrix, who – in Eric's own words – was not just the 'flavour of the month, but of the year', the name on everyone's lips, Clapton would have been justified in thinking that the UK was simply not big enough for the both of them.

A few months previously, Eric had moved into the Pheasantry, an impressive-looking but somewhat down-at-heel building on the King's Road in Chelsea which was reached through an ornate arch and which had been used in the eighteenth century as a place where pheasants were reared for the royal family to shoot at. His flatmate was to be Martin Sharp, with whom he had become particularly close, and they shared the place with Sharp's girlfriend Eija and Clapton's lover Charlotte Martin. Another room was taken by a painter called Philippe Mora and his girlfriend Freya. The building operated as a sort of commune and at one point during Eric's stay, a tramp called John Ivor Golding moved in. The ground floor was taken up by the studio of the artist Timothy Whidborne, while in the basement was the Pheasantry Club, which had once attracted an upper-crust set, but had, in more recent times, become a bit seedy.

While at least some of Whidborne's neighbours upstairs were experimenting with every type of weapons-grade narcotics they could get their hands on, the artist himself was hard at work on an official portrait of the Queen astride a horse called Doctor, the monarch decked out in the ceremonial uniform of her role as colonel-in-chief of the Irish Guards. 'The building was a hive of activity with models coming and going,' Whidborne says. 'Upstairs were Eric and Martin Sharp and upstairs in another studio was Germaine Greer endlessly typing away on her book *The Female Eunuch*.'

Another regular was David Litvinoff, who was a friend of Whidborne's from the early 50s and who worked part-time as his secretary. Although he lived in Kensington, the Pheasantry became a second home for Litvinoff and he became firm friends with Clapton. The colourful Litvinoff, who was gay and an expert raconteur, was an East End Jew who was as tough as he was fiercely intelligent. He was also a fast-talking thug for hire who wore a large livid scar across the right-hand side of his face that he said he'd picked up in a fight with the Krays. Whether this was true or not was anyone's guess. Likewise, his claim to Clapton that he worked for the William Hickey column on the *Daily Express* was probably exaggerated too. But his association with the Krays was real enough. Litvinoff, who had no obvious financial means, was prone to run up gambling debts in the gaming clubs of London owned by the underworld brothers. More often than not, though, his ability to spin a yarn would have even those to whom he owed money in fits of laughter and generally got him off a beating. Clapton became an immediate acolyte and the two men would spend hours wandering up and down the King's Road, with Litvinoff bitching about the local types, often to their faces.

Stories about Litvinoff were legion among the artsy set he liked to mix with. For example, not long after Clapton moved into the Pheasantry, Litvinoff and another renowned London villain, John Bindon, arranged to meet one of the more colourful figures of the flower-power generation for what they euphemistically called 'a little chat'. As was often the case, however, when the brutish duo came calling, there was precious little polite conversation on offer. Instead, the man they had come to visit, Nicky Cramer, a rather fey member of the trendy Chelsea set, with a taste for lurid make-up, would spend much of the encounter being dangled by his ankles from the upstairs window of his flat, the garish robes for which he was known billowing, like drying washing, around his ears. The hardmen had deployed their unrivalled powers of persuasion on Cramer in a bid to discover if he was the mole who had tipped off police for the notorious Redlands drugs bust, during which Mick Jagger and his bandmate Keith Richards were arrested in February 1967. The raid became a *cause célèbre* for Britain's rebellious youth against the forces of the Establishment. And, overnight, it also turned Jagger's twenty-year-old girlfriend, Marianne Faithfull, into the most infamous scarlet woman in the land.

The debauched goings-on at Redlands, the rambling house owned by Richards in West Wittering, Sussex, both scandalised and transfixed the nation. There were tales of drugs galore being found and, famously, of Miss Faithfull being discovered naked save for the fur rug she was wrapped in – not to mention a salacious, if apocryphal story involving Marianne being found in a compromising position with a Mars bar. Litvinoff, as well as being an underworld enforcer, was Jagger's pet gangster – he was later the dialogue coach and technical adviser on Mick's debut film, *Performance*. Now he had taken it upon himself to track down the police's informant. After giving the terrified Cramer – who had been a guest at the infamous house party – a thorough beating, he and Bindon declared the poor chap innocent.

Like Jagger, Clapton, who had taken a similar shine to another London hardman, Alphi O'Leary, enjoyed having a bit of muscle around, and he and Litvinoff would go on regular shopping sprees to Granny Takes a Trip, on the King's Road, which was run at the time by the artist Nigel Waymouth and was London's latest and most happening boutique. The triumvirate of Clapton, Jagger and Litvinoff would lead to whispers among anything-goes London. And, decades later, John Dunbar, the ex-husband of Marianne Faithfull, claimed to Jagger's biographer Christopher Andersen that Mick and Eric were once discovered in bed together, though Dunbar admitted the story was second-hand and he had not witnessed it himself.

The wily Litvinoff also had other uses. The iconic 'Clapton is God' graffiti may once have been a spontaneous outpouring of admiration, but Litvinoff appointed himself as Eric's unofficial PR man and ensured the epithet was scrawled all over London, including on the wall of the Pheasantry.

In August 1967, the Summer of Love was in full effect. A

few months earlier, Scott McKenzie had released the counter-culture anthem 'San Francisco (Be Sure To Wear Some Flowers In Your Hair)'; hippies were flocking to Haight-Ashbury in San Francisco; and on the East Coast, former Harvard lecturer Timothy Leary was advising America's youth to 'turn on, tune in, drop out' on LSD and magic mushrooms. It was against this heady backdrop that Cream arrived back in the US to headline the bill at the Fillmore Auditorium in San Francisco, after which they would begin an energy-sapping coast-to-coast two-month tour. The Fillmore, which occupied a former dance school on the corner of Fillmore Street and Geary Boulevard, had been opened the previous year by a West Coast promoter called Bill Graham, a Korean War veteran who was rumoured to have links to the Mafia. Now, with the Hippie Revolution at its height, Graham was catching the zeitgeist. His club may have had a capacity of little more than a thousand people, but it attracted all the big names of the flower power era: the Grateful Dead, Jefferson Airplane, the Doors, Big Brother and the Holding Company and the Byrds.

For his part, Graham was acutely aware that for most of his audience being off their faces while they danced was the whole point. Consequently, he sought out bands whose music fitted into the category 'Best Heard When Stoned'. Cream undoubtedly fitted the bill. Nor was it that important to Graham that the British trio could be seen while they played, and he arranged for a psychedelic light show to be projected on to the stage, all but blanking them out. Graham was also happy for them to play all night if the mood took them. Since Cream only had two albums' worth of material to draw on, it inevitably meant that songs needed to be padded out with long improvisational sections which could often extend to twenty minutes at a time. The combination of Graham's far-sighted approach, the prevailing appetite for songs that went beyond the traditional three-minute format and the new drugs culture made Cream a smash with audiences at the Fillmore.

Drugs use was certainly nothing new to Ginger Baker, whose use of industrial quantities of heroin meant it was not unknown for him to throw up in the middle of one of his endless drum solos. While there, they employed the services of an underground chemist called Owsley to make their acid. An acolyte of the Grateful Dead, Owsley, whose real name was Augustus Owsley Stanley III, 'cooked' huge quantities of LSD (said to have reached 1.25 million doses in the two-year period to 1967). With acid so freely available, Clapton experimented with playing shows while on a trip. During one gig, he was so high he was not able to feel his hands or even know if he was actually holding a guitar or not. On another occasion, he became convinced that by playing different notes he could transform the audience into angels or Devils.

But the freedom of playing on drugs, with an audience listening on drugs, was a double-edged sword. Bruce described appearing at the Fillmore for the first time as a revelatory experience because the audience had, in effect, given them carte blanche to play anything they wanted for as long as they wanted. In reality, it was exactly the opposite of what the band needed. In his more lucid moments, a voice was already chipping away in Clapton's brain, warning him that what these three big musical egos needed was not a free pass to jam themselves into self-indulgent oblivion with the permission of a tripped-out audience, but the structure and economy that could have turned them into a seriously good band.

Even so, publicly, Eric was extolling the virtues of the chilled-out, inclusive West Coast scene, as compared to the cut-throat world of music in London. 'England could use a little more maturity,' he opined at the time. 'In San Francisco there is more encouragement and less competition from musician to musician. The scene in London thrives wildly, often because everyone is jealous of someone else's success. In the States you are encouraged. Everyone digs everyone else and they don't hide it. It seems the English market has been bred on immaturity. What they could learn from San Francisco is to be more minded to what is not Top Forty, and grow up a little.' The subtext of all this was, of course, Britain's love of Jimi Hendrix, who had almost completely usurped him as the new guitar god on the block, and the still-disappointing sales of Cream records back home.

San Francisco crowds were discerning, Clapton argued, with the unspoken dig that British ones weren't. 'They're the best anywhere,' he said of San Franciscan audiences. 'They're so obviously critical. Every little move you make, every note you play is being noticed, devoured, accepted or rejected. You know you have to do it right. You do your best because they know if you don't. We seem to be a lot more popular in San Francisco than I'd imagined. I knew the Cream had been heard of through the underground scene, but I didn't imagine we'd be this popular.'

Their first US tour lasted seven weeks, and they went back to New York to play two weeks at the Café au Go Go and the Village Theater. While they were in Manhattan, Ahmet Ertegun asked Eric to play on a track he was recording with Aretha

Franklin called 'As Good to Me as I Am to You'. There was no time to rest. Cream came back to Britain in triumphant mood. But while their reputation was mushrooming in the States, back home, they found themselves in a quandary. Not yet big enough to play large venues, they had out-priced themselves from the middle-sized venues because of their success across the pond, and going back to the club circuit was not an option. The problem was solved by Stigwood booking them almost immediately on another mammoth five-month tour of America.

Once again back in the States and hanging out in Los Angeles meant meeting like-minded people. Clapton palled up with Stephen Stills of Buffalo Springfield, who invited him to go to his ranch in Topanga Canyon for the weekend in March 1968. Eric arrived with actress Mary Hughes, a blonde all-American girl from Southern California with a taste for rock stars. But the party came to an abrupt end when the house was raided by the cops and nineteen members of Buffalo Springfield and their hangers-on, including Clapton, were hauled off to the Malibu sheriff's office and thence to the LA county jail, accused of smoking dope. Eric was thrown in a cell with a bunch of black guys for the weekend, during which, presumably, he questioned whether his choice of a pair of bright-pink boots might not, in hindsight, have been his best move. Finally, he was bailed out by Ertegun, who as well as identifying Clapton as a solo star in the making, had taken a genuine paternal interest in his wellbeing. On 4 June, he was found not guilty on charges of being present in a room where marijuana was being smoked, after denying the charge. It was a close shave though. If he had been convicted, it would have been the end of Cream in America.

Already, the band was a huge cash cow. Stigwood was negotiating big fees for their seemingly never-ending tours, the latest of which had generated an advance for the band of £500,000, and when they returned to London that summer *Disraeli Gears* was the biggest-selling album in the US and 'Sunshine of Your Love' was a hit single.

But the pressure of energy-sapping touring only exacerbated the tension between Bruce and Baker. Now Clapton joined in the clash of egos. During one London gig, Jack stormed off stage halfway through, leaving Eric and Ginger to carry on without him. Where before they had all insisted on staying on different floors of a hotel, now they wanted separate hotels, and they took to arriving at gigs in their own limousines, just a few minutes before they were due on stage, before traipsing on in silence. Worse – much worse, as far as Clapton was concerned – they had become complacent. Later he recalled: 'I began to be quite ashamed of being in Cream, because I thought it was a con.'

Perversely perhaps, given their popularity, he came to the conclusion that they were already stagnating. What appeared to the outside world to be the band's musical highlights left him cold. A case in point was Clapton's two blistering solos on a live version of 'Crossroads', recorded at the Winterland Ballroom in San Francisco in early March 1968, which appeared on Cream's double album *Wheels of Fire*. His guitar work on the tracks reached new heights of innovation and intensity, with the expert prompting of Bruce and Baker holding him back one minute and the next, pushing him headlong into faster and more furious flurries of notes. There remains some conjecture as to whether the final track was edited down by engineer Tom Dowd – Clapton says the original may have been as long as eleven minutes. Others insist that the version that appears on the record, which comes in at just over four minutes, was exactly the way it was played on the night. Whatever the truth, the two guitar breaks – and particularly the second one – continue to be cited in every guitar magazine poll to this day as among the best solos ever committed to tape.

Even with the benefit of hindsight, Clapton himself has long struggled to understand the track's almost mythical reputation. 'There's a couple of big myths about me,' he told *Rolling Stone* in 1988. 'This thing about God and this thing about "Crossroads". I think that's a terrible solo. I really appreciate that respect for it, but I can't figure out what the hell they're talking about.' So what's so wrong with it? 'It's messy!' he argues. 'I admit it's got tons of energy, but that alone doesn't make it. I've always had that held up as like, "This is one of the great landmarks of guitar playing." But most of that solo is on the wrong beat. Instead of playing on the two and the four, I'm playing on the one and the three and thinking, "That's the offbeat." No wonder people think it's so good – because it's fucking wrong.'

For all that, Clapton remains pretty much in a minority of one on the subject. But his negativity was as much to do with the crushingly bad atmosphere within Cream as it was with his apparently dodgy timekeeping. Holed up at the Huntington Hotel in San Francisco, he began talking about his 'longing' for solitude. Meanwhile, he started comparing Cream, who were riding a crest of a wave, with the likes of B.B. King, who was acting as their support on tour, and finding the comparisons were not favourable. And matters were not helped when a review in *Rolling Stone* by critic Jon Landau, who went on to be a record producer and Bruce Springsteen's manager, described Clapton as 'the master of the blues cliché'. 'Clapton's problem', Landau added, 'is that while he has a vast creative potential, at this time he hasn't begun to fulfil it. He is a virtuoso at performing other people's ideas.' When he read it, Eric was said to have been so devastated he almost fainted. Then he rang up Stigwood to say he wanted out. His rattled manager persuaded Clapton to do one more tour.

Elsewhere, there was a general sense of things disintegrating. In a bid to show what a good time they were all having, Eric, Ginger and Jack bought a red Chevrolet in Stigwood's name in LA and proceeded to wreck it after taking a road trip to Death Valley, where they bought guns and fired wildly at passing cacti. But they were kidding no one.

During one gig at the Village Theater in New York, a disgruntled Clapton walked off stage and watched from the wings as bass player and drummer carried on, not even noticing he had gone. Around the same time, a Wall Street bond dealer called Martin Forbes found himself walking up Eighth Avenue to his apartment on West 71st Street and discovered a man sitting in a white shirt on a bench. He had a satchel on his lap and was smoking a cigarette. This being New York, he walked on, but turned back because he got the impression something was wrong. When he reached the man, he could see he was crying. Finally, the man looked up, his face suddenly illuminated by the street lamp, and Forbes could see that this tormented visage belonged to Eric Clapton, a young man with, apparently, the world at his feet. 'It got to the point', Clapton observed later, 'where we were playing so badly and the audience were still going raving mad – they thought it was a gas. But I thought, we're conning them, we're cheating them. We're taking their bread and playing them shit. I couldn't work on that basis.'

But the pressure to make more and more money kept them hard at it. They went back into the studio in London and New York with Pappalardi and Dowd to make *Wheels of Fire*, which included the excellent Jack Bruce/Pete Brown-penned 'White Room', plus the 1930s blues standard 'Sitting on Top of the World' and a remake of Albert King's Stax classic 'Born Under a Bad Sign'. Sides three and four of the album were given over to live versions of 'Crossroads', 'Spoonful', 'Toad' and 'Traintime'.

But to Clapton, the record already seemed old hat. His opinion was only reinforced when a friend, Alan Pariser, an LA businessman, played him *Music from Big Pink*, the debut album by Canadian outfit the Band. Eric was hooked on the rootsy feel and uncluttered playing. It only confirmed his feeling that Cream were in a rut. He began calling Stigwood on an almost daily basis to tell him he wanted to go home. He was sick of being a virtuoso in a band of virtuosos. He was exhausted. They were all exhausted. For his part, Stigwood was getting it in the neck from all three of them. Jack would call to complain about Ginger, Ginger would ring to whine about Jack, and Eric would be on bitching about the pair of them. But Stigwood was privately telling Clapton that if he wanted to quit, then he was the horse he was planning to back. Clapton told Ray Coleman: 'He was saying in so many words, "You're the one I pick. So if you don't like it with them, don't worry. I'll look after you. I'll take care of them later. But you've got big things ahead of you, so if you want to break the band up, don't worry about it, because we can go somewhere else."'

As *Wheels of Fire* went to number one in America and number three in Britain after its release in August 1968, Stigwood flew to New York to arrange a final tour. At the same time, the news was leaked out. Clapton gave an interview to Chris Welch of *Melody Maker* confirming their decision to go their separate ways after the tour. 'I've been on the road seven years and I'm going on a big holiday,' he said. 'I went off on a lot of different things since the Cream formed. I went off on a lot of different directions all at one, but I have floated back to what I like doing as an individual, and that is playing exploratory blues. You get really hung up trying to write pop songs or create a pop image. I went through that stage and it was a shame because I am and always will be a blues guitarist.'

That autumn, Cream embarked on a farewell tour of the States that involved them playing fifteen shows in nine cities over a month-long period. The tour, which saw them play to 22,000 people at Madison Square Garden at the beginning of November, grossed $700,000 and meant that, if nothing else, Clapton was leaving Cream a very rich 23-year-old. A week or so earlier, three songs, including 'Sitting on Top of the World' and 'I'm So Glad', were recorded at a show at the Forum in Los Angeles. They would appear on a final album, appropriately enough called *Goodbye*, which would not be released until February 1969, three months after Cream disbanded. Again, Felix Pappalardi was brought in to take on the role of producer. A sad postscript is that Pappalardi would come to a sticky end. On 17 April 1983, he was shot and killed by his wife, Gail Collins, with a .38 Derringer pistol at their apartment on New York's East River after he returned home from a night out with his mistress. Collins, who got a writing credit with Clapton and Pappalardi for 'Strange Brew', claimed the shooting was an accident that happened, bizarrely, during a 6 a.m. firearms training session. A jury convicted her of criminally negligent homicide.

Cream played two farewell gigs at the Royal Albert Hall in London. For their final show, on 26 November 1968, Clapton gave every impression that he had moved on, literally and figuratively. A few months earlier, he had appeared on stage done up to the nines in a flower-power melange of beads, flowing multi-coloured robes and bell bottoms. Now his hair was shorter and he wore an unfussy rodeo-style shirt and Levis. His outfit seemed to say that from now on, the emphasis would be on frugality, on a pared-down, simpler approach to life and music, on substance over style.

Ultimately, the Cream experience had left him conflicted. On the one hand, he appeared to have bought into the ethos of Baker and Bruce – that he was right to break free of the supposed stranglehold a strict adherence to the blues had over his creativity. Indeed, a year after the group disbanded, he was telling the *Daily Sketch*: 'I don't mind playing that stuff for my own pleasure, but blues can be awfully boring to listen to.' At the same time, however, he was lamenting that the supergroup trio had failed to live up to his – and everyone else's – expectations. 'People expected so much of us, we could not live up to it,' he said. 'Now there's a bit of disillusionment on the part of the public. What I want now is to become a bit less known as a guitarist, a bit better known as a singer.'

Later still, he observed: 'Cream was a shambling circus of diverse personalities who happened to find that catalyst together. And when it burnt out, it burnt out. We couldn't save it and probably didn't want to until later. We all had regrets over the years. I miss those good times, the companionship. I have never been, since then, with two other guys I felt so completely akin with. I also got hurt quite a lot in that band, really badly hurt, and ever since then, I have managed to keep a certain amount of distance between myself and the other musicians I've worked with. I won't let anyone get that close to me anymore.'

His new philosophy of detached self-preservation would come unstuck, however, when it came to his destructive relationship with the wife of his best friend.

# SEVEN

# Pattie

Amid the brooding, Gothic splendour of a vast baronial hall, the fires were roaring and the candles lit in readiness for the late-evening arrival of an unwanted guest. For the past hour, George Harrison had been pacing the floor of Friar Park, his labyrinthine and darkly forbidding estate in Henley-on-Thames, in readiness. En route was Eric Clapton, his foot to the metal of his Ferrari Dino as he raced through the winding roads towards George's imposing country residence. Harrison's plan for the evening was simple and age old: they would fight a duel for the hand of a beautiful woman, who would be present to witness the contest. His strategy may have been heavy with eighteenth-century melodrama, but George had chosen very modern weapons for this bout of armed combat. Instead of pistols, foils or épées, they would take each other on with electric guitars and amplifiers. To the winner would go the spoils of the battle – Harrison's beautiful wife, Pattie Boyd.

Eric and George had become friends way back in Eric's Yardbirds days. When Clapton later moved into the Pheasantry during his time with Cream, George was a regular visitor, stopping by on his way home from the studio to sit and jam together. Likewise, Clapton was often to be found at George's house, at that time a bungalow called Kinfauns in the Surrey stockbroker belt of Esher, where they would take acid and hang out. As far back as June 1967, Eric had played on 'All You Need Is Love', when the Beatles and friends performed during a live global TV extravaganza called *Our World*. The following November, George called in Clapton to perform the effortlessly tasteful guitar solo on Harrison's song 'While My Guitar Gently Weeps', from the Beatles' *White Album*. George returned the favour by co-writing 'Badge', arguably Cream's best song, on their *Goodbye* album. George, who played the famous 'rotating' rhythm guitar part on the track, was credited in the sleeve notes under the pseudonym L'Angelo Misterioso. The song's title came about when Eric misread George's writing and mistook the word 'bridge', as in 'bridge section', for 'badge'.

However, the relationship between the two men was not without its bumps in the road, even before Eric set his sights on George's wife Pattie. Once, when Cream were on tour in America, word reached Harrison that Clapton was letting all and sundry listen to an acetate, or early test copy, of *The White Album*. The Beatle immediately pulled rank and rang Clapton to give him a 'huge bollocking'. Those who know them say Clapton did not take the dressing-down well. It was allowed to fester and a hurt and humiliated Eric retreated from the friendship for some time. Clapton himself would say that from then on, he was nervous of letting his guard down around George.

At the beginning of 1969, Eric was forced to go to ground after Ginger Baker warned him he'd heard on the grapevine that the notorious Sergeant Norman Pilcher of Scotland Yard had him in his sights and he needed to get out of town. Pilcher had built a reputation for busting rock stars in the hope of pinning drugs charges on them. Mick Jagger, Keith Richards, Brian Jones and, later, Harrison all found themselves the subject of his investigations. Eric immediately made his escape and went to stay with his manager, Robert Stigwood, at his half-timbered Elizabethan mansion in Brooks Hill, Stanmore, called the Old Barn. That night, the Pheasantry was raided by the police, but Eric had not thought to warn his flatmate, Martin Sharp, and the other residents that the boys in blue were planning to pay them a call.

Anyway, with the money he was earning, it was time for Clapton to invest in a home of his own. He found it in the form of Hurtwood Edge, a beautiful, if rundown, Italian-style villa, perched on the top of a hill between Shere and Ewhurst, with a balcony, arched windows and porticos, leading to a tiled terrace, and all set in woodland that gave way to uninterrupted views across the Surrey countryside. It had been empty for two years and had no furniture. But what it had in abundance was solitude, tranquillity and peace, and Eric fell in love at first sight, paying £30,000 for it in early 1969.

Built in 1910, the house was designed by Arthur Bolton and had a living room with three sets of windows and a formal parterre planted with palm trees, poplars and redwoods, like a Mediterranean garden. Clapton moved in and parked his ancient Douglas motorbike in the living room. Eventually, he brought in David Mlinaric, an interior designer, as well antiques dealer Christopher Gibbs, and together they did the place out with Persian and Moroccan hangings and carpets and a four-poster bed. Meanwhile, Eric bought Rose and Jack a cottage a few miles away in Shamley Green.

That just left his girlfriend of two years, Charlotte Martin. As she was making her mind up about whether to quit Chelsea for a life of bucolic bliss, Clapton wrote to her calling off the affair and announced he had 'pressing NEW arrangements'. Increasingly they involved Harrison and his stunning wife. Having been unceremoniously dumped, Charlotte left for Paris and went on to have a long relationship with Led Zeppelin guitarist Jimmy Page. Now single, Eric had more and more time to make the thirty-minute drive to Esher to visit with the Harrisons. However, he found that he would often come away with a gnawing sense of emptiness. 'I was certain I was never going to meet a woman quite that beautiful for myself,' he told writer Ray Coleman. 'I knew that. I knew I was in love. I fell in love with her at first sight – and it got heavier and heavier for me.'

That first encounter had taken place backstage at a Cream gig at the Saville Theatre in London a couple of years earlier, where the Beatles' manager, Brian Epstein, who had recently bought the theatre, was throwing a party. In his 2007 autobiography, Clapton wrote of her effect on him: 'It was her entire being, and the way she carried herself that captivated me. I had never met a woman who was so complete. I was overwhelmed.' For her part, Pattie thought Eric was exciting to watch on stage and very sexy. But when they were introduced, he was reticent and very unlike a rock star. The more he saw Pattie, the more he laid on a puppy-dog routine, finding an excuse to sit next to her, complimenting her on the food she cooked or her clothes. It worked too, because what Clapton could not have known was that this was the kind of thing that her husband George no longer did.

As far as Clapton was concerned, Pattie fitted his criteria for the perfect woman to a tee. Posh, pert and blonde, she had a sexy gap-toothed smile and little-girl looks. The daughter of a fighter pilot and eldest of six children, she was born in March 1944 in Taunton, Somerset. Like Eric, she was from a broken home and after her parents divorced she'd had little contact with her father from the age of nine. The family later moved to Kenya and on her return, Pattie was enrolled in a private boarding school, which she left at seventeen without taking her A levels. At eighteen, she became a model, landing the role of the 'Smith's crisps girl' in a TV advert. A year later, in 1964, she met Harrison on the set of Dick Lester's *A Hard Day's Night*, when she was cast as one of a trio of schoolgirl fans smitten by the Beatles. She and George married at Esher Register Office in January 1966.

Pattie may have been the primary reason to be jealous of Harrison, but Clapton's feelings of envy also extended to George's cars, his money and the power that went with being a Beatle. And while their friendship was based on mutual respect and warmth, there was something else in the relationship for both men: Harrison offered Clapton an entrée to his inner circle and the chance to hang out with the likes of Bob Dylan and Jimi Hendrix, and in return Eric would give the Beatle informal guitar lessons, showing him how to bend a string properly, when they hung out at Hurtwood. Indeed, George wrote 'Here Comes the Sun' in the garden at Clapton's new house in April 1969, after 'sagging off' from the Beatles' Apple headquarters to visit his friend. Hurtwood soon proved itself a muse for Eric too, and he wrote the spiritual 'Presence of the Lord' about finding the house.

What he really needed, however, was a group to perform the song with. In the wake of Cream's demise, Eric had kept his hand in by joining other people's bands for ad hoc performances, including the Rolling Stones, when they recorded *The Rolling Stones Rock and Roll Circus* at a studio in Wembley in December 1968. The film, made for the BBC, was not released for another twenty-eight years because the Stones, who were unhappy with their performance, refused to allow it to be aired.

Now his thoughts turned to assembling a band of his own once more. Having been vetoed by the other members of Cream over recruiting Steve Winwood (in fact, in the latter days of the band, he had again tried in vain to persuade Jack and Ginger of the merits of hiring Winwood, in the hope it might keep Cream together longer), Eric now sought out the singer and keyboard player about starting a new group. He began hanging out at Winwood's house in Berkshire, where they played songs to each other. But word got out, because one day, Ginger Baker arrived out of the blue. Eric was not happy to see him.

Given the nightmare of infighting and angst that Cream had been, Ginger was, of course, the last person Clapton wanted in the new group. In reality, neither he nor Winwood had a say in the matter. Ginger simply pitched up uninvited at the band's first official meeting, announced he was in and asked when they would be kicking off. It was out of a mixture of embarrassment and pure fear that they didn't have the heart – or the guts – to tell the pugnacious Ginger he was not wanted. Deep down, Eric knew he should have spoken up, but he was so set on working with Winwood that he did not let on that every fibre of his being was telling him that, given the turbulence and angst of the Cream years, working with Ginger again would be doomed to failure.

Baker was far from the only problem. From the very outset, Clapton, who brought in bass player Rick Grech to join them, was concerned about the obvious anxiety that being in the next supergroup – to be called Blind Faith – was causing Winwood. Indeed, with Baker on board, the music press was already labelling the band 'Cream Mark 2'. And once they started touring, Eric was instantly aware of how ill-prepared they were. In fact, the group's amusingly prophetic name was possibly one of the only things that any real thought had been given to. 'Steve and I were just trying to get to know each other,' Clapton recalls. 'And the next thing, we were on stage. We didn't know what we wanted to sound like. We were enjoying each other's company musically, but we hadn't got an act for anyone to see.'

Which only made the decision to make their first live appearance in that most low-profile of ways – a free concert for 100,000 people in Hyde Park – all the more head-scratching. The gig, the first rock show to be held in the London park, took place on 7 June 1969, and would be their only major British appearance. From the beginning, things did not go well. Before the show, in Stigwood's office that day, a furious Eric suspected Ginger was back on heroin, which he knew the drummer used as a crutch in stressful situations. For his part, Clapton has few memories of the gig on that sunny afternoon, admitting he 'zoned out'. Matters were made worse by the fact that they did not have enough amplification and sounded weak and underpowered. Nobody really seemed to know what they were doing. At one point, one member of the crowd bellowed: 'It's not Cream, Eric, it's Blind Faith, play what you want,' in the hope of goading him into action. By the time he came off stage, Clapton was shaking with rage and humiliation. And his resentment towards Ginger only intensified as they went straight from the gig to a tour of Scandinavia.

The problems did not stop there. Clapton hired photographer Bob Seidemann to shoot the cover for the band's eponymous album. Instead of a picture of the band, it featured an eleven-year-old schoolgirl called Mariora Goschen, who was pictured topless and holding a silver model plane designed by Eric's friend, the jeweller Micko Milligan. Clapton loved the shot so much he said they should only put the band's name on the wrapper, so that underneath would be the 'virgin' photograph. But the cover caused a massive outcry, particularly in America, where it was described as 'obscene and salacious'. A worried Stigwood was told that 70 per cent of US record dealers were refusing to stock it. With 250,000 advance orders placed, a rapid retreat was made and at the last moment they had to change the cover to a picture of the band in the living room at Hurtwood.

Clapton had envisaged the new group being a British version of the Band, of whom he was a big fan. But despite his long-held desire to be a singer, in the event, he lost his nerve and summarily abdicated the vocal duties to Winwood, even on 'Presence of the Lord', which had been one of Eric's first serious attempts at songwriting. Eric's excuse was that because he wrote it in the key of C, it was too high for him. But the reality was that he was overwhelmed by the multi-talented Winwood's presence as a singer. 'I don't think I could have stood in the studio and sung it while he was there,' Clapton admitted later. Nonetheless, the album was not without its high points, especially Winwood's touching 'Can't Find My Way Home'.

And, like Cream, Blind Faith was making them a fortune. When the album was released that August, it went to number one in the UK, Canada and America, where it also went platinum. Meanwhile, 20,000 fans showed up for their first New York concert at Madison Square Garden on 12 July, at the start of a seven-week tour which saw them earn $20,000 a night. Astonishingly, however, they had only an hour's worth of material and frequently submitted to shouted requests from the audience to do Cream and Traffic songs. In America, particularly in New York and Los Angeles, there was violence in the crowds. But worse than that, all too soon, it had become obvious that Blind Faith was guilty of what Clapton had sworn he would never do – selling himself and the fans short. In hindsight, Clapton admitted mournfully that Blind Faith was 'my only regret. It wasn't given time to work.'

Steve Winwood remembered: 'The management and the record company joined our own greed. You can't really blame them or us. There was a multi-million-dollar time bomb out there. We wanted to work, so we said, "Oh, let's go and earn the bucks!"' But while the money was rolling in, Clapton was already planning his way out. On tour in the US, Blind Faith's support band was a duo called Delaney & Bonnie, which consisted of husband and wife Delaney and Bonnie Bramlett, plus their backing musicians. They had the distinction of being the first white group to be signed by the legendary Memphis-based record label Stax, on which Otis Redding had recorded.

Eric was immediately a huge fan of their album *The Original Delaney and Bonnie – Accept No Substitute*. Nor did he relish going on stage each night after them, because he thought they were 'miles better'. The couple were backed by a team of expert Southern musicians, including Carl Radle on bass, Jim Gordon on drums, keyboard player Bobby Whitlock, Jim Price on trumpet and sax player Bobby Keys, with Rita Coolidge joining Bonnie on vocals.

Soon, rather than travelling with Winwood, Baker and co., Eric was travelling between gigs on Delaney & Bonnie's tour bus, sitting on the back seat strumming guitars and kicking back. And the musical attraction was mutual. The duo began courting him. Before long, Delaney was whispering in Clapton's ear that he must start singing and have his own band. By the time Blind Faith reached Honolulu at the end of August 1969 for their last gig, the idea of going solo had already begun to ferment.

The charismatic Delaney Bramlett had been born in tiny Pontotoc, Mississippi, in 1939 and began playing the guitar at the age of eight, before later joining the navy and arriving in Los Angeles in the early 60s. He lived there until his death in 2008 at the age of sixty-nine, and – oddly – his Southern twang only appeared to get stronger there. He formed a band called Shindogs, and they were playing at an LA bowling alley in 1967 when he met Bonnie Lynn O'Farrell. They were married the following week.

On his return to England, Clapton converted a top-floor room at Hurtwood into a rehearsal room to begin work on songs with Delaney & Bonnie for a tour, under the banner Delaney & Bonnie and Friends. With Delaney in the guise of part father figure, part mentor, part confessor and part evangelical faith healer, they began a tour of Germany, Britain and Scandinavia, and were joined by George Harrison, who was keen to sign Delaney & Bonnie to the Beatles' record label, Apple.

For Clapton, the new band was a breath of fresh air; organic, uncluttered and not motivated, so he thought, by the usual music-business greed for cash. During gigs, Clapton refused to do more than a couple of songs per show, much to the chagrin of audiences. And whereas Cream had stayed in five-star luxury on their later tours of the States, he happily bunked down at Delaney and Bonnie's small house in Sherman Oaks, California, which was also home to Delaney's mother. All the while, Delaney was positioning himself to produce Clapton's first solo album.

Through Delaney, he met Southern musicians like Leon Russell, who had a studio in North Hollywood, and together they introduced him to the music of singer and guitarist J. J. Cale – of which Eric was an instant fan. As far as Eric was concerned, he heard in the Oklahoma-born Cale everything he wanted to be as a musician. Cale was authentic, rootsy, passionate and unshowy. A master of his trade, he avoided the limelight to concentrate on what mattered most – the music. Delaney played him the original version of Cale's song 'After Midnight', which would appear on Clapton's debut solo album. The plan was to emulate Cale, to refine and simplify, to play enough and no more. Later, Eric said of the period post-Cream: 'I lost confidence because I thought I'd done it all. People were really infatuated with Cream, and, for me, it was just a passing stage. That's why I didn't play as much lead guitar on those albums in the seventies. I was very, very nervous that I'd said it all.'

In November 1969, recording began in earnest at Amigo Studios in Los Angeles. In keeping with the prevailing laid-back ethos, little serious preparation was done. Eric had already written one song, 'Let It Rain', but the rest he and Delaney made up in the car on the way to the studio. They would then record live almost without rehearsal. In many respects, the record they produced, the eponymously titled *Eric Clapton*, was actually a Delaney Bramlett album in disguise. As Clapton's time in Cream had illustrated, he was still nowhere near confident enough to impose himself as a bandleader in the way the experienced and truculent Bramlett could. (Bonnie was known to proclaim matter-of-factly that if she riled her fiery husband, he was quite likely to smack her in the mouth.) From Eric's point of view, he was quite happy to accept being led by the nose. Only later would he say: 'In a way, it was a vehicle for Delaney's frustrations with himself. He may have been projecting himself on me a lot. And that comes across on the record. I don't mind it at all. I enjoyed it and learnt a lot in the process.' (Nothing much changes. Thirty-six years later, when he made another album, *The Road to Escondido*, with J. J. Cale, he would once again more or less hand over the responsibility for the sound of one of his records to someone he admired and was somewhat in awe of.)

By way of explanation, Clapton says: 'If there is a forceful character in the mix, I will let it come out rather than try to alter the direction of things so I'm in the front. I don't like to compete musically. If you put me on stage with another guitar player and he starts showing off, I won't compete. I'll let him go. When it's my turn, I'll play what I'm going to play anyway.' Certainly, Delaney's role went way beyond simply de facto musical director. Throughout the recording of the album, he kept up a mantra, instilling in his disciple the belief that his gift was God-given and if he did not use it properly, it would be taken away again. While Clapton was fairly immune to the religious aspect of Bramlett's teachings, he was wide open to being coached in a way to live his life in music.

With Pattie Harrison apparently happily married to his best friend and very much off the agenda for now, Eric began dating the unimpeachably aristocratic Alice Ormsby-Gore, to whom he was introduced by his interior designer, David Mlinaric. The younger daughter of Lord David Harlech, the former British ambassador to the United States, she was beautiful, ethereal – and barely sixteen. She was also a virgin whose experience of the opposite sex was at best limited. Nonetheless, she moved into Hurtwood almost immediately, wafting around on the outdoor terrace in flowing Arabic-inspired clothes. If the seven-year age gap bothered him, Eric was not showing it, although he would later insist that sex was not a big part of their lives and, for the most part, they were like brother and sister, happy to hang around smoking dope and listening to music.

And love was out of the question, given that he was already madly obsessed with Pattie. Which only really left one possibility – that he was using the impressionable Alice until the woman he really wanted became available. Certainly, the thought that Alice was already his victim had not escaped his mind. With the benefit of hindsight, he wrote in his memoirs: 'I had a terrible fear that getting attached to an upper-class girl like her was part of a childhood resentment, connected to my feelings about my mother, to bring down women, and that deep inside I was thinking, "Here's an Ormsby-Gore, and I'm going to make her suffer."'

Not that having Alice on the scene put paid to his pursuit of Pattie. In December 1969, Pattie and George, plus Ringo Starr and his wife Maureen, went to see Eric play with Delaney & Bonnie at the Albert Hall, followed by a heavy late-night drinking session at the Speakeasy. Within the space of a few days, they would all meet again, when Pattie took her younger sister, Paula, who was seventeen at the time, to Liverpool to see Delaney & Bonnie and Friends again, this time with George joining them and Eric on stage.

Paula, the prettiest of the Boyd sisters, was a proto-wild child with her sights set on becoming an actress, but who caused her mother nightmares with her taste for overly short skirts and too much make-up. She'd been sent off to boarding school in the hope that it would sort her out, but to no avail. Following the Liverpool Empire gig, they all crowded into a restaurant and proceeded to get riotously drunk. As the rest trooped off to bed, Eric and Paula stayed behind dancing, much to the anger of George, who, Pattie would later say, felt a big brotherly protection towards his wife's little sister. Clapton, however, remembers the events of the evening slightly differently. According to him, George drunkenly proposed to Eric that he should spend the night with Pattie so he could get it on with Paula. Clapton, unsurprisingly, was not averse to the idea and took the suggestion in his stride. But when push came to shove, Harrison backed out, and Eric and Paula spent the night together. The following night, Pattie and Paula were in

Croydon to watch Eric and co. again, before piling back to Hurtwood for another party. When, a few days later, Clapton had a row with Alice, she took off to her ancestral home, Glyn Cywarch, near Gwynedd, and he moved Paula in. But the younger Boyd girl was very much the consolation prize.

It was at this time that a friend from his Pheasantry days, Ian Dallas, persuaded Eric to read the Persian love story *Layla and Majnun*. Originally a traditional poem, the story was later embellished and published by the twelfth-century Persian poet Nizami Ganjavi. It tells the tale of a young man who falls in love with the beautiful Layla. Forbidden to marry the girl of his dreams by her father, he goes mad. The story had deep resonance for Eric who cast himself in the role of Majnun – 'the possessed one' – with Pattie as the unattainable Layla.

The following month, George purchased the 120-room Friar Park in the Oxfordshire town of Henley-on-Thames. Until Harrison bought the Gothic revival house for £140,000, it had been owned by the Salesian Sisters of St John Bosco, who had run a Catholic teaching order there for more than twenty years. By the time he and Pattie moved in, the school had been shut down and half a dozen nuns and a lone monk were rattling around the building. With twenty-five bedrooms, a ballroom and library, spires, turrets, a miniature Matterhorn in the grounds made from 20,000 tons of Yorkshire granite, plus a replica of the Blue Grotto of Capri, it was spectacularly over the top.

Eric, already juggling his on-off relationship with Alice and his flirtation with Paula, began turning up. From the outside, it appeared the object of his affections was not Pattie, but yet another female – a blonde American whom George had hired to be a live-in personal assistant. Chris O'Dell was a Goldie Hawn lookalike and had worked for the Beatles' company, Apple, until George brought her home late one night, not long after he and Pattie had moved into Friar Park, announcing that she was moving in to help around the place. Pattie, who suspected the priapic George was cheating on her with no end of women, was not happy. But she and Chris quickly developed a close bond and agreed a pact that if George came on to her, which inevitably he did, Chris would rebuff him in order to maintain their friendship.

And Chris was certainly rock-star girlfriend material, having formerly dated another Clapton cohort, Leon Russell, who had written the song 'Blues Power' for Eric. But even she was in the dark about Eric's intentions towards Harrison's wife. 'I thought Eric liked me and was coming over to Friar Park all the time to see me,' says Chris. 'I liked him very much during that period and I didn't know about Eric and Pattie for a long time. I was the best friend who knew nothing. Eric would just show up and ask me if I wanted to come back to his house, so we became friends. He would call and I would go and spend a night or two at his place, but not in a romantic way. We'd go to a movie and he was really nice. But I did think it was a bit odd that he wasn't making a move on me.

'There was only one phone at Friar Park and it was in a little room by itself, which was very private, and sometimes Eric would call and talk to Pattie, or he would show up and he and George would hang. But it was during that time that I realised there wasn't really any hope for me and it was Pattie he was basically after.'

Finally, Eric plucked up the courage to tell Pattie how he

felt about her. The conversation did not go as planned. Pattie told him flatly that a relationship would be impossible. However, she agreed to him going over to Friar Park one evening while George was away, where they drank wine and ended up kissing. On the way back in his Ferrari Dino, a bit drunk, Eric took a bend too fast in Clandon, near Guildford, and turned it over. He crawled out from the wreckage shocked but unhurt and ran off because he did not have a driving licence, having not bothered to take his test, and hid out in a graveyard, before eventually returning to the twisted mass of metal that had once been his gleaming Italian sports car. Someone called an ambulance and Clapton was taken to Guildford hospital for a check-up. Fortunately for him, the police did not get involved.

A few days later, in the cavernous old kitchen at Friar Park, Pattie opened a letter which was marked 'express' and 'urgent'. It was from Eric, addressed to 'dearest l', and was written solely in lower case, with the odd spelling mistake. He described his domestic situation as a 'galloping farce' and went on to ask her if she still loved George or whether she had another lover. More pertinently, he inquired, did she have any feelings for him? If so, she was to write, not phone, and let him know one way or the other, so 'my mind will be at rest'. He signed it simply, 'love E'.

Pattie assumed the note was from one of the loonies who regularly wrote her either fan mail or hate letters – the latter mainly from Harrison's female fans, who were still smarting over the fact that she had bagged their favourite soon-to-be-ex-Beatle ahead of them. She even showed the letter to George, and they had a laugh about it, neither thinking for a minute that they actually knew the author. It wasn't until Clapton rang her that evening and asked if she'd got his letter that the penny dropped. It is telling, perhaps, that Pattie had no idea it was from Eric. Clearly, he had not been on her mind. But as was so often the case, Clapton's timing was perfect. While she may not have been overly interested in him before that point, she was a woman desperately seeking attention from her increasingly distant and unresponsive husband. The passion of the note piqued her interest and suddenly gave the flirtation with Eric more zing. However, as far as she was concerned, it was never going to amount to anything more than that.

Yet, as he made a play for Pattie, Eric was telling the press at the same time that there was a 'more than 50-50 chance' he and Alice, now back in situ at Hurtwood, would get married, despite the age difference. Meanwhile, Lord Harlech was publicly saying he had no objections to the seventeen-year-old Alice getting hitched to her musician lover. The goodwill was reciprocated by Eric, who insisted on calling his girlfriend's titled father Big H.

Around the same time, Clapton got a call from Carl Radle, the bass player in Delaney & Bonnie and Friends to say they had split up and did he want to get a band together with him and another couple of its ex-members, Bobby Whitlock and Jim Gordon? Eric was immediately interested. In his opinion, Radle and Gordon were the most powerful rhythm section he had played with, and Gordon the best rock and roll drummer ever. Indeed, he was happy to concede that his appreciation of their talents verged on awe. They moved into Hurtwood en masse and began jamming morning, noon and night, staying awake on a potent combo of coke and Mandrax sleeping pills.

'Mandies', as they were known, had become the drug of choice among the chemically minded, because if they were taken and the urge to sleep was stifled by taking a hit of a stimulant like coke, the result was to create an even better high. All this was topped up with lashings of brandy and vodka. Regular visits to the house were also made by Eric's drug dealer, who would insist on him buying smack – heroin – every time he scored coke, in a sort of two-for-one special offer. But with little interest in the heroin, Clapton would put it in a drawer and forget about it.

In May 1970, Harrison began work in London on his debut solo album *All Things Must Pass*, the cover of which had him sitting in Wellington boots on the lawn of Friar Park. Clapton and the rest of the 'Tulsa guys' – Radle, Whitlock and Gordon – effectively became George's backing band for the early parts of the sessions (Clapton's term for them was actually a misnomer, since only Radle actually hailed from Tulsa). In return, the record's producer, Phil Spector, agreed to oversee the making of two songs, 'Tell the Truth' and 'Roll It Over', at Abbey Road Studios for Clapton's next LP. In the event, neither of Spector's versions made it onto the album, though the Spector-produced 'Tell the Truth' was released as a single later that year.

With George focused on his new record, not to mention meditating morning, noon and night, he was increasingly a peripheral presence in his own marriage. Chris O'Dell, for whom George wrote the song 'Miss O'Dell', says: 'George was so involved in the house and Hare Krishna that he wasn't very emotionally available at that time. He was a distant figure. The Krishnas moved in and they were in the chapel all the time and there was a lot of competition that Pattie had to deal with, so Eric chose the perfect time to invade her life.'

Eric and Pattie began seeing each other. For such a high-profile couple, it was dating on a very traditional level. Clapton took her to see the Ken Loach film *Kes*, about a troubled teenager who forms a close bond with a wild kestrel. As they walked down Oxford Street afterwards, Eric asked her: 'Do you like me, then, or are you just seeing me because I'm famous?' Pattie replied that she thought he was only seeing her because *she* was famous. The complications of the situation were lost on nobody, however. Not just because of Pattie's marriage to George, but Eric was still juggling Alice and Pattie's sister Paula. To complicate matters further, Alice and Paula knew each other and were friends.

In truth, by this time, Clapton's obsession with Pattie had long since reached the point of no return. It had taken over his every waking moment and driven him to the point of madness. Eric was in love with her and desperately wanted her to call time on her marriage and run away with him.

Now even the ostrich-like George had begun to get an inkling that something was going on. So it was that he invited his rival over for their bout of musical duelling. Not that Eric was in the best shape for the encounter. He arrived at the Oxfordshire pile of the ex-Beatle somewhat the worse for wear, having sunk the best part of a bottle of brandy prior to leaving for what Harrison had billed as a 'little discussion'. Nor was George exactly preparing for a good clean fight. Not only had he set up an inferior instrument ready for his adversary, but knowing Eric's voracious taste for Courvoisier cognac, drunk inelegantly with lemonade, he would keep topping him up for the rest of the evening as they played. George, meanwhile, kept a clear head by sipping nothing stronger than tea that Pattie served with trays of cakes to keep them fortified. He would also need an impartial observer on hand, so joining the party of four was British actor John Hurt.

For two hours, as the fires crackled and the candles flickered in the otherwise dark hall, the two guitarists went head-to-head as they traded ever more impassioned licks, each attempting to slay the other with a barrage of frenzied notes. Throughout, they spoke not a word as they hunched over their instruments, barely making eye contact with their opponent. When, at last, there was silence, a clear winner had emerged, though there would be no handshakes and magnanimous back-slapping. In spite of, or possibly because of, the booze, Clapton had emerged victorious, Harrison the vanquished loser.

'George dearly needed a small audience,' Hurt later recalled. 'He got down two guitars and two amplifiers and put them in the hall. It was an extraordinary contest because George had quite clearly given him the inferior guitar and inferior amplifier. But Eric was unbeatable. Harrison got rattled and tried to be too clever, whereas Clapton concentrated on playing a few meaningful notes in contrast to Harrison's instrumental gymnastics.'

Clapton may have won the musical skirmish, but his battle to win Pattie's heart was far from over, and it would be infinitely more protracted and painful.

# EIGHT

# Exile

Faced with an increasingly tangled home life, it was no surprise that Eric started looking for an escape. He asked George's ex-PA, Chris O'Dell, who was then just leaving Apple, to find a flat in town as a base for him and his musicians. She rented a beautifully appointed two-storey flat above an estate agent, opposite South Kensington tube station. It had high ceilings, an upright piano and a crystal chandelier. For the next two months, Chris moved in to look after Clapton and his band. She says Eric would arrive at the flat, gloomy and complaining that he couldn't be with the woman he loved. 'He'd talk to me about Pattie and he told me how much in love with her he was,' says Chris. 'I think he wanted it to be finally out in the open about them.'

Occasionally, Pattie would arrive and sit on the sofa next to Eric, their knees touching, and they would look longingly into each other's eyes. It put Chris in an uncomfortable situation. 'I wasn't at all happy about it because Pattie and George were like my family,' she says. 'George was like a brother to me, but Pattie was also my friend. But I wasn't going to say I didn't want to be a part of it because it wasn't my flat. I just felt sorry for George, even though I knew he wasn't an angel either. He had his own little things going on. It wasn't like he was this committed puritan.

'But what was happening between Pattie and Eric seemed much more threatening than what George was up to. Pattie was at a point where she was so tired of George's infidelities and his non-emotional behaviour to her. He was not paying much attention to her and then along comes someone who was paying all this attention and declaring undying love. Of course she was going to be swayed by that. I think there was an element with Pattie that this was a way to get George's attention because she still loved him. I would go so far as to say that George was the true love of her life. I think she hoped that George would get jealous and start acting more intimately with her.'

Certainly, Pattie was giving no sign to Eric that she was considering leaving her husband for him. Increasingly, Eric would spend evenings in a foul mood, moaning about his lot and about being in love with his friend's wife to the others. His anger over his plight erupted one night at the house. Chris says Eric picked up a glass and threw it against the wall, forcing her to duck to avoid flying glass and put her hands over her eyes. After seconds of shocked silence, Jim Gordon, already a heroin addict, threw his plate of egg and beans on toast at the ceiling and it collected in the chandelier. They all broke into fits of hysterical laughter and Eric threw another glass. Finally, the place trashed, they settled down to get drunk and take some coke. Then, on their last night at the flat, Eric and the others came back from an Indian restaurant drunk and thoroughly wrecked the place, throwing glasses full of red wine at the walls and smashing every piece of crockery in the kitchen. Back in the living room, Clapton bowled a full ashtray, cricket-style, at the wall and smashed up the crystal from the wine cabinet. Someone threw a glass at the TV and the screen exploded. Chris says she was left to face the estate agent the following day. 'Eric was letting out his anger and I think everyone else just followed suit,' she remembers. 'Eric's frustration was really intense at that point because Pattie was not moving in with him. She was staying with George and that was fairly apparent. So it was a very tough time for Eric. He was really hurt. His mood would affect everyone and it wasn't helped by the fact that Jim Gordon, whom I was dating at the time, was high on heroin and Carl Radle definitely was too.'

Clapton began a tour with his band, which he had named the Dominos, on the understanding that they would play 'incognito' to crowds of fifty or so people in small clubs and town halls. At the end of August, they flew to Miami to begin work on a double album, under the name Derek And the Dominos, which would arguably go on to become his finest ever work. It finds him mining the seams of his desolation over the seemingly hopeless quest to get Pattie to stunning artistic effect, producing the most tortured, heartfelt singing and playing of his career.

Meanwhile, Eric asked Chris O'Dell to move into Hurtwood while he was away. 'It was such a beautiful house,' she says. 'Eric had a housekeeper, a husband and wife who lived in the front lodge, and they took care of the place. He'd had a decorator in and it was well fitted out, with lovely curtains in the living room and main sitting room, and there was a den with a TV in it. The bedrooms all had beautiful furniture. But the kitchen was really old fashioned, a bit boring, so while he was away, I painted it orange and yellow to liven it up because it was just so drab!'

On the surface, the omens for the record, *Layla and Other Assorted Love Songs*, did not look that promising. Not least because none of those involved in the making of it were in the best possible shape. During the recording at Criteria Studios, the preparation for nights ingesting vast quantities of weapons-grade narcotics was approached with a boot camp-like mentality. By some unspoken diktat, it was decided that in order to get so monumentally wasted during late nights in the studio and still be able to make music, all the musicians should concentrate on getting as fit as possible for the fray. So, by day, a healthy regime of energetic swimming sessions, saunas and sunbathing was called for. When the sun went down, it was a different matter. The hotel where they were staying on Miami Beach had a new take on room service; the girl in the gift shop would take drug orders and deliver them in a paper bag later the same day. So, on a nightly basis, Clapton and co. were collecting their daily doses of smack, coke and the hallucinogenic PCP.

To impose some order on the proceedings, Clapton called in Tom Dowd, the engineer on Cream's albums, to produce. And not long after their arrival in Florida, they brought in 23-year-old slide guitarist Duane Allman because they were so impressed with him when Dowd took them to see the Allman Brothers play at the Coconut Grove. Eric agreed that Duane's guitar playing was great, despite falling asleep, stoned, during the show, and they took him back to the studio that night to jam. The two had an instant affinity. 'Between the two of us, we injected the substance into the *Layla* sessions that had seemed to be missing so far,' Clapton said later. 'He was like a musical brother.'

Allman's recruitment was, consciously or otherwise, in keeping with Clapton's attempts to take as much of a back seat as possible. Paradoxically, however, this was also his most personal album. In some way or other, all of the songs were either about or for Pattie (he wrote 'Bell Bottom Blues' because Pattie had asked him to buy jeans for her in America). Meanwhile, 'Have You Ever Loved a Woman', a cover of the song recorded by Freddie King in 1960, included the anguished line, 'She belongs to your very best friend,' and ends, 'Something deep inside of you won't let you wreck your best friend's home.' Likewise, the title track was a plaintive and desperate plea to Pattie to give up George for him. But for all that the album, and 'Layla' in particular, was a primal cry of anguish laid out in all its rawness, there was still an element of self-protection going on. 'It wasn't Eric Clapton singing those songs. It was Derek, of the Dominos,' Eric reasoned. 'So I'd already shifted one move to protect myself. And it also wasn't Eric singing about Pattie, it was Derek singing about Layla. There were a lot of subconscious shifts to protect my ego, to protect my mind.'

When he'd arrived in Florida, the track was unfinished. The iconic 'Layla' riff, added later, was actually a fairly literal recreation of the notes of the vocal motif in the Albert King song 'As the Years Go Passing By' from the Mississippi-born bluesman's 1976 album *Born Under a Bad Sign*, just speeded up a bit. For his part, Clapton was always happy to flag up where the inspiration for the guitar part came from. The second part of the song, a piano coda credited to Jim Gordon, featured

Allman's moving, almost whimpering – and occasionally out of tune – guitar.

Clapton's choice of guitar was also notable. In a marked change from his days in Cream, he recorded most of the album using a 1956 two-tone sunburst Fender Stratocaster, with a maple neck and fretboard, which he christened 'Brownie'. It would mark the beginning of maple-neck 'Strats' becoming the guitar he was most associated with for the rest of his career. He had purchased Brownie second-hand at Sound City in London on 7 May 1967, a few days before Cream flew to New York to record *Disraeli Gears*. He had been promising himself one since seeing Buddy Holly playing a maple-neck Stratocaster on television as a boy, and had been blown away by Buddy Guy's use of a Strat on an album called *Folk Festival of the Blues*, which was released in 1963. Later, he went to see Guy at the Marquee in London, and around the same time saw Steve Winwood playing the same instrument. Significantly, the guitar was also the weapon of choice for Jimi Hendrix. But Clapton was not taken with the rosewood fingerboards that Fender had begun putting on all Stratocasters from 1959, a trend that continued up to the mid-60s, saying the deeper grain of the wood made string bending harder, and he decided to find a second-hand model. The sound was markedly different from the Gibsons he was used to. Firstly, Fenders were routinely fitted with single-coil pickups, which produced a 'thinner', brighter sound than the 'fatter', warmer tone most associated with a Les Paul.

Eric invited Paula Boyd, whom he had kept dangling on a string, out to Miami and played her 'Layla' in the studio, and she knew at once it was about Pattie. Broken-hearted, Paula, who was deeply in love with him, packed her bags and left. She returned to England with her confidence shattered.

Emboldened by their capacity for mammoth drug-taking sessions during the six weeks it took to make the album, Clapton and his bandmates scored a massive amount of cocaine and heroin before they left Florida, in preparation for going on the road in the US. But by now, the joins were beginning to show. 'I don't know how we got through it with the amount we were taking.' Eric remembers of the tour. 'It definitely wore the band down and introduced a lot of hostility that wasn't naturally there.'

Amid the old-money confines of the elegant George V Hotel in Paris, a distinctly nouveau crowd gathered in the early autumn of 1970 to pay homage at the court of Mick Jagger and the other members of the Rolling Stones. On the guest list for a party to celebrate the release of the Stones' live album *Get Yer Ya-Ya's Out!* was Pattie Harrison. She may have been married to an ex-Beatle, but that wasn't going to stop the priapic Jagger making a play for her. 'Mick had a crush on Pattie and he called and asked me to bring Pattie to Paris, where the Stones were on a European tour, and hang out with them,' says Chris O'Dell, who would later work as a PA to Jagger. Certainly, it was no longer a secret that the Harrisons' marriage was in trouble. But in a welcome signal that Clapton's love might not have been in vain after all, it was not Mick that Pattie was interested in hooking up with. Chris goes on: 'When we got there, Pattie told me Eric was also going to be in town on his tour and she was going to see him. That's when their relationship was fully out in the open.'

Not one to waste time worrying about what might have been, Jagger spotted 25-year-old Bianca Perez-Mora Macias, who had arrived on the arm of her on-off boyfriend of five years, ageing French record label boss Eddie Barclay. Within a year, Bianca would become Jagger's first wife. The slight was not forgotten, however, and many years later, Jagger would take his revenge on Clapton for beating him to Pattie.

'Mick seemed pretty cool about it at the time,' says Chris. 'Pattie walked into Mick's suite at the George V with Eric, and Mick already had Bianca sitting on the sofa with him. People saw Eric and Pattie together for sure, but George still didn't know they were an item.'

The Dominos returned to England at the beginning of October 1970 to play at a charity gig at the Lyceum Theatre in London. After the show, Eric met Dr John, who had been in the audience. The Mississippi-born Cajun musician, real name Malcolm John Rebennack, had made an album a couple of years earlier called *Gris-Gris* and fancied himself as a voodoo doctor. Eric asked him for a love potion because he was in love with the wife of another man. Dr John gave him a small box made out of straw and told him to keep it in his pocket and follow various weird instructions to the letter. Clapton did as he was told.

Not long afterwards, Eric met Pattie at one of their assignations and he played her 'Layla'. He played it two or three times, watching her keenly to gauge her reaction. Pattie panicked, unsure whether she wanted to be led in the direction he was clearly intent on taking them. But it was also deeply flattering that such a song had been written about her. During their previous meetings, Pattie had resisted his physical advances. Now, seduced by the outpouring of passion in the song, she gave in and they slept together for the first time.

Steve Turner's 1976 book *Conversations with Eric Clapton* gives an insight into the dysfunctional dynamic of his relationship with Harrison and Pattie. Of the Beatle, Clapton said: 'We have had some really strange scenes. I'd go over to his house sometimes and he ends up throwing me out and then he comes over here and ends up throwing himself out. You see, he grabbed one of my chicks and so I thought I'd get even with him one day. And it grew from that. All Pattie wanted was for him to say, "I love you," and all he was doing was meditating. I feel now that she may have been trying to attract his attention, trying to make him jealous – and using me. And I fell madly in love with her.' Asked about what Pattie thought when she heard 'Layla', he added bluntly: 'I don't think she gave a damn.'

Following the consummation of their relationship, that night Eric, whether by accident or design, found himself at the bawdy Kenneth Tynan show *Oh! Calcutta!*, with its scenes of full-frontal nakedness that shocked Middle England. Pattie was there too and when she got back after the interval, Eric was sitting in the next seat, having asked the occupant to swap with him. Later that night, they went separately to a party at Robert Stigwood's house in Stanmore. George arrived very late and found Clapton and Pattie in the garden, just as dawn was about to break. He asked them what was going on and Eric replied: 'I have to tell you, man, that I'm in love with your wife.'

It did not elicit the reaction he'd anticipated. 'Pattie was mortified,' says Chris O'Dell, who was also a guest at the party.

'Pattie said to me that when Eric told George he was in love with her, she just wanted to die.' A furious Harrison asked Pattie if she was going home with him or leaving with Clapton. She replied: 'George, I'm coming home.' When they got back, Harrison skulked off to his recording studio, while Pattie went to bed. They never spoke about it again. 'It wasn't a comfortable position for Pattie because it's not in her personality to hurt someone,' says Chris O'Dell. 'She does not like confrontation. She felt very much in the middle and that they were competing over her and she was like an object to some degree in all of this. And I think George was very hurt. He might have appeared blasé about it, but of course it was hurtful to him. But he wouldn't show it; he would throw it off and say, "Oh well," but that's not how he was feeling.'

Despite the setback, Eric was not going to give up easily. For ten days, he ran a campaign of persuasion and pleading. One evening, he arrived out of the blue at Friar Park when Harrison was away and, over a glass of wine, desperately tried again to persuade her to leave George for him. Pattie explained that she was married and would not contemplate it. Theatrically, Eric produced a packet of heroin from his pocket and said: 'Well, if you're not going to come away with me, I'm going to take this.' Pattie tried to wrestle it off him, but he grabbed it and thrust it back into his pocket. 'That's it,' he said, 'I'm off.' Pattie would barely see him again for three years. Her rejection of him was the signal for Clapton to begin a retreat from the world and set a course towards seemingly inevitable self-destruction.

There was also bad news on the music front. For reasons that were not obvious, the first Derek and the Dominos single, the Phil Spector-produced 'Tell the Truth', was hurriedly recalled soon after its release, and when *Layla and Other Assorted Love Songs* came out in November, it bombed. The single version of 'Layla' only reached number fifty-one in the Billboard chart in America the following March. Part of the problem was that Clapton insisted on staying in character as his alter ego Derek and refused to do any interviews with the press for the album's launch. Stigwood and the UK record company, Polydor, realising they had a big flop on their hands, demanded badges be stuck on the cover of the LPs, proclaiming, 'Derek is Eric', which did rather give the game away. With the cat out of the bag, the album went gold in the US and silver in Britain. And when 'Layla', the single, was re-released the following year after appearing on a compilation, *The History of Eric Clapton*, it reached number seven in the UK and number ten in the US.

Understandably, Clapton viewed this belated success with some ambivalence. Had it originally died a death because the album simply wasn't that good? And when it did begin selling by the bucketload, was it on merit, or simply because people had got to know that Derek really was Eric? After much pondering, he decided he'd rather not know.

By this time, Eric's band – the Dominos – were on the rocks. It was not just dope that Clapton blames for the increasing infighting that was ultimately the death knell for the Dominos; money and women had also combined to form an unholy trinity. Things came to a head when Jim Gordon heard on the band grapevine that Eric had been speaking appreciatively about another drummer. While recording their aborted second album, he got up from his drum kit one day and told Clapton

**Above:** The two-up, two-down former almshouse in Ripley, Surrey, where Eric was born in 1945 and brought up by his grandparents Rose and Jack Clapp.

**Below:** Eric and his beloved Rose who casts a proud eye over her grandson and her silver tea set in 1971.

**Right:** Eric (left) with his first band the Roosters in 1963. Clapton fitted in rehearsals and gigs around his job on a building site working as his grandfather's gofer. But the group, which had Terry Brennan on vocals, lasted only six months.

**Left:** In the days before Armani and Versace, a 19-year-old Clapton (centre) shows off a clean-cut image – and several inches of pale calf – as he poses with the Yardbirds in June 1964.

**Left:** Eric, seen here playing a Fender Telecaster, built a growing reputation as a virtuoso guitarist during his stint in the Yardbirds, but his vehement opposition to commercialism left him isolated from his bandmates.

**Below:** A moody-looking Eric with fellow members of the Bluesbreakers in 1966 (left to right, John Mayall, John McVie and Hughie Flint). The previous year Clapton left Mayall in the lurch by disappearing off to Europe with a ragtag collection of musicians and friends in a shambolic band called the Glands.

**Above:** A bizarrely bespectacled Clapton with Jack Bruce (centre) and Ginger Baker in Cream (1966). The combative Jack once threw his double bass at the equally volatil drummer mid-way through a gig.

**Left:** Sporting a perm and an exotically painted Gibson SG, Clapton goes all psychedelic on stage with Cream in 1967.

OPPOSITE PAGE
**Top:** With Jimi Hendrix in London in 1967. When the American guitarist sat in with Cream the previous year, a shocked Clapto told Jimi's manager Chas Chandler: 'You ne told me he was that fucking good.'

**Bottom:** Eric plays drums during a break in rehearsals with Blind Faith at Hurtwood Ed in 1969. Singer Steve Winwood (left) and Ric Grech (seated) joined Eric and Ginger Bake (holding a guitar) in the group dubbed 'Crea Mark 2'.

Marshall

**Top:** The guitarist locked himself away behind the gates of his imposing and brooding Surrey home Hurtwood as he succumbed to his heroin addictic

**Left:** The highborn Alice Ormsby-Gore (pictured with Clapton in September 1969) became his live-i girlfriend and was tasked with scoring his heroin fixes. Years later, the drug would cost Alice her life.

**Below:** Suffering from the effects of drug withdraw Clapton puts in a shaky performance alongside George Harrison at the Concert for Bangladesh at Madison Square Garden in August 1971.

**Above:** Eric sizes up George Harrison while chilling out with Delaney and Bonnie Bramlett backstage at Birmingham Town Hall in December 1969.

**Left:** Eric as 'Derek' with his Dominos (left to right) Bobby Whitlock, Jim Gordon and Carl Radle in 1970. Rows and their taste for industrial quantities of booze and narcotics caused the band's premature demise.

**ight:** Clapton's comeback concert at the Rainbow theatre in London in January 1973, was masterminded by Pete Townshend (right) and eatured an all-star line-up which included Ronnie Wood and Rick Grech.

**Above:** Model Pattie Boyd was a 1960s goddess and Eric's perfect woman – posh, pert and blonde. Maddeningly, she was also married to his best friend George Harrison.

**Right:** Eric was envious of everything from George's status as a Beatle to his fabulous Ferrari, but it was his covetousness of Pattie that threatened their friendship.

in no uncertain terms that if that was the way he felt, he could go and get the unnamed rival in and he would happily hand over his sticks. After all, Gordon sneered sarcastically, 'He could play it better than I could.' Clapton stormed out and they never went back into the studio again.

Even though Eric was left with a feeling of sadness and futility, he knew there was no possibility of a reconciliation. The unfinished tapes remained in the studio and he would never listen to them again, until the box set retrospective *Crossroads* was released in 1988, which featured several previously unreleased tracks, including the Clapton-penned 'Got to Get Better in a Little While', the Willie Dixon song 'Evil', another Clapton number called 'One More Chance', 'Mean Old Frisco', the Arthur Crudup song, and a Clapton/Whitlock composition entitled 'Snake Lake Blues'. Keyboard player Bobby Whitlock says of the group's demise: 'Cocaine and heroin and whisky will make you one crazy dude. Eric and I managed to come out relatively unscathed. But Jim's alcohol and drug intake was way over the top. It was pretty scary.'

Later still, however, Clapton would concede that the talk about rows destroying them might have been overplayed. 'When the Dominos tried to make another album, we folded, we couldn't cover it,' he said. 'We made up a lot of excuses about personal rifts, but we knew we didn't have the fire anymore. We'd burnt out on one album.' But of the demise of his fellow members of the Dominos, he added: 'I hold myself responsible for a lot of that. And I live with it.'

The old adage of 'where there's a hit, there's a writ' continues to ring true. In 1999, nearly thirty years after 'Layla' was released, the daughter of Duane Allman attempted to sue

PolyGram Records for $1 million, claiming that her father had come up with the opening riff. In the lawsuit, filed in Manhattan, Galadrielle Allman claimed he had an oral agreement entitling him to 2 per cent royalties on its sales. Allman was not around to argue. He was killed less than a year after the *Layla* album came out, at the age of twenty-four. He died on 29 October 1971, when his motorbike skidded to avoid a lorry in Macon, Georgia.

He was not the only one of the Dominos who would meet a sticky end. Bass player Carl Radle died of liver poisoning and kidney failure, aged thirty-seven, in 1980. Then, on 3 June 1983, after hearing voices, Jim Gordon drove to the Hollywood home of his 72-year-old mother, Osa, and attacked her with a hammer, before stabbing her to death. Diagnosed as a paranoid schizophrenic, he was committed to a mental hospital in California. While in jail, in the mid-80s, he began an expensive, and ultimately fruitless, bid to sue Clapton through the New York courts for an extra £10 million he claimed to be owed in royalties. When Clapton won a Best Rock Song Grammy for his 'Unplugged' version of 'Layla' in February 1993, Gordon, who was watching the event from his secure unit, is said to have let out a sound like an animal howling at the moon, before going on a rampage, banging on walls, smashing furniture and spitting on windows, before being sedated.

Whitlock's assertion that Eric had his drug-taking under control when the Dominos disbanded was stretching credulity. In fact, for all that he had threatened Pattie he would become an addict if she rejected him, the truth was that he was already well on the way. Indeed, Tom Dowd was so concerned about what he had seen going on in Miami that he asked Ahmet

Ertegun, the boss of Clapton's US record label, to speak to him one-on-one, in a bid to get him to ease back on the self-destructive path he seemed set on. The paternal Ertegun broke down in tears as he begged his protégé to clean his act up, warning him that he had witnessed Ray Charles become a slave to hard drugs and the devastation it had caused. He was desperate that Eric should not go the same way. Clapton listened to his mentor's impassioned plea, but it left him utterly unmoved. He was already too far gone.

Nor was he a complete novice when it came to the subject of heroin, despite the impression he had given Pattie at their last meeting. Thanks to Jim Gordon's taste for smack, the drug had been ubiquitous on the Dominos recent tour of the States. In fact, the first time Clapton took heroin was several months earlier, at Hurtwood. One of those who joined him that night in taking her first hit of 'H' was Catherine James, a beautiful Diane Keaton lookalike who had first met Clapton in New York during Cream's first visit to the Big Apple. Now in London, she already had a son, Damian, with her on-off guitarist boyfriend, Denny Laine. Coincidentally, American Catherine was also singing backing vocals at the time in Ginger Baker's new band, Air Force, of which Denny Laine was a member. But her relationship with Laine was volatile and after a huge bust-up, she went to the Speakeasy, where she bumped into Clapton. 'Eric was there and he said, "Why don't you come up with your son and spend the summer at Hurtwood Edge?" He had my cases picked up and I went to Surrey. I was there about four months,' recalls Catherine.

The grounds of Hurtwood were manicured in places, she remembers, but mostly wild. The house itself had marble floors and wainscoted walls and her toddler son, Damian, would ride his tricycle up and down the wide hallways. Clapton, she says, had just formed Derek and the Dominos and the band was there working on material that summer. But, she adds, 'There was a feel of a Shakespearean tragedy brewing in the manor. Eric was writing "Layla" and it was obvious he was in love with Pattie.'

As the only girl in the house, she became the cook. The extent of Clapton's drug-taking at the time, she remembers, consisted in the main of snorting cocaine, smoking hash and taking Mandies. On one evening, Clapton's dealer paid a visit. Catherine takes up the story: 'The dealer, who always brought the coke, came and said that this time he had something special and we were, like, "OK. Let's see what it is." He said it was something called China white.' She says none of them had tried heroin before and didn't know how much to take. Even so, they sniffed it through rolled-up £10 notes. Those who took it, including Eric, sat on the sofa in front of the fireplace in a catatonic state. 'We all tried it, there were about four or five of us. We fell on the couch from about nine o'clock till six in the morning. It was like being dead with vital signs. We didn't do anything,' she says.

Catherine adds: 'I took heroin once in my whole life and that was the first time Eric took it too. But he liked it and I didn't like it. It made everybody sick. We all threw up. I didn't want to do it again because it made me feel really awful. I felt I had no emotions. I felt dead, but I was alive. Nothing would have bothered me. The place could have been on fire and I wouldn't have got up.'

She says that at a party for Jim Gordon's birthday in July, at

Hurtwood, someone spiked the punch with the hallucinogenic mescaline. George arrived with Pattie and played a new song he had written, 'My Sweet Lord', for Eric. Mick Jagger also turned up in a white Bentley convertible and made a play for Catherine. Not that Clapton appeared to notice or care. Catherine says: 'Once Eric started doing heroin, I moved out pretty much after that because by then I'd met Mick. He kept coming up to see Eric. But Eric would get short shrift and Mick spent the time chatting to me. But Eric was in love with Pattie so it didn't make any difference. I was going to go back to California, but Mick said, "Why don't you just stay here?" So I moved in with him.' It would not be the last time Jagger would steal one of Eric's women.

One evening in September 1970, Clapton marched up the steps of the Lyceum Theatre, just off the Strand in London, carrying a white Fender Stratocaster. The guitar, a rare left-handed model, was a gift for Jimi Hendrix. It was a magnanimous gesture, considering how comprehensively Hendrix had snatched away Clapton's crown as the world's undisputed guitar god in the preceding four years. A few hours later, Hendrix would be dead. The exact facts of the intervening period have been a subject of some dispute ever since. But what we know for sure is that the following morning, Hendrix was found by his lover, Monika Dannemann, a German skating instructor, in her room at the Samarkand Hotel in Notting Hill. Officially, a coroner ruled that the 27-year-old Hendrix had died of barbiturate intoxication and inhalation of vomit, and returned an open verdict. Since then, however, there have been conflicting wild conspiracy theories as to how he died, everything from suicide to claims that his manager, Michael

Jeffery, killed him for the $2 million life insurance he'd taken out on him, or that Jimi was bumped off by the FBI because of his support for the Black Panthers.

Clapton's name has also come up in relation to the contested details of the events of the previous night. In 2011, Welsh folk singer Meic Stevens, who was a friend of Hendrix, claimed on BBC Radio 4 that in the evening, he, Jimi and Eric had been drinking at the infamous Scotch of St James bar in Mayfair. But, all round, memories are a bit hazy.

Even Eric's recollection of what happened that night seems to have changed over the years. Nine years after the American guitarist's death, Clapton gave an interview to a BBC film crew in which he claimed that the night that Jimi died, he was supposed to meet him at the Lyceum, to watch American funk rockers Sly and the Family Stone play. He said he had found a left-handed Stratocaster, which he had never seen before, at Orange Music in London, and he took it with him to present to Jimi. But once at the theatre, he saw Hendrix on the other side of the venue and never got to hand over the gift. He explained: 'He was in a box over there and I was in a box over here and I could see him, but we never got together. The next day, whack, he was gone and I was left with that left-handed Stratocaster.'

Yet, nearly forty years later, when Clapton wrote his memoirs, his recollection had changed. He wrote that he had bought the white Stratocaster 'on impulse' in the West End to give to Jimi, knowing he would be seeing him at the concert that night. He took the guitar to the Lyceum, but Jimi never turned up and the next day he heard he had died.

What would have made him say he had seen Jimi on that fateful night if he hadn't? Well, in the 1979 interview for the

BBC documentary, Eric was clearly not in good shape. At the height of his alcoholism, he was glassy-eyed, looked totally out-of-it and was emotional throughout, seemingly blinking back tears. Of Hendrix's death, he spoke of feeling bereft and isolated. 'It was a lonely feeling to be left alone and after that I kept running into people who were shoving him [Jimi] down my throat,' he slurred. 'I knew him and I played with him and I loved his music, but I don't ever want to hear anything said about him again.'

Certainly, it seemed that Clapton was experiencing conflicting emotions where Hendrix was concerned. A week after his death, Clapton was telling reporters that losing his friend had made him change his mind about giving up the guitar. 'I felt I just couldn't go much further,' he said. 'But now Jimi Hendrix is dead, I must go on and try to fill the gap he's left. He was the king.' Later, he would say that his first reaction on hearing of his death was unbridled anger, quickly replaced by the feeling that he was 'the loneliest man in the world.' Later still, he would describe a complete absence of emotion. 'My experience of death with people who have been close to me, people I've loved or admired, has been, for the most part, a lack of feeling,' he said. 'It's only when I rationalise what it meant to me intellectually that I'm able to tap into an emotion. If someone tells me, "So-and-so's dead." I go, "Oh, really?" And then I go away and think – and I'm being as honest as I can here – "What should I feel?" Because I don't know how you're meant to feel. I still don't know how to react. What is supposed to happen? I think maybe the fear is so great, you go into an anaesthetised state. With Jimi, it's been recorded that I was very angry. It seemed to me so fucking careless. But the real truth is, I was already really angry with Jimi because he'd come on with this bullshit about, "Oh, people only come to see me play guitar with my teeth." He developed this real hang-up that his audiences were ignorant and that they wanted him to sell out with a gimmick. But he did it anyway! That was his choice.' Clapton was unimpressed by Jimi's 'carelessness' when it came to women and drugs, because he thought they were getting in the way of his music.

And for all the talk that they were kindred spirits, he has been candid enough to admit that he, for one, felt the rivalry between them keenly. 'If the cards were down in reality, I would have to admit, even then, that what I was doing was nowhere compared with what he was doing,' he concedes. 'But I kidded myself that we were on a par.'

For all that, Chris O'Dell says Clapton's competitiveness towards Hendrix should not be overstated. 'When Jimi died, Eric was very deeply affected by it and I remember him saying to me, "How could he leave me like that?"' she says. 'It was as though he had someone that he really related to in Jimi, and now he was gone. I never got the impression, when I was around Eric, that there was too much competition. In a way, it was admiration, respect, and perhaps the competitive side showed itself in the fact that being around Jimi pushed him to be better at what he did.' And, as Clapton can attest, it is nigh on impossible to compete with dead icons. 'There's no doubt in my mind that Jimi was as great a guitar player as everyone said, but there has been a lot of mystique added to it by his early death,' Eric said in 2006. 'I suppose I've reacted to that over the years, and tended to put it away. I think you can get stuck in the past in a way that's unhealthy.'

His comments about Jimi wasting his talents because of his taste for drugs and women are particularly telling given the path to self-destruction Clapton himself was embarking on at the time of Hendrix's death. Certainly, it would have been natural that he should have felt guilty for surviving drugs when Jimi didn't. But was there something more going on? A fellow musician who worked with Eric in the early 80s says that as he fell deeper into the clutches of his various addictions, he would on occasion muse about why he had survived when others had died. 'The subject of Robert Johnson came up again and again,' he says. 'Eric was captivated by the story of Johnson selling his soul at the crossroads. He related it to his own life in as much as he felt there was some presence watching over him, but he wasn't sure if it was a force of good or evil.' So did Clapton, in his drink- and drug-addled mind, believe he had sold his soul like his hero Johnson and the pay-off was that he lived while his rival Hendrix succumbed? Did it haunt him that he had been, so he claimed (though he later retracted the story), in Jimi Hendrix's presence that fateful night? Who knows what goes through the mind of a man tormented by demons, chemical or otherwise, during his darker moments, as he reflects on things that were, in reality, totally out of his control.

Coincidentally, the details of Hendrix's untimely end had tragic echoes in the death, twenty years later, of another great guitarist, Stevie Ray Vaughan. Like Hendrix, Vaughan had established himself as Clapton's superior as an electric blues player. And, astonishingly, Eric was with him too the night he died in a helicopter crash after a gig they played together – a helicopter that Eric could so easily have shared with him if fate had twisted in a different direction.

Either way, Hendrix's death was one of the triggers for the beginning of a steep decline which would see Clapton come perilously close to losing his own life. The following month, Stigwood called Eric in the States, where he was touring with the Dominos, to say his grandfather was ill in Guildford Hospital with suspected cancer. Eric pulled out of a press reception for the band and flew home. Jack Clapp had been in ill health. A year earlier, he'd had a stroke which left him with little movement down one side. Illogically, Eric felt responsible because he had bought him and Rose a house, which meant Jack could afford to retire. He tortured himself that by helping him out financially, he had robbed the proud and industrious Jack of his dignity and caused his illnesses. Shortly afterwards, his grandfather died, aged sixty. It was a traumatic experience, particularly for Rose, who was devastated, but also for Eric himself, whose relationship with Jack had grown distant in the previous years. When he had gone to live with John Mayall five years earlier, he had broken all links to his grandparents and Ripley. Now the guilt began to kick in.

To start with, Clapton's taking of heroin was a strictly on-off thing, an adjunct to the large quantities of coke and alcohol – brandy and vodka – that he was getting through. Once every two weeks became once a week, and then twice a week, until, gradually, taking hits of heroin became a daily occurrence. He got high to forget: to forget Pattie, Jimi and Jack. Ironically, one of those who sought to snap him out of his downward spiral was George Harrison.

Harrison was shocked and worried by the state he found him in when he arrived one night at Hurtwood with Leon Russell to find his friend and love rival 'smacked out of his head'. But George's pep talk fell on deaf ears. Likewise, Russell's angry words about what he was doing to himself were brushed off. Instead, Eric told him ominously that he was on a 'journey into darkness'. He had been seduced by the ill-fated lives of people like Robert Johnson, the people he wanted to emulate.

A few years later, Clapton told author Steve Turner: 'I always argue that all of my heroes were junkies. Ray Charles, Billie Holiday, Charlie Parker, you name 'em. They all either die on it, or they're hooked on it, or they're controlled by the Mafia on it, or something. So my argument is that it stimulates your playing – maybe not for long, because sooner or later you hit the downward trail, but for a while it actually inspires you. If it wasn't heroin, it'd be whisky or women. There's got to be something, something that's bugging me. If I'm satisfied with everything then I've no reason to pick up the guitar and play.' Looking back, he would add: 'There was definitely a heroic aspect to it. I was trying to prove I could do it and come out alive. At no time did I consider it was being suicidal or shutting down on life.'

The point about whether it improved his playing, even in the short term, is deeply questionable. But what is undeniable is that smack had stopped his ability to have any feeling for the concern of others about what he was doing to himself. And the simple fact was, he was enjoying heroin. Increasingly, those like Harrison who tried to reason with him were given a wide berth. Very quickly, he retreated inside Hurtwood. The phone rang off the hook, the gates were left open, but when friends came knocking at the door, he ignored them. The only person he allowed to be in his presence was Alice Ormsby-Gore, who, with Pattie and Paula off the scene, had been granted readmittance to his drug-addled orbit.

Two months after his ultimatum that he would become a heroin addict, Eric wrote to Pattie on the title page of an edition of John Steinbeck's *Of Mice and Men*. Addressed to 'Dear Layla', the letter, written when on a holiday in Wales, beseeched her poetically to tell him why she had rejected him. Was it because he was ugly, a bad lover, too strong or too weak? She wrote back saying she would like to come and visit him. To her surprise, he replied by return of post, saying somewhat protractedly that he had decided he was better off alone.

Things went downhill very quickly. Before long, his stash of two-for-one heroin, which he had stockpiled in a drawer, never meaning to use, was gone. As he became more hooked, Clapton began scoring strong, pure heroin from Gerrard Street in Soho. The realisation of how completely he was hooked came when Alice made a trip home to Wales and he promised to drive up to see her. However, the small part of his brain functioning logically told him that to get in his Ferrari in that state would be suicidal. So he went cold turkey, lying for three days in agony in the foetal position, howling liking a banshee as muscle spasms coursed through his body. He was horrified to discover that he felt worse clean. With Alice back, soon she too was sharing his heroin and succumbing to the same addiction. Their home life was punctuated by often daily mutual bouts of petulance. After one row, in early 1971, the eighteen-year-old Alice walked out and took off to Tel Aviv, where she got a job dancing in a production of the musical *Hair*, which had scandalised late 60s London with its full-frontal nudity and profanity. Soon, however, she was back.

Did Clapton have any thoughts for her wellbeing? Did he

try to steer her away from the route he was taking into oblivion? Patently, if he did try, he didn't try very hard. But, then, his mind was already numb to suffering – his own as much as anyone else's. And it made sense to have a playmate, not least because Alice soon took on the role of enabler and delivery boy, being sent out on almost daily errands to find and score more and more heroin. Some years later, Alice would say: 'I remember thinking how stupid it was of me, even then. I did that for him, and for myself, for three years. It was probably childish to be over-protective, but I thought it helped him not to have to face the full horror himself, of scoring his own heroin supply. It might have been better, I can see now, to let him do it and learn the difficulty of it first-hand. Then he'd know, like I learned, the degradation of the dealing. But then, you see, Eric's able to give himself into other people's hands for a limited spell of time, and give himself totally, if he thinks it will tide him over a problem. If it hadn't been me doing the scoring for him, it would have been someone else. And if you love someone, as I did, you do anything.'

If there could be an upside to such a dire situation, it was that because of a lifelong fear of needles, Eric had steadfastly refused to inject and instead snorted the drug. The downside, however, was that he needed to use far more than if he had been an intravenous user. And the more he became tolerant of the drug, the more he needed just to get the same level of hit. With his addiction kicking in hard, his dealer put up his prices, as dealers will do, from £150 for half an ounce to £300. Before long, Clapton was spending £1,500 a week, nearly twice the price of a small family car, to feed his habit.

By the summer of 1971, his self-imposed incarceration had

been in operation for more than a year. In the hope that he could tempt him out of his exile, George rang to ask Eric to appear at Madison Square Garden that August, for a charity event to raise cash for the Bangladesh famine. To his surprise, Eric agreed, but only on the condition that George kept him supplied with enough heroin for the week of rehearsals and the show. No smack, no show. George said he would. True to his word, when Clapton and Alice got to New York, instead of a fruit basket, there was a plentiful supply waiting for them in their room. Snorting a big hit of it, Eric waited for the effects to kick in: nothing. He tried another hit, but it made absolutely no difference. The heroin George had scored for him was low-grade, probably cut with baby formula or something else to reduce its potency. Whatever it was, it was not the rock-star-standard junk he was used to (Clapton's personal preference was for the finest heroin, which came in small nuggets that looked like brown sugar, which he would grind up and snort). As a result, he went cold turkey by default for three days and missed rehearsals, while Alice was forced to trawl fruitlessly around the crumbier areas of a city which she hardly knew, trying to buy her boyfriend a better quality of self-destruction. Nor was Alice in the best frame of mind either, because when they had got to Heathrow Airport for the flight to the States, Pattie – whom Eric had not seen in more than twelve months – was there to see him off. Understandably, a seriously annoyed Alice assumed wrongly that they had been carrying on behind her back.

With Clapton's appearance on the bill in grave doubt, the one-time Beatles' manager Allen Klein gave him an ulcer remedy he had been prescribed and, bizarrely, it did the trick.

Even so, George was not sure Eric would make it and there were fears he actually could die on stage of withdrawal. When he did show up, thin, white-faced and shuffling, Clapton was joined on stage by George, Bob Dylan, Ravi Shankar, Ringo Starr, Leon Russell and Billy Preston. In the intervening forty-odd years, Clapton says he has only once watched footage of the shows, because he was so ashamed. And he'd be well advised to wait another forty before catching another re-run. Most of his contribution was edited out of the footage that was released from the two gigs. One 'highlight' that did survive for posterity was George's rendition of 'While My Guitar Gently Weeps', with Eric reprising his *White Album* guitar part. When the time came for Clapton to come in with his first guitar fill, a nervous-looking Harrison felt it was necessary to gesture over to him, to ensure Eric, who spent most of the performance seemingly unable to open his eyes, didn't miss his cue. And when a spaced-out Clapton played the outro solo, George was forced to join in, soloing on his Stratocaster, to fill out the strangely thin sound of Eric's Gibson Byrdland. At the end of the song, Eric, who had tucked his cigarette under the strings on the guitar's headstock in trademark fashion, tried to take a drag and missed his mouth completely. All in all, then, it wasn't good.

Chris O'Dell, who had helped Harrison to arrange the event from the house where he and Pattie had been staying in Nichols Canyon, Los Angeles, moved into George and Pattie's hotel suite in New York for the concerts. She says: 'I sat with Pattie in the audience for the second show. It was obvious to her, and all of us, the state Eric was in. I remember we went to the rehearsal the night before at the Garden and all the talk was about whether Eric was going to make it. There was a great concern about whether he could even get on the plane from London to get all the way to New York because that was a lot of time up in the air without any drugs.'

Back at Hurtwood, he and Alice quietly slipped back into the same routine. Despite the fact that Rose had been recently widowed, she was avoided. Having seen George try and fail to coax him out of his seclusion by getting him back on stage, Ginger tried an altogether more Ginger-like approach. He formulated a plan to take Eric hostage and whisk him off to the Sahara in a Land Rover, away from drugs and temptation, where they'd live like two Bedouins until he had beaten his craving. But the elaborate plan failed because when Ginger arrived at the house ready to cart him off, Eric didn't come to the door.

Eventually, Clapton disconnected the doorbell and slept in until late afternoon, before sitting around playing the guitar. He also took to building model cars and planes, and renewed an interest in drawing. But in time, it was all he could do to sit watching endless drivel on the TV, while gorging on chocolate and junk food.

The consolation for everyone else was that he didn't go out while he was on heroin. He was fat, bloated, constipated, a strange shade of yellow, covered in spots and foul-smelling from the chemicals in his system, added to the fact that he didn't bother to wash. Thankfully, he also had zero libido.

As months turned into years, Hurtwood went into lockdown, with Eric cast in the role of his own jailer. When Ben Palmer, his dearest friend, who was now living in Wales, came round, he could not get an answer at the door, even though he knew they were in. The next time he tried, Alice let him in, but he says Eric made him feel like an 'intruder'. One of the few people who was granted admission was Pete Townshend of the Who. He had persuaded Clapton to let him help him sift through some of the unfinished tapes that were left over after the breakup of the Dominos. While Eric was stoned out of his mind upstairs, unbeknown to him, Pete would also show up to talk to Alice about him, or she would phone Pete in hysterics, pleading with him to come over to listen to her troubles. Eventually, Townshend also got in touch with Alice's father, Lord Harlech, to ask for his help. Harlech was, naturally enough, beside himself with worry for his daughter and keen to help. He was also a big music fan, with a love of jazz, and together he and Townshend came up with a plan to snap Eric out of it by arranging a concert at the Rainbow Theatre in London to celebrate Britain's entry into the Common Market. The show was to be called Eric Clapton's Rainbow Concert and also on the bill were Townshend, former Blind Faith cohorts Steve Winwood and Rick Grech, Ronnie Wood and former Traffic drummer Jim Capaldi.

Somehow they persuaded Clapton to take part and the rehearsals took place at Wood's house. The problem was that while Eric was obviously trying his best, given the state he was in, what was coming out of his amplifier was fairly sub-standard stuff. Nor did it help that when it came time for the concert, on 13 January 1973, he and Alice arrived smacked out of their minds and late because she'd had to let out the waist of his trousers because of all the chocolate he'd been eating. George, Ringo and Elton John were in the audience to hear him put on a rather ring-rusty showing. But just as with the

Bangladesh gig, afterwards he went straight back to his reclusive, druggy ways.

Now, to add to his growing list of problems, he began running out of money. As is the junkie's way, he was successful in keeping the depth of his financial problems secret from Stigwood for a long time. But gradually his manager discovered just how broke Clapton was and sent him word that because he wasn't earning, while spending huge amounts on drugs, he was broke and would have to start selling things to get straight. Reluctantly, Eric began selling his guitars to anyone who was prepared to buy them. Meanwhile, he started taking Alice's heroin too and she had to make up for it by drinking two bottles of vodka a day. In an interview with Simon Bates on Radio 1 in August 1987, Clapton said of Alice: 'She had become like a slave. It was really depraved. I was destroying Alice's life.'

At his wits' end because of his daughter's plight, Lord Harlech now decided his best bet was to play hardball. He sent Clapton a letter, telling him how much he loved them both, but adding in no uncertain terms that he would go to the police and inform on them if they did not stop. As out of it as he was, Eric knew he meant business. He rang Harlech, telling him that he was aware they both needed help and that he wanted to get clean, as much for Alice as for himself, but that he was scared and didn't know how they could possibly kick their habits. Harlech told him he had been doing some research and had come across Dr Meg Patterson, a Scottish neurosurgeon who, at the Harley Street clinic she shared with her husband George, had developed a form of electronic acupuncture to help heroin withdrawal which she called neuroelectric therapy.

It involved a small black box with wires connected to

needles which were placed in the earlobes of patients, and the tingling effect produced was supposed to send them into a relaxed semi-sleep. Harlech had already arranged with the Pattersons that they would come and live at Hurtwood for a week, to administer the three-hour sessions each day. However, things got off to a slow start because neither Clapton nor Alice could sleep as withdrawal symptoms began to kick in, and after five days with no breakthrough, Dr Patterson told Eric that she needed to separate him and Alice. He was to go and live with them at their house in Harley Street, with their two sons and a daughter, and Alice would go elsewhere. Alice was dispatched to a nursing home. But, then, Alice did not have the celebrity cachet that weaning Eric Clapton off heroin would give the Pattersons and their patented 'black box' treatment. Once chez Patterson, he was kept under close supervision to ensure he didn't relapse and was given daily lectures about God from the devoutly Christian Mr Patterson. But one day, when he was finally allowed out on his own, Eric scored some methadone, and when Dr Patterson found out, she outed him humiliatingly in front of the family. Even so, the treatment was successful to a degree. Being off heroin allowed him to begin reconnecting with music and to shake off the stifling numbness that came from his deadly habit.

The plan was that Eric would recuperate, with the help of the country air, on a farm near Oswestry and the Welsh border which was run by Lord Harlech's son, Frank Ormsby-Gore. The problem was, he was about to part-exchange one addiction for another.

# NINE

# Booze

The bucolic idyll of Oswestry was a welcome antidote to the pervading reek of decay and self-pity at Hurtwood. Clapton arrived there in early 1974, in a second-hand Mini, albeit the 'Magical Mystery Tour' Mini from the Beatles' film which George Harrison had specially painted with gaudy Indian art before giving it to Eric. His mode of arrival might not have been exactly low-key, then, but once there, the emphasis was on a lifestyle diametrically opposed to the rock-star existence to which Clapton had become accustomed.

Frank Ormsby-Gore was, at twenty, nine years younger than his new famous lodger, but instantly the two men found they had much in common. Frank was a music aficionado, with a big collection of vinyl, and they were soon sitting around sharing their passion for records. Beyond a few clothes, the only thing Eric took with him on his country sojourn was an acoustic guitar and a few LPs. The plan was that he would not only get some fresh air, but get fit too. So he was expected to muck in, getting up at first light to chop logs, bail hay and clean out the cows. Nor were his digs in the stately home category. Frank's place was a small two-bed cottage, with a living room and kitchen downstairs, where Eric would noodle around on the guitar while his host cooked.

The Ormsby-Gores presided over a cursed Camelot, at once glamorous, but also tainted by tragedy. The patriarch, David Ormsby-Gore, the fifth Baron Harlech, was an Eton- and Oxford-educated war hero who had been the MP for Oswestry after the war, before being made British ambassador to the US following the election of President Kennedy, with whom he was close. But he'd only inherited the Harlech title because his elder brother had died in a car crash in 1935, aged nineteen. Following JFK's death, Harlech began a relationship with Kennedy's widow Jackie and she accepted his marriage proposal in 1967, not long after the death of Harlech's first wife Sylvia – Alice's mother – in a car crash. But Jackie eventually threw him over for Greek shipping magnate Aristotle Onassis. Harlech went on to become the founder of Harlech Television. But in 1974, his eldest son, male model Julian – the heir to the 124-year-old title and the substantial fortune that went with it – shot himself through the head with a Smith and Wesson in a flat in Fulham, after succumbing to depression and an addiction to booze and heroin. His sister Alice discovered his body.

Yet more misfortune and misery was to follow the clan. In 1985, Lord Harlech was killed in a car crash near Shrewsbury, when he swerved to avoid a sheepdog. Frank not only inherited the title and the family seat, the Palladian stately home, Brogyntyn, near Oswestry, but a heap of problems. Faced by crippling death duties, he was forced to sell off paintings and furniture. Finally, as Brogyntyn fell into disrepair, he sold up to a developer in 2001. Frank, who has suffered mental illness, was banned from driving in 1994, after admitting drink-driving and carrying firearms in his car, and was cautioned for possessing cannabis. Five years later, he was fined £300 for carrying heroin. At one time, he was reduced to working as a lorry driver.

And while Clapton was able to kick his addiction to heroin, Alice never could. Brought up amid the splendour of Brogyntyn, she died with a syringe stuck in her arm in 1995, in a grotty Bournemouth bedsit, furnished only with a bed, a cooker, a rusty fridge and a broken-down table. At the time, her rent was paid by social services and everything she possessed was in two plastic bin liners. She was said to have injected herself with an almost pure strain of the drug. A few years before her death, Alice gave author Ray Coleman a telling insight into Clapton's relationship with drink and drugs: 'As it was with heroin, so it was with drink,' she said. 'Eric always waits for the other person, or in this case it was the other article, smack or alcohol, to make a mistake. In the case of heroin, the drug's failure for Eric was not to live up to his expectations in helping him create some work of genius, or help him towards some profound recognition of life. So when heroin did not provide any answers, he could kick it and say, "I've conquered it! I've won. Because I've met heroin head on and I've come out on top – and I can *still* create!" So, yes, heroin was a major reason he went down the road. Because deep inside him, he knew that he could find a way back.' Tragically for Alice, she never could.

Before long, Eric was increasingly fit and healthy, his skin glowing from his outdoor life. But it was another daily routine he joined Frank in that was the problem. Every night, after dinner, the two would go on a tour of the pubs in Oswestry and proceed to get completely smashed out of their brains. However, even this destructive behaviour seemed infinitely healthier to him than a solitary, slow death at Hurtwood. As far as Clapton was concerned, the two of them might have been making drunken spectacles of themselves every night, but at least they were doing it in the real world. And on the plus side, Eric was tentatively beginning to write songs again, strumming chord progressions in the kitchen of a night.

At around the same time, his ex-Dominos bandmate Carl Radle sent him some tapes of a band he was playing in which included Jamie Oldaker, a fellow native of Tulsa, Oklahoma, on drums and Dick Sims on keyboards. Throughout their correspondence, Radle was cajoling him to give up his rural sojourn and role as celebrity farmhand and get on a flight to America to resume his career. In truth, the concept was not one that needed much selling as far as Eric was concerned. More and more, he was feeling the gravitational pull of America, not only home to his musical heroes, but also a country where, even more than his homeland, he was treated with the reverence he deserved.

There was also the issue of money. After a three-year hiatus, the royalty cheques that had once been coming in thick and fast had started to dry up and he badly needed to get back to work. In fact, he did return to work of sorts during this period, spending a day at Pinewood Studios in Buckinghamshire to play the part of a Marilyn Monroe-obsessed preacher in the weird Pete Townshend 'rock opera' *Tommy*. On the plus side, he also got to play the old blues song 'Eyesight to the Blind', written by Sonny Boy Williamson.

In the meantime, George and Pattie turned up and threw a

spanner in the works. During his time as a recluse, the plan was that a mountain of drugs would take his mind off his Pattie dilemma, and it had worked, for the most part. But now, out of the blue, she turned up at the farm with George to check on his progress. To all intents and purposes, she and George gave the impression that their marriage was holding up well enough, but when all three of them went to the pub, there was something about her demeanour that made Clapton think he might be back in with a chance. What Eric didn't know was that Pattie's marriage to George had become an even more distant affair, with Harrison disappearing to his studio in the dead of night, or staying up for hours on end meditating alone. In his own way, Harrison was, like Eric, hiding away too, his own jailer in his vast Gothic pile, afraid to go out in public because he hated being recognised. He took to chanting all day for months at a time. When he wasn't following the path of spirituality, he was chasing other women. And as early as the previous year, George had announced to Pattie at a New Year's Eve party at Ringo Starr's house that he wanted a divorce in the coming twelve months.

Pattie's re-emergence signalled the end of Eric's relationship with Alice, who had made a fleeting visit to see him during his recovery. Now, with his break on the farm at an end, Eric retuned to Hurtwood and began making regular pilgrimages to Friar Park to see Pattie, in the hope that she would relent and agree to leave George for him. For her part, Pattie was not sure what her husband's attitude was to his friend's re-appearance. George had been stoned when Eric had told him he loved Pattie at Stigwood's party four years previously, and she wondered if he might simply have forgotten. And Pattie had given no hint that Eric was on her mind during the time he hid himself away at Hurtwood.

'When Eric went into his reclusive phase, I saw Pattie and George all the time,' says her friend Chris O'Dell. 'I would go to stay at Friar Park and they would come to LA where I was living. But the interesting thing was that Pattie never talked about Eric. It was as though the whole thing didn't exist anymore. There was a part of her that was putting it on ice because it was so complicated.'

Stigwood was also keen to get Eric working – and earning – again. When Clapton told him he was interested in taking up Carl Radle's offer of recording together, his manager was already one step ahead of him. He announced he had booked a studio in Miami and lined up Tom Dowd to produce the record. Stigwood had also rented a white house with a palm tree in the garden, overlooking the sea in Golden Beach. The address was 461 Ocean Boulevard (the house, outside which Eric posed for photographer David Gahr on the iconic cover of the album, is still there, though it's now painted a pinky terracotta, and the palm tree died soon after Eric and his band moved out).

First, Stigwood took Eric to London, to show him off to the press. If Clapton was glad to be back after three years in the shadows, he wasn't exactly showing it. At a reception thrown by Stigwood at a Chinese restaurant in Soho in April 1974 to announce his comeback, Eric, flanked by Pete Townshend and Elton John, sat morosely eating spring rolls and deep-fried prawns and drinking wine, and pointedly refused to talk to the invited media.

A few days later, he flew to Florida to renew his relationship with Radle and meet his new bandmates, Oldaker and Sims. If the others were match-sharp and at the top of their games, Clapton was most certainly not. In the years he had been away, his ability to play the frenetic solos for which he was known had become seriously diminished through lack of practice. With his limitations apparent for all to see in the studio, a new approach was necessitated. As the one-time guitar god re-acquainted himself with the instrument, songs were kept simple, stripped back and bare, for the most part, of anything but short, simple solos. But quite apart from the fact that he simply no longer had the wherewithal to tear it up musically, this distinctly less-is-more approach also suited Clapton's mood. Certainly, he was playing – and singing – within his limits, but, paradoxically, that only added to the album's appeal; his fragile, delicate voice providing unmistakeable echoes of all those recent hard times, still so fresh in his memory, but also hinting at a mellower future.

For the recording, he would also be using the guitar he has become most associated with, a Fender Stratocaster, nicknamed 'Blackie'. It was actually a hybrid of three guitars he had bought second-hand a few years earlier, in 1970, at Sho-Bud music shop in Nashville, where he'd purchased six or seven vintage Strats for about $100 each. Then, back in England, he gave one to George, one to Pete Townshend, and another to Steve Winwood. The others he kept, taking the best bits and turning them into one guitar, a black-bodied, maple-neck instrument circa 1956 and 1957.

The sessions, in the familiar confines of Criteria Studios, were joined by a Florida-based guitar player called George Terry and the Hawaiian-raised singer Yvonne Elliman, who had appeared as Mary Magdalene in *Jesus Christ Superstar* and had a big hit in 1971 with a ballad from the show, 'I Don't Know How to Love Him'. As well as having a stunning voice, she knew how to party hard and had a particular liking for alcohol and marijuana. Almost immediately, she and Clapton 'fell in lust' and began an affair.

Whether by accident or design, the opening track was a version of the blues standard 'Motherless Children', first recorded in 1927 by Blind Willie Johnson, which offered a commentary on Clapton's own childhood and continued distant relationship with Pat. Whatever the case, the slide-guitar-dominated number was to become a fixture of his live set for years to come. Another blues track, Robert Johnson's 'Steady Rollin' Man' was added, as well as 'Let It Grow', a song Clapton had started writing in Oswestry. The laid-back and mainly acoustic track features a solo that amounts to no more than a handful of notes and has an arpeggio progression played on an electric. It was only much later that Clapton realised, to his horror, that he had, inadvertently, in his own words, 'totally ripped off' the Led Zeppelin classic 'Stairway to Heaven'.

Elsewhere on the album was the George Terry-penned and rockier 'Mainline Florida'. It was Terry who brought into the studio an album called *Burnin'* by Bob Marley and the Wailers, a band that Clapton knew nothing about. Terry suggested they record Marley's song 'I Shot the Sheriff'. The hardcore reggae track was a huge departure for Clapton and, once they had recorded the track, he felt that it was not good enough when set against the original version, and he argued it should be left off the album. However, Stigwood and the record label were convinced the song would be a hit and insisted it was not only included, but released as the first single from the sessions. 'I Shot the Sheriff' went to number one in the US, as did the album, *461 Ocean Boulevard*, when it was released in July 1974. It was also a hit in Britain, going gold. This, finally, was the album where Clapton had, at long last, found himself comfortable with his role as frontman and bandleader. Crucially, too, it was the record that laid out his future as a pop star for a mass market, thanks to its crossover appeal – a blend of radio-friendly rock, blues, reggae, country and soul.

Back in the UK, the jungle drums were beating that Pattie's marriage to George was in a dire state. In fact, although word had reached Eric about how bad things were between the couple, he could not have realised just how bad. Harrison had begun an affair with Ringo's wife Maureen, which he made no attempt to hide from his own long-suffering wife. Maureen would arrive at Friar Park at midnight and disappear into George's studio with him. Meanwhile, George bought Maureen a stunning necklace, which she took great delight in wearing in front of Pattie. They became so brazen about the affair that, once, they locked themselves in a bedroom at the house, with Pattie outside banging on the door and demanding to know what was going on. When they eventually came out, a laughing George made some half-hearted excuse that Maureen was tired and was having a lie-down. Not only was Pattie devastated by the betrayal, but so was Ringo, to whom George revealed the affair in the kitchen one day. Though Ringo's response, 'Better you than someone we don't know,' was apparently sanguine, he was traumatised and fell into the arms of Pattie's friend Chris O'Dell, with whom Starr would have a short-lived rebound affair.

Chris says of that time: 'George would talk to me about their relationship and Pattie would talk to me, but they didn't often talk to each other. George began to totally emotionally detach himself. At one point, very close to the end, just before Pattie left him to go to Eric, it was Christmas time and I went to stay with them at Friar Park. George came in and asked me if I'd go and buy Pattie a Christmas present. I thought, "Are you kidding?" He was already involved with Maureen.'

Suddenly, it seemed as if the stars were aligning for Eric and Pattie. Pattie began ringing Chris O'Dell to discuss leaving George and getting an apartment with her in LA, where Chris was living. In June, Clapton was in the studio with Pete Townshend, finishing the track he had recorded for *Tommy*. Pete suggested he, Eric and a singer called Graham Bell, whom Pete was working with on an album, should go over to see George at Friar Park. Pattie arrived to find the mood at the house oddly jovial. She cooked dinner for everyone. The meal was consumed amid increasing forced laughter and fake merriment. Finally, George took Townshend and Bell off to show them his studio, and Eric sat with Pattie in the kitchen. His sales pitch was well rehearsed. He spoke quietly for what seemed like hours, trying desperately to convince her that now really was the time for her to call it a day with George and come away with him. In her memoirs, *Wonderful Tonight*, she wrote: 'I had to make a choice. Would I go to Eric, who had written the most beautiful song for me, who had been to hell and back in the last three years because of me and who had worn me down with his protestations of love? Or would I choose George, my husband, whom I had loved, but who had been cold and indifferent towards me for so long that I could barely remember the last time he'd shown me any affection or told me he loved me?'

However, Clapton left with the situation unresolved and immediately flew off to the US on tour. On 3 July, Pattie confronted George and told him she was leaving him and going to America. That night, he pleaded with her not to go, but the following morning a tearful Pattie packed her bags and walked out. She later wrote: 'Half of me wanted to stay and to believe him when he said he would make it better, but I was at the end of my tether. What I had felt for George was a great, deep love. What Eric and I had was an intoxicating, overpowering passion. It was so intense, so urgent, so heady, I felt almost out of control.'

George wasn't alone for long. After the split from Pattie, he took off to Grenada in the West Indies with 24-year-old model Kathy Simmonds, who was an old flame of Rod Stewart.

Stigwood, who had his hands full with the Bee Gees, among other things, told Clapton he was appointing Roger Forrester to look after him on a full-time basis. Forrester was tough, a quick-witted northerner who worked for Stigwood's company RSO. A balding former wrestling promoter at working men's clubs, he, nonetheless, had a taste for dapper clothes. He and Eric hit it off at once and his relationship with his new charge would very soon be akin to brother, partner in crime and father confessor. For a quarter of a century, Forrester became his enabler, facilitator and resident bad cop. If Eric agreed to appear on someone's record or TV show and later had a change of heart, he'd tell Roger to get him out of it. But Roger was still the senior partner and Eric would do nothing without his new manager's approval. More importantly, he was, for long stretches, the most significant person in Clapton's life. Oh, and he would also save him from almost certain death.

For someone emerging from years of hibernation, and nursing a brand-new addiction to drink, embarking on a six-month coast-to-coast stadium tour of America, encompassing twenty-eight cities, was a tall order – and would have been even for the most emotionally and physically robust of entertainers. The tour was preceded by rehearsals in Barbados, where Stigwood had rented him and the band a luxurious villa on the beach, which a drunken Clapton soon trashed in a food fight, throwing plates of spaghetti at the wall just for something to do. It was an indication of the way of things to come. Stigwood's reasoning was that with his client riding high on the back of the huge success of *461 Ocean Boulevard*, they should make hay while the sun shone, particularly as fans were prepared to come out in their droves to see him, as 70,000 did for the first gig in Newhaven, Connecticut, in June 1974. But Forrester was dead set against the idea. In his opinion, Eric was vulnerable, far from healthy and still in grave danger of relapsing into the same trough of despair that had resulted in the lost previous years. Also, anyone with half a brain could see his drinking had reached worrying levels, even before the tour kicked off. Forrester would eventually take over Clapton's management contract from Stigwood in 1979, but for now he was overruled by his boss.

Eric began the way he meant to continue, getting smashed on brandy, which he mixed with lemonade or ginger ale because, despite his growing reliance on it, he actually did not like the taste of alcohol. And just as he had gone on stage high at the Bangladesh concert a few years earlier, now he was appearing in auditoriums every night drunk as a skunk. Sometimes he would walk off halfway through a number and have to be cajoled by Forrester or the road crew to go back on. Despite his serious reservations about the length and breadth of the tour, Forrester did his job of keeping Clapton functioning brilliantly.

Realising that playing the mother-superior role would only alienate Eric and probably end up with him getting the sack sooner rather than later, Forrester expertly walked a potentially treacherous tightrope. One minute he was barroom buddy and fellow reprobate, getting into scrapes, high jinx and practical jokes, often with Stigwood cast in the role of stooge, the next he was indulging Eric's tantrums and mercurialness. But when it came down to it, Roger did what he was there for: he got Clapton on stage in the evenings, usually in just good enough shape to perform. And, unlike Stigwood, who had branched out into film production and stage shows like *Hair* and *Jesus Christ Superstar*, Roger was available 24/7, always along the corridor in a hotel room, or on the end of the phone at 3 a.m., when Eric needed something that simply couldn't wait until the morning. Best of all, he was loyal to a fault, defensive of him and protective no matter what, and constantly reassured Clapton's fragile ego that he was indeed the best, the biggest, the most talented. Quietly, he took the balance of power in the relationship. Those people who once worked for Eric now worked for Roger. It gave him a tremendous sphere of influence. And his influence now extended to making Eric's wish of getting Pattie come true.

Roger got word that Pattie had left George and gone to stay with her sister Jenny in Los Angeles. And Jenny knew the score because she was a rock chick herself, having married Fleetwood Mac drummer Mick Fleetwood in 1970. With Eric constantly banging on about Pattie, Roger decided it was time for action rather than talk and cajoled him into ringing Pattie up and inviting her to join him on his US tour. She agreed, arriving in Buffalo, New York, on 6 July with the plan to begin a new life with the man of her dreams. That was the theory, anyway. The reality was less Mills & Boon and more Irvine Welsh. Eric was drunk and red-eyed because he was suffering from a severe case of conjunctivitis, caught from Yvonne Elliman, who had joined the band on the road and with whom he was still sleeping. Before that night's show, he went on a booze spree with members of the Band, who were also in town, and had to sprint, wheezing and skidding, on to the stage, where, near-blind, he ran headfirst into a massive pot plant. Even before he was formally introduced by the MC for the evening, 'Legs' Larry Smith, there was a shout from the audience of 'Clean up yer act!' Clapton set off on a rambling rendition of 'Going Down to Brownsville', which was interrupted by someone setting off a firework. He responded with an angry, slurred tirade: 'To be serious . . . one more of them, I'll tell you, and YOU'RE OUT OF HERE! One more of them silly fucking fireworks and you are out of here! Behaviour!' Things only got worse. Later, stating the bleeding obvious, after a near incoherent version of 'Let It Grow', Clapton shouted: 'I am drunk and I am ready for fuckin' trouble!' Then, as special guest Freddie King took the stage, Eric began a running commentary: 'He's strapping on his guitar, moving to the guest spot . . . And if you haven't heard of him, you don't fucking deserve him! His name is Freddie . . .' He never reached the end of the sentence because someone in the audience shouted, 'Wanker!'

Then, during a joint performance of 'Hideaway', as King played on stoically, all that could be heard from Clapton's guitar was incessant feedback. During 'Have You Ever Loved a Woman', and after the line, 'It's a shame and a sin,' Eric interjected: 'Don't believe them! There's no shame, there's no sin.' Later, he began an incoherent monologue, during which he blurted out: 'Meanwhile, in Birmingham – England, that is, not here, in Alabama – they're making Persian carpets at 19,000 quid apiece. There's only ten Pakistanis here! That can't be bad. Who am I?' Finally, members of the Band came on stage to join him for a ramshackle version of their song 'Chest Fever', before helping to haul him off. One fan who wrote to *Rolling Stone* to complain about the gig, commented: 'Eric Clapton stunk when he came to Buffalo. First, he walked out on stage so drunk he couldn't sing worth shit. He was constantly cursing the crowd. Many of the fans left before the show was over, only to miss the Band lift Clapton up and carry his drunken corpse off stage.'

Pattie quickly worked out that Roger Forrester had developed a policy of allowing Eric to drink all day. But at four in the afternoon on the day of a gig, he would stage an intervention and stop him, giving him soft drinks and cold tea. After the show, he was free to drink himself into oblivion again.

As far as Eric and Pattie's nascent relationship was concerned, it was not, in any sense, the love story of rock legend. In truth, it was a rather childish affair, conducted for the most part in an alcoholic haze, as Pattie increasingly joined her lover on his voyages to the bottom of a bottle. There were also elements of the relationship about which a shrink would have had a field day. For starters, Clapton showed every sign that he was in some sort of denial about the fact that Pattie was still married to George. Indeed, he even changed her name – giving her the new monikers Nell, Nelly, or Nello – as though it was his plan to create a new woman, leaving Pattie and her history as the wife of a Beatle behind. It could, of course, also have been subconsciously because she and his mother shared the same name. But weren't his nicknames for Pattie the sort you would imagine belonging to a guest-house landlady in Torquay, or a fishmonger, rather than a beautiful ex-model and thoroughly middle-class pilot's daughter? It was as if Eric needed to reduce her, if only in his own mind, in order to feel he could possibly be worthy of such a goddess, one who for years he had put on a pedestal and worshipped from afar. His controlling nature towards her also manifested itself in displays of petulance and jealousy when it came to her family and friends. Indeed, Pattie says Eric was madly jealous of anyone to whom she gave her attention and didn't even like her talking to her own family on the phone.

When the tour reached Denver, just a few weeks after Pattie had left George, she was having second thoughts. Coincidentally, Chris O'Dell found she was staying in the same hotel. She immediately rang Eric in his room and Pattie answered, delighted to hear from her old friend. But it soon became clear that Eric was not so thrilled she was in town. They spent what Chris describes as a 'strange night' in each other's company. Eric had seemed happy to see Chris at first, but the longer the night went on, the more he became distant. 'It was obvious he wanted Pattie all to himself,' says Chris. 'He was possessive of her and jealous of me. I couldn't put my finger on it, but something strange was going on between them. Eric was drinking a lot, maybe that was the problem. And he was a mean drunk. When he was drinking, he was just nasty. It was different when he was high on heroin, because he couldn't do anything, he was not functioning. But when he was on alcohol, he was just mean. He would pick on people and told me later that he just didn't like it that Pattie and I were so close because it left him out. He did the same thing to Pattie's sister Jenny. He would be difficult to her and that was all alcohol related too. Eric is a good person, but when he was drunk and on drugs, he wasn't a good person.'

The tour, now extended to Europe and Japan, played forty-nine sell-out shows. But there were complaints from some of the harder-core fans that Clapton was not playing solos. The reality was that he felt so rusty, he was trying to avoid them. To some extent, he was simply not physically able to perform those incendiary guitar parts anymore. 'For most of the seventies,' he said later, 'I was content to lie back and do what I had to do with the least amount of effort. I was very grateful to be alive. I didn't want to push it. I was an intensely dedicated musician in my early twenties. It was something I wouldn't care to live through again because I missed so much of the rest of my life. Music can become an obsessive thing with me, really obsessive. A lot of that has since dropped away. Whether my music has suffered or not is not the point. My life is a lot better for it.

'I was also tired of gymnastic guitar playing. And not only was I tired of it in myself, it seemed the advent of Cream and Led Zeppelin had woken up a whole spectre of guitar players who just wanted to burn themselves into infinity. The more I heard about that, the more I wanted to back off. I started to identify with like-minded people like J. J. Cale. When I listened to J. J. Cale records, I was impressed by the subtlety, by what *wasn't* being played.'

Sometimes, however, Eric wasn't playing simply because he was drunk and flat out on his back on stage, having sneakily swapped the cold tea Roger insisted he drink during shows with his favourite tipple, Courvoisier and 7Up. And when Forrester tried to warn him to ease up on the drinking, he would invariably get a verbal volley.

At the end of the US leg of the tour, Pattie flew home as planned. Without breaking his stride, Eric was quickly back to sharing his bed with as many women as he could, on an often daily, and usually fairly indiscriminate, basis. It was decidedly odd, given how long and hard he had campaigned for Pattie to leave George, that he was now, seemingly, prepared to risk losing her if she were to find out about his carousel of meaningless one-night stands.

In the meantime, his management were keen to cash in further now that Eric was hot again. A plan was hatched to follow up the massive hit that 'I Shot the Sheriff' had become by sending Clapton to Jamaica, where the idea was that he would immerse himself in Jamaican culture and music and come up with a similar reggae-style hit. So, in the autumn of 1974, he and Pattie, who had joined him once more, landed in the capital, Kingston. Artistically, it wasn't a success. For one thing, Eric found it hard to keep up with the enormous amounts of ganja the local musicians, who arrived for sessions with him at the island's Dynamic Sounds Studios, were smoking. Also, being put under pressure by Forrester and Tom Dowd to come up with a hit to order put Eric in a bad frame of mind from the off. The harder he tried, the less appealing the idea of repeating himself seemed.

Nor was the plan to make the trip an unofficial 'honeymoon' with Pattie altogether without hiccups either. At the Terra Nova Hotel, Chris O'Dell came to pay them a visit, and she and Pattie sat in the studio as Eric put down vocals for his new album, *There's One in Every Crowd*. As he worked on through the evening, Pattie and Chris got steadily drunker on pitchers of Brandy Alexanders, brought over from the hotel bar. Finally, they were told to leave by Eric because they were making too much noise and they went back to the hotel, where they ordered yet more Brandy Alexanders. In Pattie's room, they began reminiscing about Friar Park and George, and Chris suggested they call him up. 'Really, do you think we should? It would be nice to talk to him,' Pattie replied. It was about nine in the morning in the UK as Pattie drunkenly dialled the number. George was delighted to hear from her, despite the relatively early hour, and they chatted happily, as though their split had not happened. After a while, Pattie handed the phone to Chris and she was talking animatedly to her old boss when Eric walked in and stood in the doorway glowering.

'What are you doing?' he asked.

'Oh, we're talking to George,' Pattie replied, unruffled. Fury took over him, he flung the bag he was carrying on the bed next to them and stormed into the bathroom, slamming the door. Sensing that trouble was brewing, Chris quickly hung up and she and Pattie hugged goodbye. She was about to leave when Clapton flung open the bathroom door and came back into the room, stomping over to Pattie, who was sitting on the bed.

'Why the fuck did you call him?' he raged. Pattie, desperately trying to placate him, said lightly that they just wanted to talk. Without turning to Chris, Eric told her: 'Get out of my room!'

So what was Harrison's reaction to this spat between his best friend and estranged wife? He certainly wasn't unhappy that he had been the cause of a ruck between the lovebirds. Chris says: 'George knew something was going on because we had to tell him, "Eric's here and we've got to hang up." Afterwards, I called George from my room and asked if I could go and stay with him and he said yes right away. He was happy because there definitely was competitiveness between him and Eric.' She adds: 'There was also a part of Pattie wondering if she had done the right thing. Pattie always will have a connection to George which is stronger than the one she had to Eric.'

But the following day, at breakfast, it was as though nothing had happened, with Eric cheerfully inviting Chris over to join their table. Nonetheless, the incident was enough for her to cut her holiday with them short and fly straight back to London. For his part, Harrison mocked his ex and Eric in a new take on the Everly Brothers' song 'Bye Bye Love' on his 1975 album *Dark Horse*, which included the lines: 'There goes our lady with a you know who. I hope she's happy and old Clapper too.' Famously, after the split, he had said publicly of Pattie taking up with Clapton, 'She is better off with him than with some dope.' But his apparently sanguine attitude was far from the full story.

For Eric and Pattie, it was just the beginning of trouble in the couple's already turbulent relationship. Not long afterwards, they had a 'playful' fight that resulted in Pattie locking herself in the bathroom while staying in the Jamaican resort of Ocho Rios, and ended with Eric breaking his toe and being taken to Kingston Hospital after trying to kick the door down.

This sense of frustration extended to the finished album, *There's One in Every Crowd*. It had flashes of reggae, mainly in the lamentable 'Swing Low Sweet Chariot' and the George Terry song 'Don't Blame Me', which had Clapton doing a deeply suspect *Black And White Minstrel Show*-style Jamaican accent. Indeed, rather than sounding like Bob Marley, which was clearly the idea, he ended up doing a fairly passable impression of a cantankerous first-generation Afro-Caribbean pensioner complaining about the price of ackees on Brixton Market.

Overall, the record sounded like a rather rattled-off rehash of *461 Ocean Boulevard*, despite the introduction to the band of the very talented singer Marcy Levy, who, as Marcella Detroit, would go on to have success in the early 90s as part of Shakespears Sister. But for the most part, it was a vaguely half-hearted affair, exemplified by a near comatose rendition of the Elmore James classic 'The Sky Is Crying'. The record-buying public seemed to agree because after Clapton's previous LP had topped the charts in the US, the follow-up – released just nine months later – only managed to climb as high as twenty-one, and fifteen in Britain. And when 'Swing Low Sweet Chariot' was released as a single in the UK, it barely broke into the top twenty.

There was more bad news on the horizon. Word reached Eric from Canada that his half-brother Brian, whom he had hardly seen in fifteen years, had been killed in a motorcycle accident. Hasty arrangements were made by Roger so Clapton and Pattie could attend the funeral. But on the flight over, Eric got horribly drunk. He later said that he felt numb and was unable to console his mother, who was beside herself with grief.

Thanks to his touring and recording commitments, his relationship with Pattie was a peripatetic one from the outset. But they had a chance, finally, to settle down in one place when Forrester told Eric he needed to become a tax exile because of the big bucks he was earning since his comeback. The plan was for them to spend a year in the Bahamas. His manager rented an estate that belonged to an international financier for Clapton on Paradise Island, just off the coast of Nassau.

As with his decampment to Oswestry, the open-air experience was initially good for Eric. He and Pattie swam and sunbathed, and for a while his drinking became more manageable, the weather and the beach acting as enough of a distraction. But the sun-bleached idyll would not last long. Soon Clapton was retreating indoors all day, alone, drinking the brandy and vodka that was available very cheaply on the island. Somewhat illogically, given how much money he was earning, the fact that the booze was inexpensive did make a difference. When it comes to the subject of cold, hard cash, Clapton has never forgotten his financially straitened childhood and jumps at the opportunity to make small savings; on his regular trips on Concorde, for example, it was a familiar sight to see Eric stocking up on duty-free cigarettes while on board.

His year in the Bahamas, during which he wrote the miserable song 'Black Summer Rain', may have saved him a fortune in unpaid taxes, but it also served to transform him into a full-tilt, 24-carat alcoholic. A tour of Australia followed and he took to inviting complete strangers in bars to take him on in pissed-up bouts of arm-wrestling. Otherwise, he was simply boorish and embarrassing to Pattie. In Adelaide, she found him and Roger in their hotel suite, lying on the bed, watching a couple of strippers, whom they had picked up on the street outside, perform. As usual, Eric blamed the whole unseemly spectacle on his manager and, as usual, Forrester accepted the flak.

Drink made Clapton, a self-confessed coward when it comes to physical combat, start picking fights with innocent strangers and he brooded endlessly about perceived slights. Authority figures – police, immigration clerks and customs officials – were a particular bugbear. Luckily, Forrester had hired a 6ft 4in, perm-haired hardman called Alphi O'Leary, who had once run celebrity hangout the Speakeasy in London with his brother Laurie, to act as Eric's 'PA', though the main responsibility of the deceptively gentle giant was to act as minder and protector against those Eric rubbed up the wrong way. And where O'Leary did his talking with his fists, the smart-talking Roger became adept at smoothing things over when they turned ugly.

The sojourn in the Bahamas did not take Clapton away from being available for ad hoc gigs, however, if the fancy took him. He agreed to appear twice with the Rolling Stones, playing in LA and New York on their American tour. Indeed, after guitarist Mick Taylor quit the Stones in December 1974, Jagger sounded out Clapton about joining the band in his place. Eric was also invited to play on a session in New York for Bob Dylan's album *Desire*, which was recorded in the summer of

1975. It was not a pleasant experience. A mildly taciturn Dylan had lined up a cavalcade of musicians, including half a dozen guitar players. They were expected just to go in and play. It was a pointless exercise because, in the end, none of what Clapton recorded was used on the final version.

But just physically getting to gigs was proving problematic, given Eric's ability to seek out and find trouble. As an example of how much of a pain he had become, on a flight from Miami to Tulsa, where he was due to play a gig at Cain's Ballroom, he was so drunk and troublesome that the pilot called ahead and police were waiting for him on the tarmac, where, just to wind them up further, he then proceeded to drop two suitcases from the first floor of the terminal building. They arrested him, despite the fact that he tried to claim his drunkenness was actually the ill-effects of the flight. Clapton was hauled off to the county jail and when he got stroppy about a cop using his middle name, he was carted off to a 4ft x 6ft drunk tank to sober up. They didn't believe he was who he said he was, so he told the cops to get a guitar, which they did, and after he played it, they let him go. The following day, a picture appeared of him in the *Tulsa Tribune*, dressed in a striped shirt and standing next to a uniformed guard, staring miserably through the bars of the prison cell.

Back in England, he took to getting behind the wheel hammered. At the end of April 1975, he was taken to hospital with cuts, bruises, concussion and a busted eardrum, after crashing his £20,000 Ferrari at 90mph head-on into a van and needing to be cut out of the wreckage by firemen. He'd jumped in the car straight after landing on a flight back from Australia, during which he had been drinking heavily. The van turned over and the driver, 29-year-old David Birch of Steyning, West Sussex, who was delivering dry-cleaning, was treated for minor injuries. 'Dave rang me up from the hospital and said, "Guess who's in the next bed to me,"' says Mr Birch's widow, Frances. 'He'd been stationary in the truck and he said Eric Clapton had driven straight at him. Dave thought he was drunk or on drugs, but the whole thing was hushed up and we heard that Clapton's lawyers paid Dave's firm for the damage. When Dave died in 2013, I must say I considered playing "Tears in Heaven" at his funeral.' Clapton eventually used a picture of the wrecked Ferrari on the inside cover of his *Slowhand* album.

His lifelong obsession with collecting Ferraris was inspired by George Harrison, who turned up one day at his house in a blue Ferrari 356 GTC. Naturally, Eric wanted one too, even though he didn't have a licence (in her memoirs, Pattie claimed Clapton eventually got someone who looked like him to take his driving test for him). He bought his first Ferrari for £4,000 and learnt to drive it on the driveway at Hurtwood. He changed them regularly because he had only enough space in his garage to keep two at once. But even at the best of times, Hurtwood was far from ideally situated for the merely careless – never mind drug- and drink-addled – driver. It was reached by what seemed like hours of motoring along tight rock-wall-lined lanes, with trees overhanging, like some sort of wooded cave from Middle-earth.

When Pattie had first arrived at Hurtwood, she found a house that, rather than being the rock-star mansion she may have been expecting, was little more than a six-bedroom hovel. During his heroin haze with Alice, they had let their two dogs mess all over the floors and never bothered to clean it up.

There were bats in the main bedroom, a resident mouse in the kitchen and she discovered that Eric stored his jumpers and shirts in the bath. Bizarrely, however, Pattie, who set about the task of doing the place up, had to get permission from Roger for any work she wanted to do and he would often veto her spending money on projects in the garden. The house quickly became a menagerie, with Eric's Weimaraner, Willow, Fast Eddy, the ginger cat, an Airedale called Trouper and a donkey called Matthew that Pattie gave Eric one Christmas.

She also found uncashed cheques for thousands of pounds that Eric routinely stuffed in a drawer with the unpaid bills. Showing a singular lack of basic economics, he'd operated a policy of refusing ever to cash cheques he was sent directly because, he reasoned, he didn't want to give his money to the bank. Eric's domestic and financial ignorance was largely due to the fact that he had everything done for him. Every week, he was given a fairly modest £200 in cash as his wages by Gladys, Roger's bookkeeper. And Pattie says that when they got together, Forrester refused to let them have a joint account, while insisting on sanctioning large items personally. Pattie got £120,000 in her divorce from George and a red Mercedes he'd bought her. But a jealous Eric did not like her riding around in Harrison's car, so he got rid of it and bought her another.

Even so, George continued to visit the house to see Eric and to give him a first listen to his new songs. But it was clear that, from Harrison's point of view, the slight was not forgotten and their friendship was not always a comfortable one. Even so, he offered to do the decent thing and arrange a divorce. Eric was horrified. If George was to divorce Pattie, he pointed out unchivalrously, then that would mean he'd now have to marry her.

Despite his less than successful last attempt at a collaboration with Dylan, Eric still invited him to appear with him on his next LP, *No Reason to Cry*, which was recorded at the Band's Shangri-La Studios in Malibu, and which followed the live album *E. C. Was Here*, which had been released in the autumn of 1975. From the outset, however, the studio sessions were an ill-thought-out affair, with Clapton more interested in getting drunk in the pleasant surroundings than doing much work. Meanwhile, Dylan, who for some reason was living in a tent in the garden of the studios, would arrive on an only ad-hoc basis to record. One of the tracks Dylan brought in was 'Sign Language', on which they duetted and which appeared on the album when it was released in August 1976. The song, which featured the Band's Robbie Robertson on guitar, is unwittingly very similar to Pink Floyd's 'Wish You Were Here', which had been recorded the previous year. Fittingly, perhaps, given his obvious thirst during the making of it, Clapton is pictured on the cover of the album wearing a Panama hat and surrounded by bottles of booze.

But there is nothing, of course, that dissolves so thoroughly in alcohol as propriety.

Lurching up to the microphone following his opening song at a gig at the Birmingham Odeon in August 1976, Clapton began his address to the audience in unfamiliar fashion. Instead of the usual platitudes about how great it was to be there again, or what a wonderful crowd they were, he began with a question: 'Do we have any foreigners in the audience tonight? If so, put up your hands . . . I think we should vote for Enoch

Powell.' Others say his rant went on for more than two minutes and some of what he is claimed to have said is so jaw-dropping, it should come with a health warning.

It is hard to know how much is true. What is indisputable, however, is that the episode has dogged Clapton ever since. In the mind of some, he will forever be tarred with the brush of being a racist and a bigot. The incident was partly responsible for the formation of Rock Against Racism two years later. Just uttering Powell's name was enough to provoke the catcalls that began in the audience that night and continue to this day. He was the former Tory minister who had made the infamous 'Rivers of Blood' speech in 1968, condemning immigration into the UK. Clapton's support for Powell was all the more incendiary because the politician's speech had also been made in Birmingham, which had become a power base for the racist National Front party.

But if Clapton was regretting his remarks the following morning, he wasn't showing it. At the city's Albany Hotel, he told the assembled press unapologetically: 'I think Enoch is a prophet. His diplomacy is wrong and he's got no idea how to present things. His ideas are right. You go to Heathrow Airport any day and you'll see thousands of Indian people sitting there waiting to know whether or not they can come into the country. And you go to Jamaica and there are adverts on TV saying, "Come to lovely England."

'I don't think Enoch Powell is a racist. I don't think he cares about colour of any kind. His whole idea is for us to stop being unfair to immigrants because it's getting out of order. A husband comes over, lives off the dole to try to save enough to bring his wife and kids over. It's splitting up families. The government is being incredibly unfair to people abroad to lure them to the promised land, where there is actually no work. Racist aggravation starts when white guys see immigrants getting jobs and they're not. Yeah, I'm getting a lot of stick for what I said, but so did Enoch. He was the only bloke telling the truth for the good of the country. I believe he is a very religious man and you can't be religious and racist at the same time. The two things are incompatible.'

If his comments seemed illogical and mealy mouthed, it is because they were. And while there was no conceivable defence for his on-stage diatribe, later he did offer a plea in mitigation. He claimed that, earlier that day, he and his entourage had travelled up from London and in the lobby of the Churchill Hotel, an Arab man had made a sexual comment to Pattie. Clapton said he was incensed and looked around to see that there were signs all over the place in Arabic. Ten years later, he was still reluctant to retract his remarks. 'Even through my drunken haze, there was a note of warning in what he [Powell] was saying that I thought people were ignoring,' he said. 'It wasn't racialist. It was just that things were getting out of control if people weren't careful, that ghettoes would spring up all over England, which they have done. He was trying to put the brakes on, for good or bad. I don't know what his real motivations were. I feel remorse because unless you know what you're talking about, you should always keep your mouth shut. What I was doing was reacting to an instinct. I still do that, but I try to keep the lid on now.'

Even so, he was still inclined on occasion to fulminate about Arab money being thrown around in London. And the incident came back to haunt him from time to time over the years, most notably on 11 June 1988, when Clapton turned up to play with Dire Straits at the seventieth birthday tribute to Nelson Mandela at Wembley Stadium. On the day, he was invited by the event's organiser, Jerry Dammers of the Specials, to go on television and publicly retract his remarks. A furious Clapton refused and later went public, branding Dammers 'a fucking jerk'.

Clapton's attitude towards his impromptu Enoch speech seems to be somewhat ambivalent. After his earlier partial statements of regret, his opinion seemed to harden with age. When he was questioned about it, for the umpteenth time, in 2004, he gave the impression of digging his heels in. 'My feelings about this haven't really changed. It was fuelled by an outrage at what was happening in London, with the Saudis buying up the West End,' he said. 'And that connected with what Enoch was saying about how our immigration policies had failed. Obviously, there's no way I could be a racist. But there was something about him that I thought was outrageously brave. He was doing what he thought was the best thing for the country. He got shot down for it. But he spoke from the heart and I recognised that.'

Of course, it may just have been that Clapton got increasingly annoyed by being questioned, in his late fifties, about something that he had said in his very early thirties. And perhaps, regardless of your point of view on his one-time support for Powell, he could be forgiven for getting the hump with journalists who refused to leave the subject alone decades later.

Certainly, the dichotomy of his comments when set against his avowed love of black music was inescapable. And particularly, as his friend Pete Townshend once observed, apparently in all seriousness: 'Eric really should have been born black.' And there could be no doubt that the reverence and respect Clapton showed his black musical heroes, like Muddy Waters, B.B. King and Buddy Guy, when they appeared on stage together, was unquestionably genuine. Also, it is a statement of irrefutable fact that few have done more down the years so generously to promote black artists than Clapton.

But for all that he had been scrupulous in ensuring that those black musicians who inspired him, and whose songs he covered, got their rightful recognition, he was also aware that some of them still had reason to be disgruntled that a white boy had stepped in and made a killing from the music they'd invented. 'The older guys are very polite, but there's a certain amount of reserve there,' Eric noted. 'There's a lot of bitterness over money. Chuck Berry, for instance. He's a very dark horse. He very definitely does have the feeling that people ripped him off and stole all his licks.' By way of payback, perhaps, when a host of celebrity musicians, including Clapton and Keith Richards, met in October 1986 to celebrate Berry's sixtieth birthday with two shows in St Louis – later released as a film entitled *Hail! Hail! Rock 'n' Roll* – some found that when they borrowed amplifiers from the great man during rehearsals, Berry billed them for the hire of them.

Perhaps, in part, because of the Birmingham debacle, the days when Eric could do no wrong in the eyes of the critics were long gone. Reviewing *No Reason to Cry*, which included the track 'Black Summer Rain', in September 1976, the *Daily Mail* complained that his songwriting was 'insular and limp' and his once incendiary playing had been replaced by 'short, largely subdued and often self-conscious guitar solos which leave you with the impression that he can't wait to get them out of the way'. Even so, the record reached a respectable number eight in Britain and fifteen in the States.

In hindsight, Clapton himself agreed that his mid-70s output, despite some obvious highlights, left much to be desired. 'If it were me now, in a fit, clear state of mind, I would have to say I could make them better without a doubt,' he has said. 'But when I look back and see the state I was in – emotionally, physically, the amount of substances I was consuming – I can't see how they *could* be any better. I know people who even now go into the studio and don't get that much done and don't consume half of what we were consuming. Every one of those records has an ingredient of some kind that can move me. And the tracks that embarrass me, I don't play.'

The truth was, at home at least, for the time being, his days as a huge box-office draw were sadly in the past. His management team took to booking him into smaller venues, including Pontins holiday camp at Camber Sands, Sussex. To add insult to injury, his appearance there was summarily vetoed on the orders of the camp's septuagenarian owner, Sir Fred Pontin, who declared he'd never heard of Eric Clapton. 'Anyway,' the no-nonsense Pontin added, 'we don't want to show established stars. Peters and Lee [the *Opportunity Knocks* TV talent show winners] started with us – and you can't get much higher than that.'

Increasingly, Clapton was seen as a dinosaur. He hated the emerging punk rock and said so. 'There's nothing there,' he remarked at the time. 'I don't think there's any merit in not being able to play and making that your profession.' Some years later, he mused, 'I was, I felt, very threatened by the whole thing because as an elder statesman, even then, I was one of the obstacles. I was one of the people who should have been swept away by punk.'

Which is not to say he wasn't capable of some fairly anarchic behaviour of his own. Drunk and egged on by his hangers-on, he took to streaking naked, including up the aisle of a crowded passenger plane. 'Sometimes I was drunk,' he explained. 'Other times slightly drunk and semi-provoked by a bourgeois situation or something.' When Eric appeared at a charity event in County Kildare organised by film producer Kevin McClory, his drunken pranks annoyed actress Shirley MacLaine so much she is said to have responded by calling him a 'creep'. In fact, Clapton had such a good time drinking in the hotel, called Barberstown Castle, where they were staying, in the village of Straffan, that he returned with Roger and they bought the place.

Sometimes his drinking put him in mortal danger. In Honolulu, in 1977, he climbed naked, save for a Samurai sword he had bought in Japan, over the balconies of the high-rise hotel where he was staying to climb into drummer Jamie Oldaker's room for a wheeze. Two cops with guns arrived at the door and trained their weapons on him, thinking he was some sort of trained killer – albeit one with a taste for murder *sans culottes*. The press picked up on it and headlines began appearing that Clapton was cancelling shows because he was too drunk to play.

At home, his drinking was invariably done in the Windmill, the pub at the top of the drive, which became the centre of his and Pattie's social world, as did the cricket club in Ripley. He introduced 'Nell' to his old school friends Guy and Gordon and the showbiz couple took to throwing boozy dinner parties for locals and going out with other couples. They also founded the Ripley Spoons Orchestra, which involved going to the cricket club, where they and their friends would all play the spoons and sing, while local musician Chris Stainton accompanied them on the piano.

Despite it all, Eric remained capable of conjuring up classics. Waiting downstairs at Hurtwood for Pattie to get ready for a party one night, he wrote 'Wonderful Tonight'. It was not quite the paean to a goddess that it appeared, however. In fact, they were late and he was annoyed she was taking so long, as she tried on dress after dress, leaving them discarded in a pile on the floor, while he fumed. Eric, who had been spending a lot of time listening to the simple lyrics of Texan country singer Don Williams, rather sheepishly admits he was in a 'foul temper' when he wrote the song. It appeared on his next album, *Slowhand*, for which he employed the services of a new producer, Glyn Johns, who had worked with the Stones and the Eagles, when recording began in early 1977. The record also featured the J. J. Cale song 'Cocaine', which would become a staple of future Clapton shows, as would 'Lay Down Sally', a number written by Marcy Levy and George Terry. The album, released later that year, was a much bigger hit in America, where it reached number two in the charts. In Britain, it only got as far as number twenty-three.

Partly because of Clapton's dislike of flying – and his habit of getting into trouble on planes and in airports – it was decided he, his band and Pattie should travel around the cities of his summer tour of Europe in 1977 by Orient Express. But once the novelty of being woken up every morning by a waiter with a glass of Champagne wore off, boredom and misbehaviour soon set in. A reporter, invited along for the ride, was thrown off without his passport. Time was passed on the train betting on anything from pontoon and accumulators to predicting whether the lunchtime potatoes would be sautéed or fried. Meanwhile, Eric and his friend, ex-Small Faces bassist Ronnie Lane, who was part of the travelling contingent with his band Slim Chance, took to busking on the boat train to Bremen and on the station platform at Heidelberg, with violinist Charlie Hart and drummer Hughie Flint.

Pattie's divorce from George finally came through while they were on board. She and Ronnie's wife, Kate, performed a five-minute interlude each night, dancing the can-can under the stage name the Harlots. Heading back on the coach to their beautifully appointed private train carriage of an evening, the contingent would round off the night with a four-part harmony rendition of 'My Old Man Says Follow the Van' and 'Maybe It's Because I'm a Londoner'.

Clapton repeated the train jaunt across Europe the following autumn, when someone came up with the bright idea that this time they should also allow a BBC film crew along to record events for posterity. The purpose of the fly-on-the-wall documentary was to promote Clapton's sixth solo album, *Backless* – which once again booze and cocaine had featured prominently in the making of, despite the best efforts of the comparatively straitlaced and work-oriented Glyn Johns. As well as the future crowd favourite 'Tulsa Time', it also contained 'Golden Ring', about Pattie's upset when she heard the news that George was planning to get married again, to Olivia Arias. In the lyrics, Eric poses the question to Pattie that if he were to marry her, would it make her happy?

Given the condition Clapton was in, the documentary was an accident waiting to happen. Throughout the one-hour-thirteen-minute film, called *Eric Clapton and his Rolling Hotel*, which, bizarrely, was shot on carriages that had once belonged to Hermann Goering, he was drunk and glassy-eyed. It opened with Clapton, bare-chested save for an open waistcoat and granddad scarf, singing a half-cut a cappella version of 'Smile' while Roger Forrester, wearing a flat cap and an inane smile, held up a table lamp to illuminate him. Elsewhere, Eric was seen taunting a squirming Stigwood about money and, more specifically, his obsession at the time, that he had 'creamed off' most of the profits from Cream to finance the Bee Gees. To forced laughter, he confronted Stigwood in front of a roomful of people, telling him: 'If it wasn't for me and Ginger and Jack, you wouldn't have been able to bring the Bee Gees over from Australia, would you?' A mortified Stigwood managed a strained, fixed smile and responded: 'After you finish filming this, I might strangle him.'

The whole exercise must have seemed like a fun wheeze at the time, but it soon became clear that the film, made by documentary-maker Rex Pyke, was a massive train wreck as far as Clapton was concerned. Amid the forced jollity of duping a confused French TV reporter into believing one of the guitarist's American minders was actually the star himself was an underlying tragedy. At the end, in a moment of sublime irony, a pissed Eric, his face puffy and eyes bloodshot, pondered how he would pass his time at home with no work to do. 'If you stayed at home, you'd have no one to play with,' he mused. 'You'd get bored. I'd probably turn into an alcoholic overnight. Because I've got a pub at the top of my drive and if I'm at home, I'm there every lunchtime . . . Come back home, pass out, get up opening time.'

It was obvious to anyone that that particular train had long since left. When the completed programme was viewed, a decision was taken that Clapton, who later described his condition during filming as 'intoxicated and deranged', emerged so badly that there was no alternative but to shelve it. As Pattie was about to find out, things were going to get yet more deranged.

# TEN

# Rehab

The Hollywood version of Eric and Pattie's forbidden love story would have ended with their wedding-day kiss, the frame dissolving into a warm glow, symbolic of the sunlit uplands awaiting them – Layla and Majnun, happy ever after. The reality was distinctly less Tinseltown. The truth was, their marriage on 27 March 1979 merely publicly ratified a rather depressing and tawdry accommodation, an unspoken, shared understanding that everything the relationship had once promised in the headiness of their early infatuation had been just fantasy. That particular pipedream had long ago been extinguished by the dregs from a thousand booze bottles. Subconsciously they must have known that they would never be enough for each other. Yet they were both prepared to go along with the charade, complicit in the deluded hope that it would work out all right in the end.

A week earlier, the relationship had been all off, the couple separated by 5000 miles and mutual bad feeling. Not only that, but Eric was living with another woman. The seeds of that break-up were sown four months earlier, in November 1978, when Pattie unsuspectingly introduced Eric to two friends, a pair of twins, both models, called Jenny and Susie

McLean. While Clapton was on tour, she had become friendly with the sisters. And Pattie had for a while been busy establishing a close network of girlfriends to fill the loneliness while Eric was away and as a support group when he cheated on her, which he did all the time. Not long after he and Pattie got together, Clapton, with the backing of Roger Forrester, had decreed that tours should be free of wives and girlfriends. The catalyst for this pronouncement dated back to a tour of America. They were sitting on a private jet when, in a flagrant breach of rock 'n' roll etiquette, Jamie Oldaker's wife began rummaging in her bag and got out her knitting. Eric was furious. The 'No WAGs' policy also gave him carte blanche to sleep with as many groupies as possible, most of whom were procured by sidekicks. Even when Pattie had been allowed to go on the road with him, Eric would mess around with women, telling her to go up to their room to warm the bed while he conducted liaisons elsewhere in the hotel. In the end, she'd go home and let him get on with it. It wasn't that there was little pretence about his philandering – there was absolutely none. When he got home, he would often painstakingly list the conquests he had made while he was away to Pattie, his logic being that these things were better out in the open. Having unburdened himself, he would then wander off to watch TV.

Elsewhere, he seemed to exist by the mantra that, for him, the term 'male chauvinist pig' was not so much an insult as a mission statement. Pattie was expected to cook his meals and present them to him at the allotted time. If they had family and friends round for dinner, he would get up and leave the table as soon as he had finished eating and go and watch television or strum the guitar in the den. Consequently, Pattie's mother couldn't stand him, partly because of the way he had treated Pattie's sister, Paula, when they were dating. He had renewed his passion for fishing and when he wasn't down the pub, he spent all day out alone, or travelling up and down the country with Roger, indulging in his love of West Bromwich Albion Football Club.

Interests soon became obsessions. Eric went through a phase of buying racehorses, then went off that too (his record as an owner, however, was impressive. A filly he bought for £500, called Via Delta, won more than £28,000 in prize money and was sold after two seasons for £50,000). He insisted on getting totally into the spirit of things and would put on whites to watch cricket on TV, or insist Pattie cook him pasta before settling down to watch *The Godfather*. And despite having more than 200 shirts, he'd go berserk if she couldn't find the exact one he wanted, even though often he had nowhere more important to go than the pub. He also installed a snooker table on the first floor of Hurtwood and when the bars closed at Sunday lunchtime, he and his chums from Ripley – some of whom seemed to get a kick out of watching a millionaire rock star make a drunken fool of himself in a down-at-heel boozer – would spend the rest of the afternoon noisily playing frame after frame.

When he and Pattie were apart due to his long touring schedule, he'd go weeks at a stretch without writing or phoning. Understandably, Pattie had long ago started to ask herself whether for Eric their relationship had been more about the thrill of the chase. Certainly, it seemed that now he had her, he had lost interest, particularly in sex, which had become another issue in their dysfunctional relationship. She dealt with the angst by self-medicating with booze and Valium. At Christmas, they split up briefly, with Clapton showing no sign publicly that the separation had caused even a moment of self-reflection. But by February, they were back together, only they were still miserable and fighting, and during one argument, Eric pulled Pattie's hair after she accused him of being 'cold'.

In early March 1979, while Eric was at home, Pattie invited Jenny McLean to dinner. When it got late, Pattie insisted that Jenny stay the night rather than drive back to her home in Hampstead, north London. Pattie, however, was unaware that Eric had set his sights on the pretty Jenny some months previously. The following morning, Pattie woke to find Eric and her friend had gone out shopping and to the pub. Pattie went out to see her sister and when she came back, Clapton and Jenny were sitting close together on the sofa. Pattie tried to say something, but a clearly drunk Eric interrupted to insist he was trying to have a very intense and intimate conversation with her friend. When an understandably confused Pattie asked him why, he replied: 'Because I'm in love with this girl. Go away and leave us alone. Just fuck off.' Pattie went upstairs and cried her heart out, before taking a few Valium to try to calm her nerves. She rang her sister, also called Jenny, and told her to come and get her. While Eric and his new girlfriend canoodled inside, Pattie stumbled, tear-stained and drenched, up the drive in the rain, staggering in and out of the bushes in the dark as she waited to be picked up.

A couple of days later, Pattie plucked up the courage to ring Clapton to tell him she needed to get away for a time. But to her dismay, rather than plead with her to come back, he readily agreed that they needed a break. Not least because he still had the attractive Miss McLean with him at Hurtwood. A desperate Pattie boarded a flight to Los Angeles and cried so much on the plane, she was asked to move seats, out of sight of the other first-class passengers, in case she put them off their Champagne. She had been invited to stay in Malibu with her friends Rob Fraboni, the owner of Shangri-la Studios, who had co-produced 'No Reason to Cry' for Eric, and his wife Myel. Meanwhile, Eric's new girlfriend, whom he had christened 'Sweet Jen', joined him on tour in Ireland for a warm-up prior to a planned US tour. In fact, he was so wrapped up in the first flush of love and lust that he clean forgot Pattie's birthday on 17 March.

Fittingly enough, Eric and Pattie's path to wedlock began with a drink. Once he had returned from Ireland, Clapton was playing pool for money at Roger's house, set in twenty acres, in Frimley Green, Surrey, with Eric fortified by a steady stream of vodka and tonics. By the end of it, Eric was so paralytic that he couldn't see straight to hit the cue ball. Haemorrhaging money, he suggested, as a last resort, a double or quits bet. Forrester had been chiding him throughout that he and Jenny needed to be more discreet or news of the affair would reach the ears of the newspapers. Clapton, doubting his value as a news story, told Roger he was talking out of his hat: no newspaper would give a damn. After much bickering back and forth, Forrester said he could get Clapton's picture in a national newspaper the next day, no problem. Eric bet him £10,000 he couldn't. Roger went directly to the phone and called the *Daily Mail*'s Nigel Dempster, the doyen of Fleet Street gossip columnists.

Given he had ten grand riding on it, Forrester spent a sleepless night waiting for the newspaper to be delivered. He breathed a huge sigh of relief to find that Dempster had repeated the story just as he had given it to him. The piece announced that rock star Eric Clapton would marry Pattie Boyd in America the following week. At Hurtwood, Eric, waking to the news, was hopping mad. He jumped in his Ferrari and floored it to his manager's west London office. Roger was chatting on the phone when he got there, but Clapton stormed in, took hold of the flex, wrapped it round Roger's neck and hit him on the head with the phone. Now he was going to have to marry Pattie, whether he liked it or not.

Once he had pacified him, Forrester insisted that the newspaper story was actually a blessing in disguise. The Pattie situation needed to be resolved one way or the other, and since she would not yet have seen the article, why didn't Eric just ring her in LA and propose? Warming to the idea, Clapton rang Pattie's host, Rob Fraboni, in LA later that day. It was early on Friday morning there and Pattie was out on the beach, recuperating from a stonking hangover she had picked up at a party the previous night. Eric told Fraboni to give Pattie a message: would she please marry him the following Tuesday in Tucson, Arizona, where he was starting a fifty-night American tour? Oh, and by the way, if she refused, she was to get 'on her bike'.

As romantic proposals go, it was unlikely to trouble the scorers. Nevertheless, Rob was dispatched to pass on the communication post-haste. He found a slightly befuddled Pattie and delivered the message verbatim. Later, Pattie rang Eric and on finding Jenny McLean was not, according to Clapton at least, on the scene anymore, said a tearful 'Yes'. 'But in the bottom of my heart I knew this wasn't right,' she later wrote in her memoirs. She rang her friend Chris O'Dell at

Chris's apartment in Brentwood, California, to tell her the happy news. It was something of a shock to Chris, who only the previous day had sat listening as Pattie complained to her that the relationship was not working and she had had enough of the way Eric treated her. 'I'd gone over to see Pattie in LA and she told me what had happened, that she had left Eric and was never going back,' says Chris. 'And the next thing I know, I get a phone call from Pattie saying. "Do you want to come to my wedding?" I was disappointed in her. I thought, "Are you really going to go back to this?" But I think if Eric hadn't been offering marriage, she wouldn't have responded. So it came down to marriage.'

In fact, Chris was so surprised that she actually felt obliged to ask Pattie exactly to whom she was getting married. Likewise, she was amazed to hear that Eric had used a go-between to make the marriage proposal. Was this really the infinitely passionate and lyrical Clapton who'd composed 'Layla' and was so tortured by his love for her he had turned himself into a heroin addict when she'd rejected him?

Both Chris and Pattie were right to have their concerns. The day before leaving for the wedding, Clapton told a reporter who asked him what had made him decide to get hitched: 'I got fed up with being turned down by birds in the pub.' And as evidence of just how little Pattie trusted him, the night before the wedding, during which they followed the tradition of remaining apart – the bride with Chris O'Dell and her sister Jenny in a shared hotel room – she had visions that Eric was shacked up with some other woman. For her part, Chris O'Dell could not bring herself to say what she was really thinking: that this was a really terrible idea. Also, the fact that everything had been arranged to fit in with Eric's tour timetable did rather kill some of the romance. Clearly, as far as his relationship with the now seemingly deliriously happy Pattie went, it was Eric – with gallons of booze fuelling his self-interest – who was in the driving seat.

Nor, once Eric had arrived in Tucson, were the omens exactly promising. He was two hours late to collect the marriage licence, forgot to pay the clerk the fee and had to stage a whip-round of his friends after realising he'd arrived without any money to pay for it. Eric's tour manager Larry McNeny told me he was also called into action to save the day and solve the problem of Eric's longstanding aversion to needles. State law in Arizona at the time insisted that the prospective husband and wife submit to a blood test before the marriage could go ahead. Eric point-blank refused. So, the bearded McNeny, who did bear a striking resemblance to his boss and was often required to act as a decoy when escaping fans after shows, was press ganged into checking into the Emergency Room of the local hospital to pose as Clapton and take the test for him.

He says he and Alphi O'Leary waited until after the normal hospital hours in the hope that there would be fewer people around who might spot the ruse. The main problem was that the Texan Larry didn't exactly sound like a Surrey-born Brit.

Thankfully the hospital was quiet. Larry says he muttered the 'occasional 'Yes' and 'No' with my poor British accent'. Alphi had explained why we were there and who I was – or was pretending to be – and that I had a bit of laryngitis. It made it much easier on me to pull off the charade.' He adds: 'I think we offered the hospital staff some tickets to the show. I signed a couple of autographs and we were back in a cab headed to the hotel.'

For the rest of the tour, the ultra-dependable McNeny would return to his daily duties, foremost among which was to carry everywhere with him, day or night, a leather attaché case containing a well-stocked bottle of Courvoisier, 7 Up and a glass.That way, Clapton would never be far from his next drink.

Nonetheless, they were finally married by a Mexican preacher on 27 March at the Apostolic Assembly of Faith in Tucson, a day before his first show of the tour. Clapton wore a white tuxedo, white cowboy boots and hat, and his bride wore a silk-satin dress and lace jacket. Rob Fraboni acted as best man, Roger gave Pattie away and she had two maids of honour, Myel Fraboni and Chris O'Dell, who traded notes with Jenny Boyd all day about how rude and mean Eric was to them.

At the wedding breakfast in a nearby hotel, Eric started a food fight, going berserk and flinging wedding cake at everyone and ruining their outfits and his own. The following night, he brought Pattie up on stage at the Tucson Community Center and serenaded her with 'Wonderful Tonight'. It was only a few days later that Roger confessed the true story to Pattie about Nigel Dempster and the bet, which Clapton – whether as retribution for Forrester's impertinence or simple tight-fistedness – welched on.

Clapton and his band, now joined by the brilliant British guitarist Albert Lee, who was brought in to replace an unavailable George Terry, took off on the road for gigs in the American south-west, with Pattie in tow, and she lovingly watched Eric from the side of the stage each night as he performed. But after the third gig, and prior to a show in New Orleans, Eric summarily announced to her that she had to fly to LA, collect her stuff and go home to England. The new Mrs Clapton reluctantly did as she was told. But it seemed an odd request, given they had been married less than a week. Soon, however, the real reason he wanted her out of the way emerged. One of the roadies got word to Pattie that Jenny McLean had checked into the hotel in New Orleans where Clapton and the band were staying. Indeed, his behaviour had so appalled members of the crew, who usually stuck to the dictum 'What happens on the road, stays on the road', that whispers of a rebellion spread and Forrester was given the job of getting rid of Eric's mistress. Even so, with Pattie gone, the newlywed Eric reverted to type and a steady stream of women began sharing his hotel beds.

Despite discovering his adultery, Pattie began arranging, in Eric's absence, a party for friends to celebrate the marriage. It took place on Saturday, 19 May at Hurtwood. A marquee was put up in the garden, a firework display booked, and a stage erected, on which Mick Jagger, Jack Bruce, Jeff Beck, Paul McCartney, George Harrison and Ringo Starr all performed. In fact, the event only just missed out on being the one and only time all the Beatles would reform on stage because John Lennon didn't know about it. He rang a few days later to say that if he'd been aware the party was taking place, he would have come. That night, Jerry Hall fell asleep on Eric and Pattie's bed, so the newlyweds had nowhere to sleep. Not that sharing the conjugal bed with Pattie was the first thing on Clapton's mind. Instead, he spent the day in an alcoholic haze, making a play for a friend of Pattie's called Belinda. Finally, he hid in a cupboard, with a drunken plan to 'pounce' on her, but he fell asleep and woke up the next day.

Another guest at the party was Eric's mother, Pat. Over the previous three years, since his half-brother Brian's death, they had started to build bridges. But the tragedy had put Pat's marriage to Frank McDonald under pressure and Pat returned to England alone. Eric bought her a house in Ripley, but his tentative steps to get to know his mother better would not be without their problems. Like him, she 'enjoyed a drink', to use the euphemism of the time, and was often demanding and tempestuous. He discovered quickly she was not one to be crossed. And given how little they had in common, Eric purposely used their mutual liking of pubs as a means to get to know her. However, more often than not, he felt safer if they were surrounded by a crowd, including Sid Perrin, a fat-faced bon vivant, to whom Pat became close. He also liked to have Pattie around, as she had formed an instant bond with her mother-in-law.

Two days after the party, Eric flew back to America to resume the tour. His support act was the 66-year-old Muddy Waters, and Clapton's reverence for the legendary bluesman was unquestioned. Once, at a gig, he was mistakenly handed Muddy's guitar as they both walked off stage. Clapton, gripped by the same voodoo that had made Robert Johnson's Devil story so compelling to him, refused to handle it, on the grounds that the instrument was touched by some ancient magic that was too powerful and dangerous to be messed with.

On the road in the States, Clapton and Albert Lee bonded over their shared humour and love of Monty Python and formed the Duck Brothers, an off-shoot band, playing for fun on duck whistles. But their friendship only brought into sharp focus how different and out of place they both were as Englishmen among Americans Radle and Sims, who were not boozers like Clapton and Lee – Eric was now drinking two bottles a day of anything, so long as it was at least 40 per cent proof – but drug users. So heavy, in fact, that Carl Radle was by now a heroin addict. Their mutual addictions and a row over Radle wanting an increased fee for the tour inevitably led to tensions in his once close friendship with Clapton. By the time the tour ended that summer, Eric had already decided to ditch the band that had been with him for the last five years.

For a while, Eric had been going to the Parrot Inn pub in Forest Green, a few miles from Hurtwood, where the landlord, Gary Brooker, the singer and pianist from Procol Harum and a fellow keen angler, used to play two or three times a week. Eric would sometimes jam with him and some other drinking buddies, including Chris Stainton, who played with Joe Cocker, bassist Dave Markee, Albert Lee and Henry Spinetti on drums. They began practising in Cranleigh Village Hall, then the band went on a tour of Europe and the Far East, recording their live shows for the double album *Just One Night*, which was released in April 1980 and went to number two in America and number three in the UK. They also played a disastrous short tour behind the Iron Curtain in Poland that resulted in a riot and Clapton and his band fleeing the country. As far as many were concerned, Clapton, at the age of thirty-five, was already all washed up musically. A review in the *Daily Mail* of his gig at the New Theatre, Oxford, in May, chucked a metaphorical bucket over him. 'Today he sounds old-fashioned and irrelevant,' it concluded. 'With the context of his own dreary and highly derivative material, he proved unutterably dull, with his bankrupt style being constantly overshadowed by his sideman Albert Lee.'

A month after the album was released, Carl Radle died, his body unable to keep up with his drug addiction. Clapton went into a steep depression over his friend's death, which was not helped by the fact that having completed his tour, he was now at home and left to his own devices. Inevitably, that meant he drank from morning till night, and he took to knocking back can after can of Special Brew lager, laced with vodka, topping it up with cocaine. Meanwhile, Pattie, who also had something of a taste for coke, fulfilled the role of what Clapton later described as his 'slave-cum-partner'. Their days followed a depressingly familiar routine, with the two of them passing the time with long drinking sessions at the bar of the Windmill or the Ship with his Ripley cronies, Eric shamelessly chatting up the barmaids or women drinkers in front of Pattie. He began inviting anyone and everyone back to their place, and even picked up tramps – or, in the Clapton lexicon, 'men of the road' – in his car on the way back because, he declared, these were 'real' people. The long-suffering Pattie would then be expected to cook dinner for them and make up an overnight bed.

The problem for Pattie, and almost everyone else who entered his sozzled orbit, was that you could never quite know which Eric you were going to get, nor how depraved his actions might become. 'Everyone used to walk round me on eggshells,' he said in an inter-view with the *Sunday Times* in 1999. 'They didn't know if I was going to be angry, sad or whatever. When I'd come back from the pub, I could come back happy or I could come back and smash the place to pieces. Or I could come back with a tramp and my wife would have to cook him dinner, and then I'd put him in a bed and he'd piss in the bed. And she was supposed to put up with this. There were times when I just took sex with my wife by force and thought that was my entitlement. I had absolutely no concern for other people at all, and I think that what happens in a family is everyone starts to doctor their own roles to make it more bearable to live that way.'

Suffice to say, he was in no sort of condition to begin a 59-date tour of the US in early 1981 to promote his latest album *Another Ticket*, particularly as his drinking was now complicated by a reliance on the painkiller Veganin, which he had begun taking for a bad back. Before long, he was taking fifty tablets a day and, while on the road, Roger was forced to bug Eric's room with a baby monitor and he and Alphi O'Leary would take turns to stay up listening, to ensure he was still breathing. Unsurprisingly perhaps, Roger had for some time needed his own supply of Valium just to cope.

It was only a matter of time before critical mass was reached, and the very fact that Clapton had already completed seven dates of the tour speaks volumes for his impressive tolerance levels. But on Friday, 13 March, Eric was complaining of abdominal pains before flying to Madison, Wisconsin, for the eighth show. Once there, he needed a pain-killing injection before he could go on stage. Afterwards, he was doubled up in agony on the plane to the next stop, St Paul, Minnesota, where a worried Forrester insisted he be rushed to hospital. Doctors diagnosed five bleeding ulcers. His manager was intent on flying him home until the doctors at the United Hospital told him, in no uncertain terms, that Clapton could die at any moment because one ulcer was pushing on his pancreas, which was in danger of bursting. As Eric lay in his hospital bed, grim-faced doctors told him the paramedics had fully expected him to die in the ambulance because one of the ulcers had ruptured. Eric was only half-listening. Throughout, his mind was pondering a far more pressing issue: 'How soon can I get out of here and get a drink?'

Yet while he remained a whisker from death in intensive care, some within his team were, somewhat laughably, claiming to the press that he had never looked better and his health problems were nothing to do with drink or drugs, just 'erratic living'. All of which was scotched rather by the fact that one ulcer was so large, it actually took up two X-rays. As he began a six-week stay in hospital, he was put on the stomach drug Tagamet, and the rest of the tour, which was due to carry on in St Paul and Duluth, was immediately cancelled. The message from his medics was a stark one: if you drink at all, you'll end up dead. But Clapton took his doctors' entreaties as merely the opening gambit of a negotiation and soon he had them agreeing to him knocking back his consumption to two or three Scotches a day. He used the time holed up in hospital to practise fly-fish casting in the corridor, after buying a stack of fishing rods when they'd let him out for a few hours. But within days of leaving, he was involved in yet another road crash, when the car he was a passenger in went through a red light, and he was admitted back into hospital in Minneapolis, this time with pleurisy.

Coming so close to death still didn't act as the wake-up call he so desperately needed. Within a few weeks of being released, he was back up to demolishing two bottles a day. And just so he was never without a drink, he began hiding half a bottle of vodka in his car under the mat by the pedals. In Greece, he nearly drowned when he drunkenly fell off a tender he was attempting to steer, having had a boozy dinner on Stigwood's yacht, *Jezebel*. Pattie began telling people not to serve him drinks, but on a visit to the home of friends in Rutland, at which the hosts dutifully kept his glass empty, he went into withdrawal, which resulted in a 'grand mal' seizure and he woke up in an ambulance. At the Wellington Hospital in London, doctors told him he had developed a late-onset form of epilepsy that would have to be treated by more drugs.

Increasingly, he had no recollection of what he had said and done during a bender. One winter's night at Hurtwood, a girl from Spain arrived out of the blue whom Eric had met on tour and given his address to. Pattie put her up for two days before sending her back home. But, in truth, she was more worried about his drinking than his unfaithfulness. Once, he climbed on the roof of the house drunk, slipping and tripping on the tiles. Then, on holiday in Spain, he was sent out to buy eggs for breakfast and came back with a bottle of vintage port, which he proceeded to drain. Sodden with booze and utterly disorientated, he would try to leave the house naked in the depth of the night and get into his car. The final straw came when they went to a Genesis concert in London, just before Christmas 1981, and suddenly Eric decided he needed a drink so badly, he literally climbed over people in their seats to get out.

For a short while, he had also been telling Pattie that he saw no point in living. With the house full of guests, he went on a bender and was found on Christmas morning lying among logs in the cellar, wearing the green fishing thermals Pattie had bought him as a present and which he had opened alone, when everyone had gone to bed, the previous night. He was laughing and crying manically. A furious and frightened Pattie locked him in his room and carried on the muted festivities without him.

But, bizarrely, having his family and friends witness his out-of-control behaviour was not to be the moment he reached rock bottom. That came when he went fishing a few days later and, after setting up his new kit, drunkenly fell over one of his rods. All this was witnessed by two professional carp fishermen on the other bank of the River Wey, who, seeing the state he was in, turned away in embarrassment. His pride as a fisherman dented, Eric says he went home and admitted for the first time to Roger on the phone that he needed help. 'The humiliation came down on me like a blanket. That was my last vestment of self-respect gone,' he has since said.

Quite how much of the decision to belatedly seek help was actually down to Clapton, however, is a matter for debate. Others maintain that the impetus, when it came, was from Roger Forrester, who was convinced that Eric was perilously close to killing himself with his addiction. Forrester's wife, Annette, is unequivocal about where the credit lies for getting Eric the help he needed. 'Probably, Eric wouldn't be alive now if it wasn't for Roger,' she says. Chris O'Dell agrees: 'It was Roger Forrester who finally said, "This is it, you have to go and get help." Roger got to the point where he couldn't take it anymore and he led that intervention.'

Indeed, in his autobiography, Clapton says he called his

manager because he was the most important person in his life. Forrester had, in fact, already booked him into the Hazelden Foundation, a rehab clinic in Center City, Minnesota. In January 1982, his manager picked a desperately sick Clapton up from Hurtwood and drove him to Gatwick. On the Northwest Orient flight to St Paul, Minnesota, Eric got blotto. Nor was he arriving in the most positive frame of mind about getting clean at last. With the sort of twisted logic that, no doubt, will make sense to many addicts, he admitted considering suicide, but what stopped him was the thought that a dead man can't drink. And the facility itself was a forbidding affair, an out-of-the-way place that could easily have passed for a maximum-security prison from the outside. To make matters worse, Clapton was told he was not even allowed to take a guitar with him. Once admitted, he was given a bed on the hospital wing and put on the sedative Librium for forty-eight hours, to help him get off the booze. But as addicts like to keep secrets, Eric did not tell his doctors he had been using Valium – bizarrely, for fear it would seem like he was taking a 'woman's drug' – and he had another grand mal seizure from the withdrawals.

It was a no-frills environment, with four people in a room. Clapton's roommates included a New York foreman who had no idea who he was. Shorn of the crutches of his booze, drugs and, crucially, his guitar, he withdrew during the four weeks of his treatment to such an extent that he developed a stammer. Just making his own bed, which he had yet to master the art of, or laying the table for meals became a huge test. The days were filled with prayers, therapy sessions, exercise, bracing walks in the sub-zero outdoors, mental tests and lectures. But, to his surprise, after ten days, Eric found he was beginning to enjoy it – particularly appealing was the Hazelden mantra that alcoholism is a disease. But while he began to respond to his treatment for drinking, his sexual addiction showed no signs of abating and, by pulling rock-star rank, he persuaded the authorities to give him a room of his own and he wasted no time in inviting in some of the female inmates.

Towards the end of his stay, Pattie flew out to join a five-day programme to help family members deal with a recovering alcoholic. But what were her feelings about the prospect of her drunken husband coming home sober at long last? According to Chris O'Dell, Pattie's attitude to his treatment included, understandably, a degree of ambivalence. 'Pattie called me and said, "Eric's going into treatment," and I was, like, "Yay!"' says Chris, now a trained therapist. 'I'd seen how he was very mean to her, the way he talked to her, because I went to stay with them not long before he went into rehab and he was getting pretty bad. He wasn't physically intimidating, it was more verbally, but he could be verbally abusive to anybody if you got him on the wrong day. Pattie was happy that he was finally getting sober, but she was also very worried, which is very common in a marriage where addiction is present. Her fear was that if Eric changed, then would he still want to be with her? That concern was definitely there for her. She was thinking that he was going to go and do this treatment and come back a different person because alcohol was a part of their relationship and she would drink with him, though never to the same degree. And, remember, it wasn't Pattie that made the decision to send him for treatment, it came from management. Pattie was grateful for it, but she was also fearful.'

On his release, and now the proud recipient of a medallion that proved he had completed the course, Clapton was also given an AA 'sponsor' who lived in Dorking, not far from Hurtwood. Eric immediately began attending 'first step' meetings several times a week, with a warning that he must, at all costs, stay clear of his old drinking cronies. But with a clear head came small, unexpected terrors and even basic tasks needed to be re-learnt. 'The first shock came when I had to go to an airport and get on a plane and then check into a hotel,' he remembers. 'And I didn't even know the first step in how to get on an aeroplane. When a guy, thirty-five years old, doesn't know how to do that, it's pretty bad.'

But if those around him had thought he would come home revitalised and rejuvenated, they were wrong. He still had the capacity to be impossibly childish and spoilt. When Pattie picked him up at the airport in his new Ferrari, which had been delivered while he was away, he was furious and insisted it must be sold immediately because someone other than him had been the first to drive it. For his part, Eric says he came home 'broken'. His sex life with Pattie suffered and, worse, he stopped communicating with her. Meanwhile, he was jealous that she carried on drinking and doing coke. Indeed, Chris O'Dell contends that Pattie not quitting booze was ultimately 'part of the downfall of the relationship'.

To fill his time, Eric spent days on end fly-fishing, which had taken over from course fishing as his new obsession. He would go out early and come back later with fish for Pattie to clean and cook for him.

On the work front, playing sober would be as much of a problem as playing drunk. And when he went out on tour four months after leaving rehab, Clapton felt that the sound of the band, at their first gig in Cedar Rapids, Iowa, was not up to scratch. He was not alone in thinking they were substandard. Once the tour was over, the band went to the Bahamas and began making a new album at Compass Point Studios. Tom Dowd, who was producing, told him that he must sack the lot of them, and only Albert Lee should stay. In their place, he wanted Donald 'Duck' Dunn, the talented bass player from Booker T. & the MG's, and Roger Hawkins, drummer of the house band at the legendary Muscle Shoals Studio in Alabama. As a sign that his newfound sobriety was helping him take responsibility for once, Clapton turned down Dowd's offer of doing the sacking and fired the band himself, over dinner. Keyboard player Chris Stainton, however, was given a reprieve.

The new album would be called *Money and Cigarettes* because, Clapton reasoned, without alcohol, they were all that he had left. With the zeal of the convert, he included a song he had written about Pattie called 'The Shape You're In', which, in distinctly unflattering terms, stuck the knife in about her continued heavy drinking. On the plus side, he also included the touching 'Pretty Girl' in tribute to her. The LP, which featured a newly smart Clapton in a tailored suit and tie, posing with a melting, red Stratocaster guitar on the cover, was his first for his new record label, Warner Bros, after his departure from Stigwood's RSO label. Disappointingly, the record, which *Rolling Stone* described as 'no great leap forward from such recent Clapton blues-pop snoozers as "Backless" and "Slowhand"', only managed to reach number sixteen in America and thirteen in Britain. To coincide with the LP's release in February 1983, Eric and his band went out on an energy-sapping tour of the US, performing twenty-two gigs in less than two months, before swinging through the UK, Germany, Holland and France during the spring, then heading back to America in June and July. A charity concert followed at the Albert Hall in September, featuring the likes of Clapton, Jeff Beck, Jimmy Page, Bill Wyman and Charlie Watts. It was in aid of Action into Research for Multiple Sclerosis, the disease that had struck Eric's old friend Ronnie Lane and which eventually cost Lane his life in 1992. After a couple of weeks off, Clapton crossed the Atlantic yet again, as his eleven-month tour rumbled on, finishing at Madison Square Garden in New York just before Christmas.

But if his plan was that by keeping busy, it would free him from the temptation to drink, he was, regretfully, deluded. Instead, the grind of life on the road inevitably took its toll. And when he eventually fell off the wagon, his drinking became worse than before. And this time, Pattie, who was, sadly, already used to the toxic effect booze had on her husband's temper and self-destructiveness, was scared he would kill one of them.

# ELEVEN

# Conor

Clapton's phoney war with booze ended with an inevitable and ignominious capitulation. Recording in Montserrat in March 1984, he went out to eat and on to a club with his fellow musicians and allowed himself two drinks. Wandering back to his room through the balmy night, he congratulated himself on his restraint. This was momentous, he reasoned, a real breakthrough. By stopping when he did, he had become just like other people – a bona fide social drinker; moderate, temperate, sensible. Once back at his rented cottage, however, he remembered that he'd been left a bottle of rum as a courtesy gift. He ignored it, pretending it wasn't there. But not for long. Soon, it was calling him. 'Go on,' it purred. 'Just one more drink, two max.' It was just there, waiting for him. It was free! He half ran into the kitchen, grabbed it and sank the lot, each stinging mouthful one part pure joy, two parts self-loathing.

But then, faced with the prospect of making an album with Phil Collins, who wouldn't hit the bottle? The theory was sound enough. Collins was hot. The frontman of Genesis had broken out into a successful solo career and earlier that year his single 'Against All Odds (Take a Look at Me Now)' had given him a US number one and would go on to win him a

Grammy. Everyone wanted to work with him, but Clapton's attitude was more circumspect. He wasn't a Genesis fan and, as far as he was concerned, Roger Forrester's suggestion of hiring Collins to be the producer of his new record was a 'pretty obvious marketing ploy'. But Phil was also a friend and neighbour in Surrey, and Eric and Pattie had been shoulders to cry on when Collins had been dealing with the break-up of his first marriage to Andrea Bertorelli.

In advance of flying out to the Caribbean to begin recording, Clapton rented a cottage in the Brecon Beacons in Wales, alone, to come up with some song ideas, then flew straight out to George Martin's AIR Studios to begin work. Collins suggested they recruit a keyboard player called Peter Robinson to play synths. And this being Phil Collins, and this being the 80s, synths would be front and centre on the record – a big departure from the pared-down sound Clapton fans knew and loved. But then, like it or not, changes were clearly being called for. Eric's last album had achieved an unwanted double whammy – lacklustre sales and lacklustre reviews. Nor was the money exactly rolling in. The previous year accounts for his company, Marshbrook, had showed he'd earned a modest – in rock-star terms – £133,000, leaving a profit after tax of under £24,000. Meanwhile, the consensus among much of the younger record-buying public seemed to be that Eric Clapton was an old fart, stuck in a terrifying 70s time warp, where people wore cords and went on telly without hair products.

So, surprisingly perhaps, Clapton found that, from the outset, it was a thoroughly enjoyable experience in the studio, with Collins an effective and proficient producer. The only problem was that Eric felt marginalised by the fact that some of those involved in making the record were drinking and doing coke and he was left out for his own good. All that ended with the marathon rum-drinking session that made him fall off the wagon. But in truth, the idea of a life without alcohol had already started to pale. Clapton's participation in 'twelve-step' recovery meetings back home had tailed off and the experience of being sober and trying to maintain his busy social life with Pattie and their hard-drinking friends had become a strain.

And, with drink now part of the equation again, he immediately revived his other addiction – for sex – and began an affair with Yvonne Kelly, the beautiful manager of the studio, who had been brought up in Doncaster, but whose father was a Montserrat musician. Given this distinctly complicated backdrop then, the prospects for this new album, which would eventually be titled *Behind the Sun*, were hardly promising. In the intervening years, the record and its follow-up, *August* – also produced by Collins – have been held up by many lifelong and knowledgeable Clapton fans as an appalling aberration, a monstrous and misguided sop to the commercialism he once so contemptuously rejected during his Yardbirds days. To them, Collins shall always be a red-horned incubus behind the control desk, overpowering Clapton's delicately human skills with the dead hand of processed orchestras, drum machines, digital delay and, horror of horrors, a Roland guitar synth.

They are wrong. For while *Behind the Sun* is unquestionably of its time, in all its over-the-top bombast, Collins produced a rare feat. He coaxed Clapton, a man still deeply beset by his many demons and in the grip – whether through fear or indifference – of an all-pervading creative inertia, to be what he hadn't been since Cream: a guitarist of real fire and passion. On this album, his playing would eclipse even the highs of more than fifteen years earlier. On one of the record's highlights, 'Just Like a Prisoner', Clapton conjured up three stunning solos, the third of which, the outro solo, is the single finest piece of studio guitar work he has ever committed to record, his playing at once a frenzy of rage, anger, self-pity and despair. Rarely can the instrument, in anyone's hands before or since, have conveyed such power and emotion; it raged and whimpered, howled and cursed. Elsewhere, there was other fabulous guitar work, particularly on the sinister 'Same Old Blues', which came in at eight minutes plus. The point that seemed to have been lost on the Phil Collins haters, who felt the collaboration was a renunciation of Clapton's musical legacy, was that he was actually playing more extended guitar solos in the studio than at any time since his days with Ginger Baker and Jack Bruce. Yes, often Clapton's Stratocaster had to compete with the trademark cannonball explosion of Collins' drumming. But here, finally, he was producing towering playing of the quality that fans of his early guitar work could have hoped for, and more. Likewise, his singing, so often laid-back to the point of narcolepsy, had a new vibrancy and intensity.

Which is not to say the record was not without its share of fluff, particularly in the pointless re-hash of the Eddie Floyd hit 'Knock on Wood' and the slushy 'Never Make You Cry', on which Clapton experimented with playing the guitar synth. But for the most part, songs like 'She's Waiting' and 'Same Old Blues' chronicled his failing marriage to Pattie.

Happy with the way the recording had gone, Eric returned home. But now his troubled domestic situation had been further complicated by the fact that Pattie, despite their myriad problems, had begun fertility treatment in a bid to get pregnant. She was desperate for a child, but blocked Fallopian tubes had so far made it impossible. In early 1984, she went to see a fertility specialist, but Eric was far from keen on having a family, to the extent that he later admitted he was secretly hoping the whole time that the treatment wouldn't work. At Hurtwood, he fell back into a pattern of behaviour that involved him avoiding his wife by spending days out of the house and drinking sporadically. For a time, his attempts at social drinking gave the impression that they were actually working, but in reality he was counting the hours until his next glass. Chris O'Dell says a sober Eric was no more fun to be around than a drunk one. She says that when she visited Pattie, they learnt to walk on eggshells, the same as if he was drinking. He would sit on the den sofa alone, watching TV and playing the guitar, or go out fishing.

As he waited for Warner Bros to give its verdict on the new record, a sensible man may have taken the opportunity to spend time with his wife, in an attempt to resolve the issues in their marriage in advance of starting the family that Pattie, at least, craved; Eric went straight back to work. He did a score for a film *The Hit*, starring John Hurt, and agreed to work with Roger Waters of Pink Floyd on a concept album entitled *The Pros and Cons of Hitch Hiking*. Afterwards, he joined Waters on a tour of Europe and the US, in June and July. By now, his social drinking had once again morphed into the anti-social kind. With booze came women. In his memoirs, Clapton admits that in the avant-garde setting of the tour, he got involved in some 'pretty crazy sexual liaisons, ménages à trois and the like', with some scary women, which was 'all rather sordid'. In Toronto, he suffered a terrifying seizure brought on by his now out-of-control boozing. In desperation, he wrote the song 'Holy Mother', calling out to a 'divine source, a female that I couldn't even identify'.

Nor was the news awaiting him back in England encouraging. Warners had pronounced the Montserrat tracks not strong enough for the proposed album. The consensus was that it needed more singles. The remedy, suggested by executives, was to the point: the album would have to be re-recorded, and some of the substandard tracks dropped. Otherwise, he was informed bluntly, he could find himself a new record company. Eric was devastated by the rejection, the first of its kind in his career, and, perversely, he equated the rejection to his sobriety when he was first working on the album. Clapton could, of course, have had the courage of his convictions and held firm, telling the record company he was convinced of the album's merit and refusing to change it. Instead, he panicked and backed down almost at once.

'I suddenly realised that the Peter Pan thing was over,' he said shortly afterwards. 'Because just before that, Van Morrison had been dropped – mightily dropped – and it rang throughout the industry. I thought, if they can drop him, they can drop me. There was my mortality staring me in the face.' He reluctantly agreed to re-record a third of the album in Los Angeles. The president of Warner Bros, Lenny Waronker, hired session men Greg Phillinganes, the keyboard player who'd worked with Michael Jackson, and bassist Nathan East to play on the new tracks, both of whom would become stalwarts in Clapton's band for years to come.

All of which must have left Collins furious. But while much was made of the Genesis singer's close friendship with Clapton and the fact that they lived only ten miles away from each other, their relationship was primarily professional in nature. When they did meet socially, the two men invariably found they didn't have much to talk about. Relations were not helped some years later, when Collins gave an interview to *Q Magazine* in which he posed the question which many others must surely have pondered: how could Clapton play the blues in a £5000 suit? A riled Clapton responded: 'Well, the point is, Phil, that the blues is a state of mind, it's got nothing to do with acquisition. Phil should understand this. I can have all the money and cars in the world and be very unhappy. It's an inside job. Once you find out that money and fame and success doesn't do it, where do you go? That's a big dilemma. I made a lot of money playing this music from an early age. And it didn't do it. When I was at the height of my drinking, and this is another answer for Phil, I had all those things: a beautiful wife, cars, home, money, friends. All the things you think a man could need and it didn't stop me drinking. I was depressed. I was suicidal.'

Warner Bros had sent Clapton three songs, 'Forever Man', 'See What Love Can Do' and 'Something's Happening', all by a Texan singer/songwriter called Jerry Lynn Williams who was under contract to the company. In LA, Ted Templeman and Lenny Waronker, who were acting as producers, brought in a string of top session men to play on the new tracks – drummer Jeff Porcaro, Steve Lukather on guitar, and another keyboard player, Michael Omartian. The hard-living Williams would not prove to be the best new buddy for a recovering addict. Nonetheless, Clapton moved into Shangri-La Studios with him, to work on some of Williams's demos and they instantly chummed up. Soon, Eric was back boozing and taking coke and prescription drugs full-time.

As if his personal life wasn't chaotic enough, he had received a letter from Yvonne Kelly on his return from his North American tour with Waters, telling him she was expecting his baby. She told him she did not want him to do anything, as she was going to try to raise the child in her own marriage, which, like Clapton's, had been under strain. Eric kept the news to himself.

Given his behaviour, who could blame Pattie, then, if she started a flirtation of her own? While Eric was away with Waters, she had been introduced to Willie Christie, through Chris O'Dell's aristocrat boyfriend, the Hon. Anthony Russell. Chris says Pattie became 'quite fascinated' with Christie, a successful photographer five years her junior who worked for *Vogue* and other high-fashion magazines. He was a handsome Old Etonian, nephew of the Marquess of Zetland, and he had previously been married to Grace Coddington, the model-turned-*Vogue*-fashion-editor. Coincidentally, he was also the brother of Roger Waters's wife, Carolyne. As Pattie was keen to get into photography, Christie gave Pattie advice on cameras and lighting.

Pattie was in the mood to warn Eric that she was more than capable of giving him a taste of his own medicine. One weekend, when Chris and Anthony Russell were staying with the Claptons at Hurtwood, Pattie persuaded Chris to speak to

Eric, to tell him that if he didn't start paying her more attention, he was going to lose her. After dinner, Chris, who was already drunk and had fortified herself with a further glass for Dutch courage, went into the den, where Eric, who was sober for once, was watching TV. Chris dutifully passed on the message from Pattie. Unsurprisingly, Clapton was not happy to hear this, least of all coming from one of his wife's friends. 'It's none of your fucking business,' he growled. At that moment, says Chris, she thought to herself: 'Yes, you're absolutely right. It is not my business.'

Embarrassed by her drunken faux pas, Chris made her exit, but Eric followed her into the kitchen and told them he couldn't stand being with any of them, Pattie, Chris or Anthony. Then he stormed out, slamming the kitchen door, and sped off down the gravel drive in his Ferrari. As the three of them discussed what to do next, all the lights in the house went out, as if an omen of things to come. As soon as they came back on, the sound of Eric's sports car could be heard roaring back up the driveway. Eric flung open the kitchen door and fixed Chris with a thousand-yard stare. Through gritted teeth, he told her he had been contemplating where he should go as he drove around, but had decided it was his house and she should be the one to leave. Chris and Anthony packed their bags and drove off. As Pattie and Eric watched them leave from the back door, Chris rolled down the window of the car, flicked him the finger, and yelled: 'Fuck you, Eric Clapton.'

Chris says: 'The longer he and Pattie were together, the more verbally abusive he became to me. He would say really nasty things. One time, they were in Philadelphia and I went down to see them from New York, and as I walked in, Eric said, "Oh no, not her!" And the next morning, I walked into the restaurant where everyone was having breakfast and he said loudly, "Oh my God, if she's here, I'm getting out of here." I hadn't said or done anything. It was embarrassing and humiliating. But in order to continue to have my friendship with Pattie, I had to learn to deal with it.'

For his part, Clapton took to disparagingly calling Pattie's glamorous contingent of girlfriends the 'Blonde Mafia' and later wrote the song 'Tearing Us Apart', about how they were coming between him and Pattie.

In September, Pattie finally walked out, leaving a note for Eric as he lay crashed out on the sofa at Hurtwood, and went to stay with her mother in Haslemere, Surrey. In her memoirs, *Wonderful Tonight*, she described how intolerable the situation had become. 'At night I went to bed before him, hoping I would be asleep before he came up, and cried. I'd pray he would pass out when he came to bed and not try to touch me. There were times when he was more like an animal than the loving, passionate husband I'd known, and reeked of brandy.'

Every day for four weeks, a contrite Eric sent her a dozen red roses, in the hope of persuading her to change her mind. Eventually, he arrived at the door, looking skinny and ill, having barely eaten a thing since she left. He begged her to return home, but Pattie turned him down. Reluctantly, Clapton agreed to a trial separation and rented her a flat in Devonshire Place, in London's West End. Pattie had begun spending more time with the easy-going and caring Willie, who gently persuaded her to see a therapist to help her deal with her own problems. And as far as her friends were concerned, they were more than happy she had chosen the considerate and protective Christie over the chauvinistic Eric. 'Will was just wonderful, successful, tall, really good-looking, and he was crazy about Pattie,' says Chris O'Dell. 'They were actually very good together. He made her laugh and they did things together. She'd really found somebody that she cared about. That's when Eric came back in and said, "I want you back." He decided he didn't want to lose her.'

Now, with Pattie in the arms of another man, the poetic and passionate letters began arriving again from Eric, the way they had when she was with George. By October, he was suicidal, drinking dangerously and taking coke as he brooded about her rejection of him and the fact that she preferred her new boyfriend to him, even though he considered the well-mannered Christie to be a 'wimp'. Clapton, too, began seeing a therapist who had been recommended by Roger Waters, but it didn't help. One evening, out of his mind with jealousy, he drove into town with the plan to drag Pattie back home 'caveman style', but she wasn't in.

In November, news leaked out of their split and *Daily Mail* diarist Nigel Dempster wrote that Pattie was seeing Christie and had been with him at a party at the Natural History Museum while Eric was away on tour. When he found out, Clapton was furious. Christie told the gossip columnist: 'Pattie and I have been friends for a long time. With Eric's approval, we used to see each other during the marriage and we continue to do so, but we're not living together.' But if Clapton had once been sanguine about the friendship, that was evidently no longer the case. Tormented by her relationship with another man, he wrote and recorded the title track of the delayed album *Behind the Sun* – named after a line in the Muddy Waters song *Louisiana Blues* – at the home of Phil Collins. The song featured just Clapton's voice and guitar and Collins's synth and was a simple and powerful entreaty to her not to give up on their marriage. The emotion of the recording was so raw and real that Collins sensibly didn't tamper with it, even leaving in Clapton's slightly fluffed guitar arpeggio near the end. Eric took the tape over to play to Pattie prior to going on tour to Australia and Hong Kong, but she told him painfully that she was no longer attracted to him and wanted to be with Christie. But just like when she had been with Harrison, Eric took her rejection as a challenge.

He went off on tour and, on arriving in Sydney, he slept with an on-off girlfriend called Valentina. But when he got back to England, he had a gift for Pattie, a necklace of ruby and diamond hearts on a chain. Still she refused to budge. Undaunted, in December, he wrote to Willie Christie in desperation, telling him in no uncertain terms the damage he was doing and that Pattie was the love of his life. At the same time, he put pressure on Pattie to agree to join him on a three-day trip to Florence, in a bid to resolve their problems. She agreed reluctantly, but the jaunt was a disaster, with Clapton concluding miserably that she found him 'sexually repulsive'. After a Christmas apart, Pattie went on a New Year's holiday to Sri Lanka and returned to find another letter from Eric pleading with her not to go back to her boyfriend and to return to Hurtwood. He also employed the nuclear option as leverage, telling her how much her beloved dog and cat were missing her. What he didn't say was that while she was away, Yvonne Kelly, about whom she knew nothing, had given birth to

Clapton's daughter, Ruth, at Doncaster Maternity Hospital on 11 January 1985.

Finally, Pattie agreed to her estranged husband's request to go on holiday to the Israeli resort of Eilat. The holiday, hastily arranged, saw Clapton and Pattie staying in a hotel on the Red Sea with British holidaymakers for ten days, instead of a private villa. Unwilling to let fellow guests know the depths of their marriage problems, they pretended to be just another couple, going out for romantic dinners and sunbathing together on the beach. While there, Eric, in an action of either desperation or lunacy, persuaded her to take ecstasy, saying it would help them recapture their feelings for each other. For her part, at least, it didn't. But in spite of the unsuccessful trip, Pattie agreed to move back into Hurtwood. Unsurprisingly, Christie took the news that she was going back to Eric badly.

In the meantime, *Behind the Sun*, with the addition of the three Jerry Lynn Williams tracks, was released in early March 1985. Given the departure the album presented in terms of style and production, it was met with a lukewarm response by the critics. *Rolling Stone* called it 'slick but inconsistent', adding: 'Perhaps Collins, who is, by any account, a fine singer, an excellent drummer and an inventive producer, was either too awed by Clapton's stature to make any changes in his songs or had used up all of his best ideas on his many other projects.' Even so, the impression remained for some that the album was as much a Collins vehicle as something authentically Clapton. Eric responded at the time by saying: 'That's how it is in the studio. At the end of the day, people will say that *Behind the Sun* is a Phil Collins record. Fine, if that's all they can hear, they're not listening properly. I'm in there with as much as I have got, but not in a competitive way. If I did, it would be a mess. It works pretty good for me to allow people to be themselves rather than trying to lay down the law.' But while he had been the first to blink in the standoff with Warner Bros, once *Behind the Sun* was released, Clapton was publicly saying how his next album would be made 'my way'. 'Because whatever I do, I am the one who has to live with it,' he said as he went on the promotional trail. 'I've always wanted to make an album that I'm 100 per cent proud of, and I don't seem to be able to do it.'

The gruelling tour that followed would take up all but two months of the rest of the year. It was in the middle of the US leg when Pete Townshend rang Clapton to ask him to play Live Aid, the charity event in aid of Ethiopian famine relief which was being arranged by Bob Geldof. Eric cancelled a gig in Las Vegas, which was due to take place the evening before, in order to make the show, which was being simultaneously broadcast from Wembley Stadium in London and the JFK Stadium in Philadelphia on 13 July. In his room at the Four Seasons, which was full of stars playing the Philadelphia gig, he could not sleep because of nerves. On the day of the show, he made the mistake of watching the other bands performing on TV, which only made him more edgy. Things were not helped by the oppressive summer heat, and both he and Duck Dunn would later confess to each other that they came close to passing out. Ominously, as he and his band moved through a tunnel from the dressing rooms to the stage, he could hear his Glaswegian guitar technician, Lee Dickson, turning the air blue over the fact that the organisers had provided the wrong amplifiers.

As Clapton began 'White Room' in front of the 90,000 in the audience, he got an electric shock off the microphone and spent the rest of the show trying to get close enough so he could hear his own voice over the monitors without getting another unwanted jolt. Back in London, the BBC were also having their own technical problems. Perhaps it was just the lateness of the hour – it was already early evening in Philadelphia – but the broadcaster completely missed the beginning of his performance, leaving Clapton fans cursing as they eventually crossed to America towards the end of the second verse. With Phil Collins, who thanks to Concorde played on both sides of the Atlantic, joining his band on drums, they went straight into 'She's Waiting', from *Behind the Sun*, and finally a barnstorming version of 'Layla'. If Clapton was, in his own words, 'a hundred times more psyched up than for a regular gig', he didn't show it. Meanwhile, his band, which included fellow Brit Tim Renwick on guitar, Jamie Oldaker, Chris Stainton, plus Marcy Levy and Shaun Murphy on backing vocals, was tight and slick, having reached fighting weight thanks to the previous weeks on the road. Despite the rocky start, it was a tremendous performance and widely accepted as one of the true highlights of the event.

It is hard to overstate the impact Live Aid was to have on Clapton's career. With 1.5 billion people viewing the event on television, Clapton was able to reach a younger audience who may previously have viewed him as a somewhat crusty figure from an earlier epoch. What they were presented with was an artist at the top of his game, looking tanned and rich in his expensive linen trousers, white shirt and Cartier watch. At once, a whole new breed of fans went out to buy his records, while older, more moneyed fans, who had his vinyl in their collections, upgraded to copies of his back catalogue on the new compact disc format. Two weeks later, two of the top three albums in the American charts were Clapton's, and *Behind the Sun*, which had so far recorded moderate sales, was given a substantial lift. Live Aid was not, as has been said, Clapton's zenith, but it was the beginning of his climb to that summit.

He had broken his 'no women on tour' rule to allow Pattie to be with him in Philadelphia. It was part of a charm offensive that included him buying her expensive presents, including fabulous Giorgio Armani outfits. The anti-social Eric had even consented to Pattie throwing a star-studded birthday party for him at Hurtwood that March, to celebrate his fortieth. But if, as she watched him proudly from the wings, Pattie thought events would mark a similar turnaround in their marital fortunes, she was wrong. A few months later, in the autumn, when his tour moved on to Italy, his promoter introduced him to Lory Del Santo, an actress and model who had appeared without her clothes in a few sex comedies and was known in her homeland by the rather colourful nickname 'Miss Wigglebottom'. She was also not averse to displaying her enviable figure by stripping down to her bra and suspenders for no apparent reason on an Italian chat show. Born in Verona, convent educated and raised poor after the death of her father at a young age, she had gone to Rome in her late teens and got parts on TV sitcoms, did some modelling and dated the bald and diminutive billionaire arms dealer Adnan Khashoggi, who was twenty-three years her senior.

Del Santo had the little-girl looks that were to Clapton's

taste, with dark bushy eyebrows and Pre-Raphaelite dark curls, but there was also a tightness of the jaw and an unblinking way she held the gaze that suggested she would not be out of her depth with any man, no matter how rich or famous. When Clapton met her, she was appearing on a well-known weekly show on Italian TV called *Drive-In*. Beautiful and self-confident, she was no shrinking violet. Eric was instantly captivated and invited her to a dinner after a gig in Milan the following night. Not everyone, however, was so enamoured of the dark-haired Lory, who at the age of twenty-seven was thirteen years Clapton's junior. His manager, Roger Forrester, and some of those in Eric's entourage had apparently thought the whole initial meeting was a set-up and few believed Miss Del Santo's claim that she had no idea who the guitar player was when they were introduced and hadn't ever listened to his music. Certainly, if that was the case, it is hard to imagine why she agreed to go out on a date with him, given that she later said of their first encounter that she found him 'a bit on the ugly side'. Whatever the reality, he was clearly more impressed with her than she was with him. While Lory says she was keen not to rush the relationship, after just a few dates, Eric rang to say he was in town. She asked him what town and he said, 'In Milan.' When she asked him why, he replied: 'Because I love you.'

Back home, Pattie was continuing to go through the stress of IVF. Because of her age, she was forty-one at the time, she was told she was too old to adopt in Britain. She would have happily taken on a baby of any colour or ethnic background from abroad, but she eventually vetoed that idea, saying in her autobiography that she was afraid Eric might say something 'offensive and horrible' while drunk and she would not expose a child to that risk. Nor would he cut down on drinking or smoking, which her doctors had warned could affect sperm count. Consequently, each time the implanted embryo failed, Pattie felt that the 'finger of inadequacy' was pointed at her. At the same time, Eric, having been adamant in his twenties and thirties that he had no desire for children, was now beginning to talk in vaguely wistful ways about wanting to extend his 'bloodline'.

With the tour finally over, he arrived back at Hurtwood, and a few days later, suggested that he and Pattie go out for dinner *à deux*. Once she'd got over the shock of being invited out by her husband, who rarely treated her to a romantic meal, Pattie excitedly made a reservation for that night at an Italian restaurant a few miles away in Cranleigh. That evening, they chatted happily over the breadsticks, but when Pattie's first course arrived, Eric announced, out of the blue, that he had something to tell her. He had met someone in Italy, he said, they had slept together a couple of times and he was in love with her. He was sorry, he told Pattie, but he had decided to leave her to be with his mistress.

It says something about his unbalanced state of mind – or sheer arrogance – that he didn't bother to discuss his plans with Lory. Maybe he assumed his ambitious new girlfriend would know a good thing when she saw one. Either way, he arrived at Lory's home in Milan unannounced the next day and told her he'd left his wife for her. Oddly, given that he had hoped that Pattie would not conceive, he also told her that he had always wanted children and they should try to start a family right away. So started a rather odd courtship that

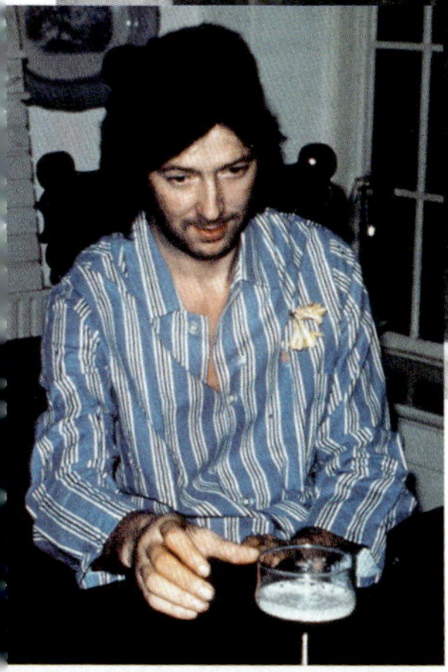

**Above:** All smiles as Clapton and Pattie get married in Tucson, Arizona, on 27 March 1979. However, within days his new bride was sent home to England and Eric resumed his affair with Pattie's friend Jenny McLean.

**Above, left:** Days at Hurtwood followed a depressingly familiar pattern. Clapton would go to the pub at the top of his drive at lunchtime, get drunk and pass out at home before getting up for opening time.

**Left:** Drinking buddies Pattie and Eric surrounded by beer glasses and cigarette packets at Hurtwood in 1975.

**Clockwise from the top:** Eric with his mentor Muddy Waters on stage in Chicag in December 1979. The bluesman called Clapton his 'adopted son'; Sharing a joke with BB King during a gig in New York in June 2003. They had been friends since first meeting in Greenwich Village 36 yea earlier; Preparing to fly to the Caribbean in March 1984 to begin work on Behind the Sun with Phil Collins. Their choice of knitwear may have been dodgy, but Colli coaxed blistering solos from Clapton's guitar; Clapton's performance at Live Aid in July 1985 was a triumph, but he spent the entire set keeping a wary distance fro the microphone after getting an electric shock singing the first line of 'White Room Philadelphia's JFK Stadium.

His daughter Ruth was born in January 1985 following an affair with studio manager Yvonne Kelly while recording in Montserrat the previous year. In June 2013 Ruth made Clapton a grandfather when she had a son Isaac.

With Lory Del Santo in 1988. The Italian said he would go days without uttering a word and insisted on complete silence.

Eric with his son Conor. Tragically, the four-year-old fell to his death from a New York skyscraper in March 1991 just as father and son were beginning to bond.

**Above:** Stevie Ray Vaughan's mesmerising performance on stage with Eric in August 1990 was evidence that the Texan had eclipsed Clapton as the world's leading guitar virtuoso. Minutes later he was dead, killed when the helicopter taking him from East Troy, Wisconsin, to Chicago crashed in fog.

**Below:** Collecting his six Grammys in Los Angeles in February 1993 marked the zenith of Clapton's career. He dedicated his awards to Conor for whom he had written the moving song 'Tears in Heaven' which won him a Grammy for Song of the Year.

OPPOSITE PAGE
CLOCKWISE FROM TOP LEFT

Clapton squired a carousel of beaut and famous women around town ir the nineties including American mc Christy Turlington.

TV presenter Davina McCall was another who found herself briefly tl object of one of Clapton's legendary charm offensives.

But he met his match in Carla Bruni (with Clapton below at a Save the Rainforest gala dinner in London). T model dumped him for Mick Jagger after persuading Eric to introduce h to the priapic Rolling Stone in Octol 1989.

Pictured in April 1993, Paula Hamilt the star of the Volkswagen Golf TV advert, was treated to lunches à deu with the guitarist.

Princess Diana was a regular at Clapton's favourite watering hole, Sa Lorenzo in Knightsbridge, where th indulged in a playful flirtation.

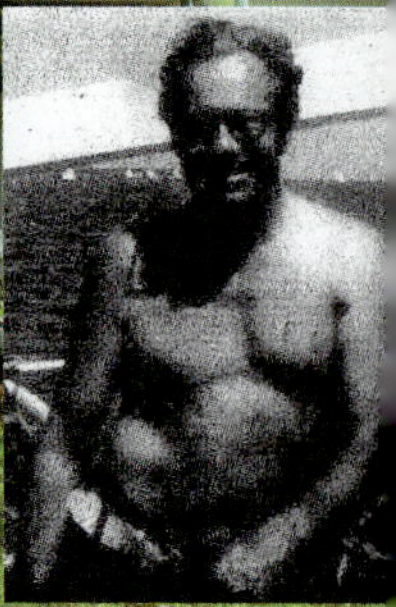

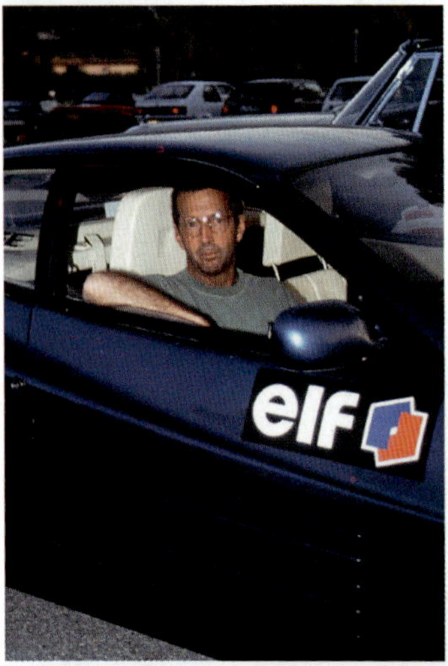


**Above:, inset** Eric never met his natural father, Canadi former serviceman Edward Fryer, who died in 1985. Li Clapton, he was a musician and womaniser.

**Above:** Eric sank millions of his own money into the Crossroads Centre in Antigua which treats drug addict and alcoholics, but his commitment to the project onl further distanced him from his manager Roger Forrest

**Left:** In one of his beloved Ferraris in 1993. In 2012 the Italian maker built a one-off special edition for him called the SP12 EC.

**Below:** Eric, Jack Bruce and Ginger Baker, put their feuding aside to reform Cream at the Royal Albert Hall in May 2005. The gigs were a critical success, but Clapton was unhappy with the quality of the band's performances at a series of shows at Madison Square Garden, New York, later that year.

e met his American wife Melia McEnery at a party in June 1999 in Los Angeles at which she
vas employed to look after guests. Despite the thirty-one year age gap, they quickly became an item and married on New Year's Day 2002.

As he approached his 70th birthday, Clapton had found contentment at last with a wife and young family. Yet he still held true to the solitary blues tradition of one man and his guitar.

mainly involved him hanging around at her flat all day while Miss Del Santo, who was launching a new career as a photographer, went out chasing business. Soon, however, Clapton was getting cold feet. In Rome, where she kept another apartment, she again left him at home one day and he went rooting around and found a stash of pictures of her with famous men, celebrities, footballers and politicians, striking the same pose and 'wearing the sort of smile that wasn't really a smile at all'. He says that at that moment he knew the relationship was doomed.

Nevertheless, in typically illogical fashion, he agreed that he and Lory should move to London together. With Pattie still in situ at Hurtwood, he found them a flat in Berkeley Square. From the start, it was an odd set-up. Lory found it strange that he never listened to music to relax and, so far as she could tell, he appeared to be searching for complete quiet. 'He needed total silence, to live in a place with no noise,' she recalled. 'I never heard him play the guitar or sing in the house. One day he told me, "Talk only when I ask you a question. Otherwise, no." He would go into silent periods for days, even weeks, and eventually come out of the silence by saying something simple like, "Do you want to eat?" That would be followed by something the next day, eventually building up to a couple of sentences a day. I would always wait for him to talk first because he expected me to be silent during those times too. Then, he would say something really beautiful to me that would make up for all the silences.' Quite how they managed to discuss having children together is clearly more of an achievement than one might expect. But talk they did, and agreed instantly it was what they both wanted. Two months later, in December, she was pregnant. She found out when they were staying with Roger Forrester and his wife Annette and Lory was ill with morning sickness.

At first, Del Santo had not realised she was involved with an alcoholic because although he drank all day, Clapton did not appear to be drunk. However, during the early part of their romance, he became abusive in a nightclub for no apparent reason, and she knew then that he had a drink problem and was drinking purely to get drunk. Also, he would disappear for a month at a time and on his return would drink only water, until, inevitably, he would start drinking again. But before she had the chance to pass on the happy news about her pregnancy, Lory says Clapton told her that their relationship was not working, that he couldn't stand the traffic noise of central London and was going back to Pattie. A furious Lory responded by dropping her own bombshell – she was pregnant. She says Clapton went into a dark mood and she reasoned that he was bothered about how a baby would impact on his ordered and structured existence. Eric drove straight to Hurtwood and Pattie. After pulling up on the drive, he peered into the kitchen window, hoping to surprise the wife he had so callously dumped just a few weeks earlier. In a joyously cruel piece of retribution, he saw Pattie and Willie Christie cooking together and looking for all the world like a couple completely in love. Christie says: 'I had my small daughter with me and we were having lunch, though I don't think Eric saw her. He walked in and there I was. It was awkward. Awkward for him.' Eric attempted to talk to Pattie, but she sent him away.

Broken, Clapton drove back to the London flat and decided that killing himself was the only way out of his predicament.

He swallowed a whole bottle of 5mg Valium tablets, fully expecting they would kill him. But he woke up 'stone-cold sober' ten hours later.

Once again, Pattie took pity on him, allowing him to move back into Hurtwood. It was an uneasy truce. In the run-up to Christmas, Eric came into the kitchen as Pattie was arranging flowers in a vase and told her Lory was pregnant. There was no question, he said, of her having an abortion because she was Catholic and wanted the baby. Cruelly, he told her how beautiful Lory was, what a wonderful photographer she was and how she hadn't known who he was when they met, a claim about which the worldly wise Pattie – like Roger – remains sceptical. Pattie responded by throwing him out of their bedroom.

The news that he was to be a father was all the more shattering to Pattie considering how desperately she had been trying for a child of her own. Her trauma was also not helped by the fact that Lory's pregnancy coincided with her best friend Chris O'Dell giving her the news that she too was expecting her first child. While she was delighted for Chris, it only brought home to her all the more her inability to conceive.

One minute Clapton wanted to be with Lory, the next he didn't. A few months later, he was telling an interviewer his mistress's allure had been too powerful to resist. 'She was very affectionate and I felt starved of affection for so long that I just fell hook, line and sinker,' he said. But the attraction, which had begun almost immediately after one of Pattie's pregnancies had collapsed, was, he admitted, 'purely chemical'. Even he conceded that it was classic mid-life-crisis stuff. 'We talked about children straight away,' he went on. 'I've always wanted children. The whole thing snowballed. The next thing we knew was that we were expecting a baby. I panicked and tried to get back in the old homestead. Of course, it was too late by then. I told Pattie everything. That was the end of it really. It was more than she could cope with. She was stunned.' He was also candid about the strain Pattie's inability to have children had put on them. 'We tried and tried and it never happened,' he sighed. 'That was another kind of stumbling block in our marriage. It became such a pressure. We tried almost too late to have children. I think it could have been dangerous for Pattie if we had really pushed it. I think our marriage suffered as a result of that. Pattie had great remorse over it. She's suffered greatly in the last year or so.'

With Lory now back in Milan, Clapton launched a campaign to win Pattie over. He finally persuaded her to give the marriage another go. But the reality of being back together was a world away from his rose-tinted expectations. A few months later, Clapton told an interviewer: 'I fought so hard to get her back that after all the effort, when she returned home, I thought, "What have I done all this for?" It didn't really seem worth it and I went on the road feeling a little discontented about everything. I was perhaps expecting too much. I had too many illusions about what it would be like. We should have realised it was over and left it.'

At Hurtwood, they had been sleeping in separate rooms and, for the most part, living separate lives. But Chris O'Dell says Pattie was prepared to put aside the fact that he was about to become a father with another woman for the sake of the marriage. 'When my son was born,' says Chris, 'we would drive out there to pick Pattie up and Eric came out to the car to look at the baby, which was surprising to me. It was as if Pattie had said to him that he should come and see the baby because he'd have one himself soon. He was sober at that point and he was very sweet.'

Throughout this period, Lory seemed to be under the misapprehension that she and Clapton were still a couple, despite living in different countries. Approached by a tabloid reporter in February 1986, she refused to believe Eric was back with Pattie, saying: 'Our relationship is something very nice and very beautiful. I am in love like never before and so is Eric.' As usual, however, Clapton had assigned the dirty work to Roger Forrester. As Lory laboured under the illusion that everything between them was OK, his manager was confirming the reunion with Pattie to the press and playing down his relationship with Miss Del Santo. 'Of course Eric knew the girl,' he said, 'but whatever there was between them is finished.' For the moment, Lory was most definitely off the scene. Sure enough, a little later, when Eric collected an award for his theme for the BBC thriller *Edge of Darkness* at the Ivor Novello Awards in London, Pattie was with him. Outside, he said of the reconciliation: 'This time, it's for good.'

Chris O'Dell remembers spending a day with the Claptons at this time and feeling desperately sorry for him. 'Pattie just decided she was going to live life her way,' says Chris. 'She came back, but on her own terms. She was protecting herself and she wasn't going to set herself up like that again. I just remember how lonely Eric looked. We went to a polo match near their home and he looked so sad. I had been on Pattie's side until that point, but I thought, "Pattie can't you see this? Your husband is really lonely." I think that, by that point, Eric had basically given up on their marriage.' Indeed, in spite of his public utterances to the contrary, it was only a matter of time before the pantomime in which they had cast themselves would come to an unscripted halt.

Sure enough, after a few weeks of this separate lives, separate beds arrangement, Eric hit the bottle. On the morning of 17 March, Pattie's forty-second birthday, he burst drunkenly into her room at 6 a.m. and threw her things out of the window. She fled to London to stay with friends, before later moving into a rented flat in Kensington. Clapton would later describe his behaviour as 'cruel and vicious' and almost immediately he was regretting it. He wrote to Pattie, begging for forgiveness. But things were moving very quickly now and were increasingly beyond his control. Soon, the secret of his on-off mistress's pregnancy would be out in the open. In May, Rome-based magazine *Novella* carried an interview with Lory, who'd had to stand strong in the face of pressure from several different sides hoping to talk her out of having the baby, where she revealed she was expecting Clapton's child and declared: 'I have met the love of my life.'

Could Eric's life get any more messed up?

The answer was yes. Around the same time, he began getting bizarre phone calls from a woman with a thick European accent who said she knew all about his marriage problems. A normal person would have hung up, but he listened. She told him she could help him get Pattie – whom, despite everything, he had now decided he could not do without – back. Stranger still, she proceeded to give him wacky instructions, which, even more weirdly, he decided to follow to the letter. These included taking a bath in various herbs and reading incantations on the stroke of midnight. And just to exacerbate the madness, he arranged to meet the woman in New York, where she lived. Once he'd clapped eyes on her, he was not impressed. She looked very peculiar and told him that in order to achieve his desire of getting his wife back, he should sleep with a virgin. When Clapton pointed out that it might be hard to find one in New York, she told him: 'I'm a virgin.' He went through with it, thinking it might bring Pattie back. Of course, the humiliating experience did not have the desired effect, and Pattie refused to agree to a reconciliation. The episode was further proof, if any were needed, about the craziness that surrounded him. Even so, he was still not prepared to accept that his marriage to Pattie was dead in the water. As for the virgin soothsayer, she would come back to haunt him soon enough.

Meanwhile, the Lory situation remained unresolved. Miss Del Santo said it would take Eric months to adjust to the idea of becoming a father, so she decided to give him his space and returned to Italy for the first six months of the pregnancy. In truth, Lory feared that some within Eric's entourage were attempting to poison his mind against her, to convince him she was a money-grabber who would use a baby to wheedle cash out of him for years to come. When she was three months pregnant, she says she received a phone call from someone in his employ, telling her 'bad things which are too painful to repeat' and trying to persuade her to end the pregnancy. She turned down the idea flat, replying: 'I can disappear, but there's no way in the world you can make me give up the baby.'

Then she received a phone call from Eric. He told her that he had tried to commit suicide for a second time by hanging himself from a tree. He had fainted and then realised he was still alive. Lory was stunned: 'I was in shock,' she says. 'Then, afterwards, I felt angry and sad because I thought, how could he try and do this when he had a family to look forward to? I was angry that myself and the baby weren't important enough to him. To think of suicide in this situation was unreal to me. When you risk dying at any time, life is too precious to waste like that.' The shocking incident only confirmed that while Clapton undeniably left a trail of destruction that affected anyone unlucky enough to come into his near vicinity, he was, above all, the hopeless, pitiful victim of his own derangement. And it is through the prism of his problems, his emotional meltdown and his degenerate alcoholism, that his actions during this period must ultimately be viewed.

None of which made him any easier to deal with. During the pregnancy, Eric was, at best, a peripheral figure, writing a heartfelt and beautiful letter one minute about how much he loved her, and then disappearing for up to two months at a time. Once, Lory says, he called to ask if she had read the letter he'd sent. She replied that she had, often. He insisted on coming over to dinner and they went out for a romantic meal, but three days later, when he left, she noticed the letter was gone too. She remembers: 'It was the only proof of him wanting our baby and he'd taken it.'

In the meantime, he had a record to make. Despite Warner Bros cool initial response to his collaboration with Phil Collins on *Behind the Sun*, they consented to the Genesis frontman taking over the reins once again as producer for a follow-up album, this time with Tom Dowd as co-producer from the outset. Clapton arrived in Los Angeles, where it was to be recorded, in bad shape. Between recording sessions, which again featured Collins playing drums, Nathan East on bass and Greg Phillinganes on keyboards, he got by on very little sleep. Nights followed a familiar format, with Clapton staying up until daybreak at his rented villa on Sunset Plaza, drinking and doing coke, then showing up at the studio by lunchtime and working through a growing hangover, before going back to the privacy of his room and doing it all again. However, his attempts to hide his drinking were clearly not successful, given that the crew made a fake licence plate to put on his rental car that read 'Captain Smirnoff'.

On his return home in May, he attempted to build bridges with Lory, making contact again after months of radio silence. Lory told him she was coming to London to have the baby. He was shocked. Why did she not want to have the child in Milan? She told him that he was the baby's father and he was English, the child should, therefore, be born in London. Once the determined Lory made it plain what she wanted, Clapton dutifully arranged everything. He found her a mews house in Chelsea and dropped by every day to visit. And when she went into labour, he arrived immediately at the hospital. According to Lory, the doctors asked him if he wanted to be present at the actual birth, to which Eric replied, 'Oh no,' before changing his mind. But his new-man conversion was clearly some way off being complete. At one point during the labour, Lory says he asked her: 'How long am I going to be here because I'm due to go on holiday and I've been working so hard?' When the baby boy, whom Lory insisted should be named Conor, was eventually born by Caesarean section on 21 August 1986 at the Lindo Wing of St Mary's Hospital, Paddington, Eric picked him up and said: 'Oh my God, I'm a father.' In reality, of course, that was a milestone he had already passed the previous year, with the birth of his daughter Ruth.

Then he did something so cruel, so pitilessly brutal, it could only have been unintentional stupidity rather than genuine malice. He rang Pattie. She was in the garden of the house in the South of France where she was staying with Genesis guitarist Mike Rutherford and his wife Angie. Eric told her excitedly that he had become a dad and how he'd been there at the birth and what a moving, miraculous experience it had been. Emotionally exhausted, and with the birth over, Clapton then went off on holiday, leaving Lory and the baby in London. Not long afterwards, he told a journalist: 'I felt I had better get away from everyone. So I had a holiday with a friend of mine – a bloke. But before I went away, I told Pattie that it was up to her to decide what she thought we should do, because my course was going to be towards my son. I'm going to try to spend as much time with him as possible. She had to decide for herself whether she could stand by me through all this or if she should have a divorce. Pattie felt the best thing was to divorce. I didn't want her to be guided by what I did. I think it's probably going to make her stronger knowing that she's made that choice for herself.'

In reality, of course, it wasn't much of a choice for Pattie. She could carry on accepting the bare bones of a marriage with a faithless, selfish, drunken husband, reminded with every mention of his son of her own barrenness. Or she could scrape together what little remained of her shredded self-respect and walk away. Commendably, she did the latter. Pattie would later say she thought Clapton was trying to break her spirit on some level and that when he realised he had failed, he backed away from the marriage. In hindsight, she regretted ever allowing him to seduce her. In hindsight, too, with the benefit of clarity and sobriety, Eric would be filled with genuine remorse over his treatment of Pattie.

For now, though, his wife's feelings were clearly not high on his agenda. On his return from holiday, Eric, Lory and Conor began to live together as a family. Shamelessly, having already abandoned his lover with her newborn for a sunshine jaunt, and having rubbed Pattie's nose in it, now Clapton bested himself. He arranged to meet Pattie to float an idea he had come up with all by himself: why didn't he, his lover and their baby all join Pattie and live together at Hurtwood. Unsurprisingly, Pattie, who was still living in her rented flat in Kensington, rejected the plan out of hand. But for a time, he and Lory moved into Hurtwood with Conor, until it rapidly became clear to Lory that he could not cope with having a baby around. 'For a start, there was no longer the silence he craved,' she remembered. 'And as Conor grew bigger, Eric just couldn't handle the mess a child makes. He resented the presence of a baby in a life which had previously been so ordered and simple.'

# TWELVE

# Clean

Eric's new album, *August*, named after Conor's birth month, was released in November and would become his biggest-selling solo album to date. However, it was hard to escape the conclusion that, increasingly, Clapton was a guest star on his own records. At the time it came out, with admirable candour, he was prepared to admit that the record and his career were firmly in the mainstream. 'I think I sold myself a long time ago,' he said, as he was wheeled out to do promotional work for the record. 'I made some kind of deal with myself to get along, to please people, just to make life easy, I think. It disturbs me a little to hear myself say that, but I have to admit it because otherwise who am I kidding?' Certainly, for all his confident talk that his next album would carry his own stamp, once again he bowed to pressure from his record company, as well as the annoying, nagging voices in his head telling him that public acceptance must come above musical satisfaction. Later, he would say of the album: 'I was very nervous that there was no longer any room left for me. I felt I was walking along a tightrope and could easily fall off if I didn't do the necessary things to stay in the public eye. So I had Phil Collins as producer and ended up making a more commercial record than I really wanted. I came very close to an unacceptable degree of personal compromise. But, afterwards, I promised myself I wouldn't be bound by those chains again.'

Which is not to say that *August*, for all its gargantuan 80s production, did not have its high points. The Clapton/Greg Phillinganes penned 'Miss You' contained an impressive guitar solo, though often it seemed Eric was being drowned out in the mix by Collins's drums, and on the moving 'Holy Mother', Clapton came up with an exceptional piece of guitar work, opening the solo by bending a single note seemingly forever. Elsewhere, however, songs like 'Behind the Mask', which was released as a single, sounded like it should have been performed by Michael Jackson, who did actually record a version of it (though it was unreleased in his lifetime). Likewise, 'Walk Away', which was written by Marcy Levy, was an excellent pop song, but not really an Eric Clapton song. Another song, co-written with Robbie Robertson, called 'It's in the Way That You Use It', was used on the soundtrack of the Tom Cruise and Paul Newman movie *The Color of Money*.

As Clapton went out on the promotional trail to sell the record, Lory was back in Milan. A plan was formulated that Eric would travel over for a few days at a time every couple of weeks to spend time with Conor. But with his drinking back to dangerous levels, any time he did have alone with the baby was spent counting the minutes till Lory came back so he could get blitzed once Conor was safely tucked up in bed. At home, his choice of companions did nothing to help his chances of staying sober. He began hanging out with cricketer Ian Botham and David English, the former president of the Robert Stigwood Organisation, with the three of them going on crazy drinking sprees. They formed the EC XI, the precursor to the Bunburys, a cricket team made up of sportsmen and musicians, and Eric regularly travelled to Worcestershire to watch 'Beefy' Botham play or followed him to matches around the country.

Publicly and privately, Clapton was in serious denial over his ongoing dependency on booze. Muddle-headedly, he began trying to convince himself – and others – that it was actually his reliance on Alcoholics Anonymous meetings that had become the problem. They were a crutch, he insisted, that needed to be jettisoned if he was to move on. With a drunk's spectacular lack of reason, he decided AA should be replaced by – you've guessed it – alcohol. In an interview with David Hepworth in *Q Magazine* at the start of 1987, he said: 'Gradually I weaned myself off that [AA] to the extent that now I drink when I want a drink and I don't get into any trouble with it.' If it sounded delusional, it was because it was. Not least because it came at a time when his drinking had reached a new nadir. Not, it has to be said, that there was much anonymity about going to meetings anyway. Sitting down with an AA group in St Paul, Minnesota, the night after playing a concert, half the room were wearing Eric Clapton T-shirts. Seeing him there, some of the younger members of the group got emotional and one girl began having a breakdown, crying and apologising to him. Through her tears, she told him that the previous night at the show, she'd speculated to her friend that he was in his changing room drinking and tooting coke. In his already fragile state, the added burden of dealing with how others viewed his addiction and how it affected complete strangers was clearly something he could do without.

As an example of his schizophrenic nature towards booze, at exactly the same time, he was telling another interviewer: 'Alcohol, I regard as twice as dangerous as drugs. Something happens to your mind when you drink and when you go over that line that makes you a drunk, you're a menace to everyone else. Alcohol is so insidious. The whole of society drinks like mad and they come out of pubs pissed and get in cars and don't think twice about it. Most drugs actually push you back into the wall, where the only danger is to yourself. I know when I was on heroin, I was no danger to anyone because I never went anywhere. I never got near to killing myself with it. Never. The thing is that I'm a guitar player with a craft and at the end of my term as a junkie I still had that to hold on to. I could still make a living out of it.'

The troubling thing for Clapton – and for his fans – was just how well he played when pissed. His appearance on a Channel 4 tribute show entitled *Carl Perkins and Friends*, a few months earlier, at Christmas 1986, was a case in point. Clapton shared the stage during the concert, which was specially recorded for TV, with a line-up including George Harrison, Ringo Starr, Dave Edmunds and Rosanne Cash. Clapton admitted not being exactly *au fait* with much of rockabilly legend Perkins's large back catalogue. Even so, a distinctly glassy-eyed Eric proceeded to tear up the place, spontaneously producing scintillating solos that had members of the backing band swapping awe-inspired glances. A few days after the show was recorded, he was admitted to hospital in Boston amid reports he was suffering from 'nervous exhaustion', although a hospital spokesman insisted he was being treated for kidney stones.

His denials about how serious his drinking had become hid a frighteningly self-destructive obsession. Bedtime had ceased to be about the succession of nubile fans willing to spend a solitary night with a half-pissed rock star. Now his nocturnal playthings were a bottle of vodka, a cassette player, a guitar – and a shotgun. 'One of the things I used to do was put shells in the gun and click it shut,' Clapton remembers of that time. 'And I'd put it in the position, with the barrel to my mouth, where you could take the top of your head off, and I thought, "Yeah, but if I did this then I'd not be able to have another drink." Now that's what I would define as insanity. It was that life and death had very little consequence to me. It was all about whether I could get a drink down my throat. Nothing else mattered. I don't know why I didn't kill myself; I was plucked from that and a lot of people didn't make it.'

Reflecting on his drinking years for a book called *Getting Sober . . . And Loving It* in 1992, he revealed how he regularly came close to ending it all. 'My liver went, my sanity had gone,' he remarked. 'I had shotguns and was practically toying with suicide. I'd load the gun after my wife had gone to bed. I knew there'd be a point in the middle of the night and I'd be thinking about killing myself every bloody night. It was a madness, it was a nightmare and I nearly died three times by my own hand.'

By the time he toured Australia, in the summer of 1987, he had the shakes. 'I was limping around on stage. My liver broke down. My skin was peeling off. I was covered in blotches,' he said later. 'The only thing I ever loved was alcohol. And when it did let me down, it was the biggest shock of my life. I couldn't trust it anymore. My friend was gone.'

Appearances may have been deceptive, but unlike when he succumbed to his first stint in rehab back in 1982, Clapton did not exactly look in terrible shape when, on 21 November 1987, he finally entered Hazelden, scene of his previous rehab treatment five years before. With pitiful irony, he was resident in the Minnesota clinic when his remake of 'After Midnight', specially recorded for a Michelob beer commercial, first aired. As it appeared on screen, Eric was left to squirm in a room full of alcoholics, as they sat around watching TV. 'Is that you?' one asked incredulously. 'Yep' was all Clapton could muster in reply. Surprisingly, however, given his suicidal thoughts, he would concede that, second time around, he had not, in his own mind at least, reached 'rock bottom', as had clearly been the case following his emergency hospitalisation in Minneapolis. Yet his wardrobe of vastly expensive Versace clothes and artfully tousled hair masked the old inner turmoil, the feelings of hopelessness, worthlessness and the sense that he had wasted his chances, particularly when it came to Pattie. 'I had everything a man could ask for in terms of material possessions – a loving wife, a loving family and good friends – and I wanted to destroy myself,' he recalled later. 'And that was a recurring reality.'

Ultimately, it was for Conor that he decided to seek help. 'I couldn't bear the idea that, as he experienced enough of life to form a picture of me, it would be a picture of the man I was then,' he went on. 'When I went back, I knew I had to surrender to this programme they talk about, the twelve-step programme, or die. When I did surrender, one of the things I had to acknowledge was that being a musician was really of little consequence – it was totally incidental to all of this. I could no longer hang on to that as an identity. It really didn't matter much, it was the icing on the cake.' With therapy came, one imagines, the need to pick the positives out of the hell of his drinking years. 'You know, I can look at my disease of alcoholism as being a stigma or being the greatest gift I ever had,' he said after leaving rehab. 'For me, it's the greatest gift because I didn't know what was wrong with me until I got sober. Until then, I thought I was crazy. I thought I was a bad, bad person. When I was told I had a disease, I thought, "OK, so I'm no worse off than someone who has cancer or diabetes." And I'm lucky because I can do something about it, and all I have to do is talk to somebody else.'

Now he was also talking to a higher power. As he prepared to leave rehab, he realised there was a danger that, on his release, he would simply go back to his old destructive ways. Terrified, he fell to his knees and pleaded for help. He describes it as 'surrender', asking for help from someone, anyone. Since that day, he always prays in the morning, on his knees, reaching out for help. At night, he does the same, this time to give thanks for his life and for remaining sober and for not once thinking about having a drink or taking drugs since getting clean. 'I'm not religious,' he said at the time. 'But I am spiritually motivated. I pray a lot, I don't know who to – maybe even myself sometimes. Everyone in a dire situation calls upon something, the higher power either outside or inside of you. I just had to keep remembering through all that that I was a person who had a gift and I was abusing it and ignoring it.' If he was not yet at the stage of his nascent recovery where he was able to acknowledge the devastating impact his drinking had on others – most notably Pattie – he was at least beginning to accept that his beloved career had been in grave danger of becoming a casualty of it.

But his transformation to considerate, reliable human being still had some way to go. For all that thoughts of Conor made him determine to get clean, it did not appear, once Clapton had left Hazelden, that he'd resolved to make much more of an effort to adapt his life to the needs of his baby son. For the most part, the arrival of Conor was viewed with vaguely detached positivity. Clapton began going on about how small children were really for women, how excited his grandmother was about the baby and how a child does not really need its father until it is three. 'When he reaches the age of three or four, maybe we can spend more time together,' Eric said when Conor was sixteen months old. It was an oddly prehistoric – but fairly typical – thing to say. He certainly was not giving the impression that the birth of his son had made any sort of profound impact on him (and, of course, he was not letting on at this point that he also had a daughter he barely knew). Nor did his dogmatic approach to how big a role he was prepared to play in Conor's life seem to make sense, given his current solitary home life. At the same time, he was bemoaning how 'very lonely' he was living alone with his Airedale terrier and four cats at Hurtwood. The possibility that spending more time with the infant could actually enrich his life did not seem to cross his mind.

Certainly, his reticence did not go down well with Lory, who at the same time was complaining to the tabloids: 'He has to decide he really wants us. He has to face up to things, life is not a joke. Eric is really a weak man who needs something important in his life, like watching the baby grow. I love him, but I will only go and live with him when I know the time is right.' Perhaps with her words ringing in his ears, when Clapton came out of treatment at Christmas, Lory and Conor were duly installed at Hurtwood. But it was Pattie that he met for pleasant lunches, and he was surprised that there was no animosity. But just as things threatened to get back on an even keel, a figure from his recent past made an unwelcome re-appearance. The virgin soothsayer began phoning him again in late 1987, and when she told him she was going to be evicted from her flat in New York, he agreed to send her some money. However, it would not be enough to stop their secret liaison being exposed. In March the following year, 27-year-old Alina Moreni, who variously claimed to be an Italian baroness or Romanian nobility, told the world's press she was expecting Clapton's baby. She said her aunt, Francesca, was married to Ginger Baker, and Miss Moreni, who claimed she had known Eric since she was fourteen, insisted she had been a virgin until Clapton 'initiated' her the previous summer. Meanwhile, she was saying he had told her he'd send her £2000 a month to support her during her pregnancy. A month later, she was telling British tabloids that after reading Eric's tarot cards, she persuaded him he needed to sleep with a virgin sharpish in order to create a magic powerful enough to win Pattie back.

Alina, a blonde part-time singer who claimed to be a reincarnation of nineteenth-century mystic Helena Petrovna Blavatsky, said she mixed her own blood into an occult potion and smeared it outside Clapton's hotel, before chanting a spell and waiting for him to fall into her clutches. Later, her 'friends' said she was suffering from toxemia, the blood-pressure condition caused by pregnancy. Meanwhile, Clapton's apparent tomcatting led one Sunday newspaper to run the tongue-in-cheek headline: 'Any more Clapton kids out there we don't know about?' But in May her story began to unravel. When she claimed to have given birth to a baby girl in St Barnabas Hospital in the Bronx, her former manager came out to say she had simply stuffed a pillow under her dress for photographers and that the Park Avenue apartment where she claimed her family lived was simply the place she worked as an au pair. Her ex-manager Lynne Robinson told the *Sun* she knew something fishy was going on when Alina's bulging stomach kept moving from day to day. Moreni later claimed she had really been pregnant, but had had the baby aborted the previous November and had carried on pretending she was expecting 'for my own self-respect'.

As she spoke, in New York, on 12 May 1988, Pattie was being granted a 'quickie' divorce in London because of Clapton's adultery with Lory Del Santo.

Suffice to say, the whole imbroglio was highly embarrassing for Eric. But just what had persuaded him, even allowing for his alcoholic state at the time of their meeting, to get involved in such a bizarre situation in the first place? An ex-Atlantic Records executive offers an insight. One night, not long after the Moreni episode, Eric was in bed in a New York Park Avenue apartment with another girlfriend and a bat flew in through the open window. Clapton apparently tore around the place in hysterics, convinced it was an occult sign from Miss Moreni spelling imminent disaster. According to Clapton himself, he chose to put a positive gloss on the whole thing and concluded that to come through it with his sobriety intact was a good sign. Nonetheless, he says that Miss Moreni didn't disappear and would on occasion confront him in the street. Eventually, though, her appearances began to diminish.

Lory, however, was still on the scene. That summer, in spite of their relationship being at best semi-detached, she was telling one reporter that she and Clapton had got engaged and were planning to marry in church, with her wearing a short, fashionable white dress. A month later, Eric was refusing to be drawn on the subject when he, Lory and Conor arrived back at Heathrow after a holiday in Antigua. Not least because, from his perspective at least, the relationship was hardly exclusive. According to one ex-girlfriend, Annie Mayhew, with whom Clapton had a brief fling during the time he was also seeing Lory, his affectionate nickname for the Italian mother of his son was 'the Hustler'. There was also talk in the Clapton camp of Lory pestering him for more money for her and the baby. In the end, Clapton insisted she sort out the financial side of things with Roger Forrester, which only served to infuriate Lory further.

Certainly, Clapton spared no expense on himself. Though he would concede that his wardrobes, bulging with Versace and, later, Armani creations, were actually an extension of his lack of self-esteem. He admits he often lavished thousands of pounds in the ateliers of his favourite designers because he felt the shop assistants wouldn't like him if he didn't. It was a two-way street. In Gianni Versace's small Knightsbridge shop at the time, Clapton's *August* album played on a virtual loop, to ensure his music would be booming out when he came in, which he did – often.

His sense of not being able to live up to the expectations others had of him extended to his music. Even at the relatively tender age of forty-three, he was saying he believed that, for many observers, his career was already all in the past. At the time, he told *Rolling Stone*'s David Fricke: 'The most difficult part for me to accept is to still be coming out with product, up-to-date material, and it won't be treated with the same kind of respect. It's almost as if it's two different people living with my name. I run into people who say, "Aw, yeah, you were in Cream. What a great band." And it's like nothing has happened since. I'm probably better off making records for people who haven't heard me before, because they'll hear it with fresh ears, rather than making records for people who have heard me over the years, constantly comparing me to the past. You can sometimes improve on the past, but you can't recapture it. And there are always going to be people saying I was better then.'

Nor would the prospect of a more stable existence, now he was finally sober, necessarily be positive for his artistic output. Indeed, cripplingly for his prospects of physical and emotional recovery, there was one chilling yet inalienable fact: he played much better when his life was in a mess. The point was illustrated with candid brutality by Bob Geldof after Clapton lent guitar parts to two tracks for Geldof's debut solo album *Deep in the Heart of Nowhere* a couple of years earlier, in 1986. 'We got him at a great time,' Geldof explained. 'It sounds callous, but he was going through big emotional things with his wife and his playing was unbelievable.' It was a truth acknowledged by Clapton himself at the time, when he said: 'I play best when I'm under strain or when I think there's nothing left for me.' It also served as inspiration for his songwriting: 'Severe crisis is what usually inspires me to write,' he added. 'I do anything best when I'm up against it. I honestly don't look for trouble, but I do seem to attract it and thrive on it at the same time.' He was also candid, however, that there had been occasions when he'd manipulated crises and personal dramas in order to stoke the fires of his creativity.

When it came to his relationship with Lory, however, there was no need to manufacture anything – there was more than enough stress to be going on with.

# THIRTEEN

# Diversions

Given that he was a married, degenerate drunk when they met, Lory could, surely, have been under no illusion that a life with Eric Clapton in it was going to be a picnic. As they carried on the pretence of a relationship, he in England and she in Milan, Eric filled his time by brazenly squiring a carousel of beautiful women around town, including model Marie Helvin. The next minute, he and Lory were taking a holiday together. In early 1989, they were back in Antigua, where he had bought a house, though it followed the pattern of the disastrous and depressing vacations that he and Pattie endured during the dying days of their marriage; it was spent largely arguing in hushed tones in local restaurants or sitting looking at their plates in stony silence. The long-distance relationship was also hardly conducive to forging a close bond with Conor. Motherhood had come utterly naturally to Lory, which only intensified Eric's feelings of inadequacy as a father. He felt out of his depth and, though they would play football on the terrace and take strolls together around the garden, the natural connection he assumed existed between fathers and sons remained worryingly elusive. He was also unusually hurt if the boy was offhand or rude to him.

So, with his confused personal life needing a period of mature reflection followed by careful and sustained attention, Eric did what he always did in these situations and went off to make a record. Somewhat worryingly for his long-term recovery, the fact that he was now clean and sober did not appear to have lessened the odds that, faced with challenges that required him to engage, he absented himself, preferring to put his problems on hold rather than deal with them head-on.

The album he started work on, *Journeyman*, was to be produced by Russ Titelman, the American who had scored a big hit three years earlier with Steve Winwood's album *Back in the High Life*. For Eric's new record, Jerry Lynn Williams would supply more songs, including 'Pretending' and 'No Alibis', on which Daryl Hall shared the vocals. Elsewhere, there were collaborations with George Harrison, and Cecil and Linda Womack. As far as Clapton was concerned, *Journeyman*, which he recorded in New York, represented an album that fulfilled his own vision of how he wanted his records to sound, unlike the Phil Collins fudge of his last two efforts. 'Whatever happens with this record,' he said when it came out in November 1989, 'I can only blame myself.' It was also, significantly, the first album he had done completely sober. Yet it only carried two songs, 'Bad Love' and 'Old Love', that were self-penned, the latter being co-written with Robert Cray, with whom he duetted on guitar.

The supremely talented Cray's presence during the sessions was responsible for lifting Eric to new levels of playing, particularly during the slow blues 'Old Love', which was recorded while Clapton was laid low with flu. Like Duane Allman, Cray filled the role of muse as much as collaborator.

The sheer joy of just playing together also resulted in two tracks, blues cover 'Hound Dog' and the Bo Diddley number 'Before You Accuse Me', appearing on the finished album, even though they were only meant to be ad hoc jamming sessions to fill time during lulls in recording. The album was a resounding success, selling two million copies in three years. At London's Tower Records, the shelf space devoted to Clapton stretched twelve and a half feet as his career continued to benefit greatly from the changeover from vinyl to CD, with older, middle-class fans with money replacing their old record collections with digital versions of his back catalogue.

But his disappearance to make the record only made the dire situation with Lory worse. The final straw in their turbulent relationship came when the couple had a major bust-up en route to a concert by the Italian singer Zucchero in Rome in October. They had a huge row in the sixteenth-century Spanish Steps Square that had tourists gawping open-mouthed as they traded insults before stalking off in separate directions. Days later, Lory was lamenting to the press that there was no hope for them and was already talking about the affair in the past tense. 'We always argued whenever we were together,' she sighed. 'Our relationship has been less than wonderful for some time. Eric claimed he missed me when he was away and he hated not being about to see Conor more. But if he was really concerned about Conor and cared about me, he would have spent more time with us and less time working. He doesn't have to work so hard. He used his work as an excuse for not being with us. Anyway, it's behind me now.'

Their problems had been exacerbated by the fact that Lory had been pushing him for several months to consider having another baby and was still angling for them to live together in England. But it was clear that Eric was not over Pattie. He had written 'Old Love', which includes the line, 'Makes me so angry to know that the flame still burns', about her. And even though they were now divorced, the couple would meet for platonic lunches. He even invited his ex-wife to Hurtwood to meet Conor. Meanwhile, according to Annie Mayhew, who had a fling with Clapton around this time, he refused to move any of Pattie's things in the hope she'd come back. And he would unselfconsciously pore over photo albums of his years with Pattie, remembering better days. Pattie's memories, however, were less rose-tinted. In their final divorce settlement over his infidelity and unreasonable behaviour that year, she agreed an out-of-court deal. She walked away, she says, with a modest flat and a modest lump sum, not the millions she reportedly won. She regrets hiring a lawyer who, she says, was too gentlemanly. Later, Clapton told her she had divorced him at exactly the wrong time, when his finances were far less healthy than they would become in future years. After one lunch post their divorce, she pointedly thanked him for taking her back to her two-bed flat.

Following the disastrous holiday, he and Lory would not see each other again for several months, with the Italian accusing him of everything from ignoring his son, to failing to learn Italian, to not being around long enough to teach the little boy English. 'I have stood by him through his drinking and borne him a child, but now, like any woman, I want more,' she complained to the press. 'He was drunk from dawn to dusk. But now that he doesn't want another child, I will have to find someone to love and give me a brother for Conor.'

There was also bad feeling about the subject of money. She told a journalist: 'I thought it would only be right to split the expense and ask Eric for money to help me bring up Conor. But he refuses to speak about money. He doesn't even ask me, when I paid my own fares to go on holiday with him, how much it costs. When I asked for money for Conor, he said to me, "Don't talk about money – speak to my agent."' And of their public row, she added: 'It was very embarrassing. People were staring at us in astonishment.'

Matters were not helped by Clapton giving an interview to the *Guardian* at the same time, in which he let slip: 'My personal life is just one disaster after another. I've actually got a lady in America, who shall remain nameless, and that hasn't reached the press yet. But I'm still carrying on. I haven't become a monk!' After the inevitable split, Clapton said of his failure to live successfully with Lory: 'We tried it a couple of times, but I think my inability to settle down prevented that from happening. It seems to be almost impossible for me to find myself in a relationship without wanting to get away at some point, wanting to run away and go and be a little boy again and play the guitar and misbehave. I'm not really sure that I'm looking for comfort or a steady relationship. I just like the company of beautiful women. I do have a weakness in that department.'

When it came to his gruelling workload, it could hardly be argued that the exasperated Lory did not have a point. As they split, he announced he was to perform a record-breaking eighteen concerts at London's Royal Albert Hall the following January. It would be the culmination of fourteen solid months of recording and touring, broken only by those disastrous holidays in Antigua. For the first time, his 1990 stint at the

Albert Hall would include three pure blues shows, with Buddy Guy and Robert Cray as guests. The annual winter residency at the iconic Kensington theatre, which began in 1987, appealed to Clapton's habitual nature and, apparently, his temptation towards the grandiose. For his 1991 stint there, he commissioned the American film-score composer Michael Kamen – with whom Clapton collaborated on the BBC thriller *Edge of Darkness* and the Mel Gibson Lethal Weapon movie series – to write a concerto for his guitar, which he performed with the National Philharmonic Orchestra. Unable to read music, Eric had to learn his part by ear. Performing with a classical orchestra had been a long-held desire. And, for the most part, he chose, when he was not working, to listen to opera. A favourite was the 'Senza Mamma' aria from Puccini's *Suor Angelica*, which, with its tale of a mother separated from her son, had obvious resonances with his own life.

It was no surprise, perhaps, given his addictive nature, that once he had overcome his compulsion to drink and do drugs, he replaced them with an insatiable craving to play live. The Albert Hall residency reached its zenith in 1991 – though his stints at the venue would continue on and off for years to come – when he played an unprecedented twenty-four nights, which became an album of the same name later that year. At the time, Eric, was saying: 'I am addicted to live concerts now. You want the buzz again and again. You *have* to have it.' But there was, by then, already a sense that it had all become rather bloated and hubristic. Playing four different sets – a four-piece formation, a nine-piece, blues and full orchestra – became a chore and left him tired and miserable.

To some extent, the annual event had also become less

about the music and more a date on the social calendar, like Henley Regatta or Ascot. Often the tickets were snapped up by big businesses, to schmooze their clients, rather than going to real fans, and Clapton became sick of looking up at the boxes on either side of the theatre and seeing the backs of those who had come to enjoy corporate hospitality rather than watch the show. He also noted that he could barely throw three new songs into the set without the audience getting twitchy and wanting the old hits. During one night there in 1990, he come off stage buzzing because he could sense the excitement of the crowd. But his bubble was burst when he was informed that the audience's animation was actually the result of someone getting a blow-job in the stalls and being asked to leave.

And when he wasn't being ignored, it was not unheard of for boorish elements of the crowd to shout 'More Eric' when the sublimely gifted singer and guitar player Robert Cray took his moments in the spotlight. Still, Cray and Buddy Guy, both regular guest stars on Clapton bills for years, have always been sensible enough to underplay when they share the stage with him, rather than risk overshadowing the star of the show. Their reticence to go full tilt is, of course, duly noted by Eric, who has on occasion bemoaned the fact that his friends are too polite and gentlemanly to go head-to-head with him. By 1992, the Albert Hall shindig had been quietly reduced to a more manageable twelve dates. By 1997, he'd knocked the whole thing on the head, though he did later begin playing gigs there again.

Clapton's elevation to national treasure status was in stark contrast to the flagging careers of his former Cream cohorts Jack Bruce and Ginger Baker. As Eric was finishing his eighteen-night residency at the Albert Hall in 1990, a weary Jack and Ginger could be found more than 3000 miles away, in Providence, Rhode Island, performing in a dump called the Living Room on the penultimate night of a gruelling ten-week road tour of some of America's scuzziest venues. The only thing that the gig in the dark, smelly bar had in common with their glory days was the inevitable aggravation. They and their back-up musicians, appearing under the banner the Jack Bruce Band, featuring Ginger Baker, were due to have gone on at 10 p.m.; by 11 there was no sign of them emerging from their 'dressing room', a filthy, windowless hole at the back of the building which had been so extensively vandalised that even the ancient microwave and broken-down furniture had been graffiti spray-painted. Out front, the punters in the less-than-sold-out crowd were asking for their $10 dollar entrance fees back. For their part, the lesser-known two-thirds of Cream were beyond caring, having spent five hours on the road and arrived at the dive late, so Jack and Ginger didn't even have time for a wash and brush-up at the hotel.

In many ways, however, nothing had changed. Baker had proved so predictably obstreperous on the nearly three months they spent holed up together, travelling up and down the country, that he had been banned from the tour bus – though officially his exile was on the grounds of his insistence on smoking a pipe on board – and had taken to travelling by car with his then fiancée-cum-manager, Karen Loucks, a 25-year-old former cocktail waitress. The groupies had long since moved on to new pastures. But whereas Clapton had become distinctly disillusioned about his Albert Hall spectaculars being hijacked by a new breed of Hooray Henrys and Henriettas who thought Muddy Waters was something churned up during the Oxford/Cambridge boat race, the crowd who turned out to see the world's onetime most illustrious rhythm section was undeniably authentic. The 400-strong contingent sinking beers in the bar were a ragtag selection of ageing rockers and Woodstock relics.

Nor did fifty-year-old Ginger give the impression that the years had been particularly kind to him. A few days earlier, when the duo and their band played in New York, the *Village Voice* had observed tartly: 'The way Baker stumbles over the drums these days reminds me of watching grandpa prove he can still de-cap beer bottles with his eye socket.' He and Bruce had reformed for the first time after more than twenty years at a time of critical, if not commercial, success for the 46-year-old bass player. His recently released album, *A Question of Time*, had garnered favourable reviews, but sold minimally. For his part, Ginger was running scared of returning to Britain for fear of a close encounter with the taxman and, at the time, he and his fiancée were living on a rented farm in the California desert with eight dogs and two horses.

So, here the two men were, forced to live on past glories and finishing each show with eighty-minutes of Cream retreads. They belted out their ear-splitting improvisations in these sweaty dives with admirable gusto and the crowds still dutifully cheered Ginger's five-and-a-half-minute drum solos. But the silence from Clapton's guitar – the only thing that had ever truly elevated their efforts beyond the gratuitously self-indulgent – was deafening. Still, the stark contrast between the state of their respective careers must have rankled. Which might have explained Bruce's rather barbed replies to the inevitable questions at the time about a possible Cream reunion. 'We haven't really talked in years,' he told the American press. 'Eric and I are on different paths. I was interested in the music, but he was always very ambitious, very intent on becoming a big star. He and our manager Robert Stigwood joined together to push him as the star of Cream. They had a problem because I was the lead singer and wrote most of the songs. They went ahead and did it anyway. That was very hurtful and sowed the seeds of resentment between the three of us.' It also clearly grated that many fans thought Clapton was the creative driving force of the band and not Bruce. 'Eric helps perpetuate that myth in his own subtle way,' Jack said.

Nor had absence made Ginger's heart grow any fonder either, when it came to the subject of their more successful ex-bandmate. 'Clapton was carried by two superior musicians,' he observed at the time. 'We lifted him to musical heights he's never achieved since. Clapton wanted to be the STAR, in capital letters. He likes being idolised. But he doesn't want to go back to being a real musician because it would be too much like hard work. It's far easier for him to carry on being a pop star. He'd rather work with people of a low standard so he stands out.' And when it came to the subject of a reunion, he was adamant. 'It will never happen,' Ginger insisted. 'I don't think Clapton would even have the nerve to think about asking me, I really don't. The majority of the world is convinced that Cream was Eric Clapton's band, and he enjoys it. Cream was *my* band. I formed it. I did most of the hard work. And I got the least out of it. I hate that stuff Clapton does now anyway.' Nor was he any more complimentary about Bruce, despite them burying the hatchet and going out on the road together again. 'I don't like Jack's new album either, to be perfectly frank,' he added, showing conclusively that none of his spikiness had dissipated in the hard intervening years.

But for all Baker's bravado, the tough talk about it being a cold day in hell before he'd consider a Cream reunion was not exactly the full story. Some time later, Ginger admitted he had gone cap in hand to Clapton after going broke in the mid-70s, to propose reforming. 'Eric said he didn't want to do it just because I was broke,' the drummer confessed. 'This really hurt me at the time, but it was also absolutely true. That is not a reason to do something.'

And Clapton had more than enough money. His huge popularity meant that, after several relatively lean years, the cash was once again rolling in. In 1990, he earned just over £5 million, nearly ten times more than the previous year, making him one of the best-paid company directors in Britain. Meanwhile, his firm, Marshbrook, turned over more than £11 million, of which £8 million came from North America. In total, the company's profits were £6.5 million, all overseen by Roger Forrester from his elegant offices in a Victorian apartment block on London's Marylebone Road.

But being as rich as Croesus did not necessarily make Clapton any less miserable. Indeed, his general sense of disenchantment extended to his considerable fortune. At the same time as his earnings skyrocketed, he was lamenting: 'Money buys you things you fantasise about and when you get them you don't want them anymore. But it's almost an in-built thing with me to spend as much as I earn, as if money is something I don't really want to have. I remember when I was twenty-two, someone asked me what I'd do if I suddenly had sixpence left in the world. I said I'd go out and buy a Mars bar, and that's still my attitude.' That said, his capacity to enjoy the simply shallow pleasures a whacking great bank balance can offer had not altogether waned. When asked by presenter Sue Lawley, on BBC Radio 4's *Desert Island Discs* in July 1990, what his luxury item might be, he suggested either an Armani suit or a Ferrari.

Likewise, being clean and sober was not all it was cracked up to be. Once he quit drinking, he began noting, with a wry smile, that while he had been boozing and drugging, he had felt fine. Now a host of niggling ailments befell him. Moreover, his general sense of disillusionment did not magically evaporate either. Nonetheless, he was keen to help others get clean and he began working four mornings a week as an unpaid 'peer supporter' at the Priory Hospital, an addiction and treatment centre in Roehampton, south-west London. He'd first got involved shortly after getting clean for a second time, when, during a private visit to see the clinic's director, he was asked to persuade a young patient who refused to get out of bed to attend a group therapy meeting.

Little did Eric know that his hard-won sobriety had yet to face its toughest challenges.

# FOURTEEN

# Loss

In the enveloping humidity of a Midwestern August evening, a helicopter waited to take off from a Chicago airfield, the downdraft from its propellers only further heating the wet air. On board, Eric Clapton and Buddy Guy were preparing for the short flight to the small town of East Troy, eighty miles away, where they were both appearing at Alpine Valley, a winter ski resort in rural Wisconsin. Clapton was reputedly earning $1 million, minus production costs, for topping the bill on two consecutive nights in front of 30,000 fans in an open-air amphitheatre. A stellar line-up of guitar players was also booked for the weekend event, including Jimmie Vaughan of the Fabulous Thunderbirds, Robert Cray, Bonnie Raitt, Canadian blues rocker Jeff Healey and Jimmie's little brother Stevie Ray Vaughan. But the substantial payday he would receive for the gigs as part of the last leg of a six-week tour of the States was the last thing on Eric's mind. His immediate concern, he told his old friend Guy, who was appearing as an unannounced special guest, was just how he was going to be able to hold his own, given that his set came immediately after Stevie Ray Vaughan's. 'How am I going to follow this guy?' Clapton moaned as the helicopter took off. Buddy shrugged.

'Well, just do the best you can,' he replied encouragingly.

The previous evening, at the first gig, Texas-born Stevie, backed by his band Double Trouble, had given a blistering performance, totally stealing the show with his brand of tough-edged blues, inspired by everyone from Albert King to Jimi Hendrix, Wes Montgomery and Lonnie Mack. After arriving for the second gig on Sunday, 26 August 1990, Eric watched Vaughan and his band open the show on a monitor in his dressing room. It did not put him in a better frame of mind because, if anything, Stevie's playing was even better. His renditions of the Guitar Slim number 'The Things That I Used To Do' and the Willie Dixon song 'Let Me Love You Baby', plus his own composition, the tasteful instrumental 'Riviera Paradise', were conclusive proof that Vaughan, at the age of thirty-five, had moved above his peers into the thin air – once breathed by Hendrix himself – at the very top of his field. His playing was a stream of consciousness, with the music seemingly flowing through him. Stevie, as Clapton would pertinently point out later, was an 'open channel', never stuck for what to play next.

Clapton's friendship with Vaughan, whom he describes as a 'musical hero', went back to 1986, when his elder brother Jimmie contacted him to say Stevie was in rehab being treated for drink and drug addiction and would he visit him. Later, Eric played a part in getting help for Stevie, whose capacity for everything that was bad for him rivalled even that of Clapton in his dark days, as he went through the process of getting clean. He had also accompanied the Texan when he came to London to seek treatment with a doctor Eric had recommended.

After Clapton's set at Alpine Valley, he came back out on

stage and, by way of closing the show, told the audience: 'I'd like to bring out to join me a big treat – the best guitar players in the entire world: Buddy Guy, Stevie Ray Vaughan, Robert Cray, Jimmie Vaughan.' As they all tuned up, standing in a semi-circle, Eric told them the song they were about to play was in the key of A, and then corrected himself quickly: 'I mean it's in E, it's in E.' They then launched into a fifteen-minute jam of the Robert Johnson song 'Sweet Home Chicago'. Following Buddy Guy, who sang the opening verse and chorus, each took a turn to solo. Whereas the others obeyed the convention of not trying to outdo anyone else, Stevie's two solos that night were symbolic of his no-holds-barred approach to his virtuosity, his performance a strutting display of stinging vibrato and huge tone, made possible by the neck of his Stratocaster being fitted with jumbo frets and telegraph-wire-thick strings, ranging between a gauge of 0.13 and 0.60. And because Vaughan literally ground the strings into the neck of his guitar with his fingers, the metal frets would have to be replaced once a year. As Stevie played his second guitar break of the night, Clapton, as master of ceremonies, nodded at him to carry on, rather than usher in the next player. It was an act of recognition and submission. 'He just sort of kicked everybody's ass and nobody seemed to fight back,' Jimmy Vaughan remembers. 'Stevie was on a cloud or something.' Even Buddy Guy, who had seen it all on stage, said later: 'I had goose bumps.' The unspoken agreement between all the players – and the vast majority of the roaring crowd – was that Stevie had officially installed himself that night as the best guitar player in the world.

As the show ended, Sunday night had become Monday

morning, and a thick bank of fog rolled in. Now, the spotlights which picked out the musicians through the pall of mist formed eerie halos above their heads as they trooped off. Backstage, there was much hugging, as a fleet of four helicopters waited to take the stars back to Chicago. Eric and Stevie stood around talking about dates they were planning for joint gigs at the Albert Hall and – ironically – spoke about travelling to Paris the following month for a tribute to Jimi Hendrix. But Stevie was keen to get going as soon as possible, so he could get the earliest flight back to Dallas, where he lived with his girlfriend, Janna Lapidus. He was supposed to be sharing a helicopter with his brother and his brother's wife, but heard that one which was about to take off had a spare seat. Stevie jumped aboard with two of Clapton's crew, Colin Smythe and Nigel Browne, and Eric's agent, Bobby Brooks, and it lifted off, with Eric's aircraft following it into the air a few moments later. The choppers were the type that looked like a Perspex bubble, and as he got in, Clapton spotted the pilot cleaning condensation from the windscreen with one of the event's promotional T-shirts. It did not fill him with confidence.

There was a low bank of fog sitting a few feet above their heads as they waited to take off, but Eric, who was concerned that something was not right, kept quiet, in case he made the others on board fearful. As they took off, Roger Forrester, who was sitting next to him, remembers seeing the 'copter carrying Stevie and the others suddenly disappear from view, though he thought nothing more of it. And seconds after the four helicopters took off, they could see that above the low-lying bank of mist was a clear night sky. After the brief flight to his hotel, Eric went to bed, but at 7 a.m., Roger rang him in his room to say Stevie's helicopter had not returned. Later, in Forrester's room, the news came through that the pilot had banked the aircraft the wrong way after take-off and had flown straight into an artificial ski slope. Clapton broke down when he was told. To this day, speculation remains about whether Eric himself had been due to be aboard the doomed aircraft, but had switched at the last minute. Although his American publicist, Ronnie Lippin, denied this immediately afterwards, Vaughan's New York PR, Charles Comer, insisted he thought Clapton had made a late switch.

The following day, Eric made a pilgrimage back to the crash site. Nigel Browne, who'd acted as his PA and minder, had a two-year-old daughter, and assistant tour manager Colin Smythe left behind a five-year-old daughter called, poignantly, Layla. Back in Britain, Forrester's wife, Annette, immediately set off to comfort their families.

Interviewed for a tribute concert and television programme six years later, Clapton said of the first time he heard Vaughan's music: 'I was in my car and I remember thinking, I have to find out, before the day is over, who that guitar player is. That doesn't happen to me very often, that I get that way about listening to music. I mean, about three or four times in my life I've felt that way, in a car, listening to the radio, where I've stopped the car, pulled over, listened, and thought, I've got to find out before the end of the day, not, you know, sooner or later, but I have to know NOW who that is.'

He added: 'I didn't get to see or hear Stevie play near often enough, but every time I did, I got chills and knew I was in the presence of greatness. Music just flowed through him. It never seemed to dry up. I have to tell this story: we played on the same bill on his last two gigs. On the first night, I watched his set for about half an hour and then I had to leave because I couldn't handle it! I knew enough to know that his playing was just going to get better and better. His set had started, he was like two or three songs in, and I suddenly got this flash that I'd experienced before so many times whenever I'd seen him play, which was that he was like a channel. One of the purest channels I've ever seen, where everything he sang and played flowed straight down from heaven. Almost like one of those mystic Sufi guys with one finger pointing up and one finger down. That's what it was like to listen to. And I had to leave, just to preserve some kind of sanity or confidence in myself.' For him, Vaughan and Hendrix were linked in terms of their skills and style. 'They both played out of their skin, every time they picked up their instruments, as if there was no tomorrow,' Clapton has said. 'And the level of commitment they both showed to their art was identical. Listening to him on the night of his last performance here on earth was almost more than I could stand, and it made me feel like there was nothing left to say. He had said it all.'

That he was half intimidated and half in awe of Vaughan was without doubt. But did it cross Clapton's mind that, by a strange coincidence, he had been with the only two guitarists who could legitimately claim to be his superiors on the evening before their respective deaths – assuming his original claim that he was in the same theatre as Hendrix on that fateful night was accurate? Why had he survived when they didn't? It is undeniable that Clapton was open to suggestion where the world of voodoo was concerned. He had sought out the voodoo-inspired Dr John to ask for a love potion to help him get Pattie, he had followed the strange rituals and incantations prescribed by the 'virgin soothsayer' only a couple of years earlier, and he had been terrified when he thought a bat that flew into the bedroom where he was sleeping was an occult sign. He had also refused to touch Muddy Waters's guitar because of its 'magic', and he was fascinated by the legend of Robert Johnson selling his soul to the Devil. Indeed, the last song Vaughan had played was a Robert Johnson song, chosen by Clapton. Now, once again, with his rival's death, he was the undisputed greatest living guitarist. Did he, even for a second, wonder if all these happenings had as much to do with gris-gris as pure chance?

In the past, Clapton had preferred to defer to others when any form of crisis materialised. Now, at last, he realised that he was 'the captain of this travelling ship' and that the members of his entourage were looking to him as to how to deal with the fallout of the crash. Should they cancel the tour or continue? Some were saying they should pack up and go home in the wake of the death of their colleagues. Eric told them he thought that, as a tribute to the dead, they should carry on with the tour that night in Kansas. After a unanimous vote involving the band and crew, the show went on. Later, Clapton speculated that had he not been sober, he would have been a 'gibbering wreck' and unable to show that sort of leadership.

The previous October, an exquisite, feline-like creature came hip-swaying into a backstage party at New York's Shea Stadium, clearing a path through the air-kissing throng in a cloud of aristocratic entitlement and Marlboro Lights. Following her nervously was Eric Clapton, dressed from head to foot by his new favourite designer, Giorgio Armani, but looking like he would rather be anywhere else than entering into Mick Jagger's lair. The young woman turning every head in the room was Carla Bruni – the 21-year-old Italian-French supermodel and new girlfriend of Clapton. They were there because she had begged Eric to introduce her to his friend Jagger at the bash to celebrate that night's Stones gig. Clapton, of course, knew Mick's reputation for tomcatting and that he had absolutely no compunction about stealing another man's woman (since his failure to make a conquest of Pattie in Paris all those years earlier, he had tried and failed several more times). So, fearing Jagger would be unable to resist making a play for the beautiful Carla, Clapton took him aside and pleaded: 'Please, Mick, not this one. I think I'm in love.'

He could have saved his breath. Within days, the high-born Carla – who would go onto become the wife of former French President Nicolas Sarkozy – was already beginning a passionate seven-year affair with Jagger that would eventually spell the end of the singer's second marriage to Jerry Hall. Clapton had met Carla, who was twenty-three years his junior, while recording *Journeyman* the previous year and they had been introduced, oddly enough, by a friend of Lory Del Santo. She seemed very taken with him and was a music fan, and when she gave him her baby-faced smile, he was hooked. Soon, ominously, Eric was, in his own words, 'obsessed' with her. The affair took place against the glamorous backdrop of New York, where she was living and he was recording the album. Every evening, Lincoln Town Car limousines were sent all over town to collect her so the two could dine *à deux* at Bilboquet, the tiny but snooty French restaurant in Midtown of which Clapton would later become a partner.

While Clapton was clearly smitten, the ice maiden Miss Bruni showed no sign that their flirtation was anything more than a passing fancy. Even before her meeting with Mick, Eric found, to his cost, how fickle she could be, after returning from a tour of Africa that July that included gigs in Swaziland, Zimbabwe, Botswana and Mozambique. He immediately flew down to visit her at her family home in St Tropez, but she was not happy to see him and gave him the cold shoulder. And just when Clapton should have remained cool, he showed his desperation, seeking out some of her ex-boyfriends in the hope of getting advice on how best to play his hand in the relationship. That he had so obviously ceded the balance of power in the love stakes to a woman was a state of affairs that was as novel as it was unwelcome. And what Clapton found out from her former suitors was not promising either. They told him pretty much the same story: that the lovely Carla had a reputation for dumping men quickly and clinically. As if to prove the point, later she began standing him up. And when, reluctantly, Eric took her to see the Stones on their *Steel Wheels* tour, her clandestine affair with Jagger began. Eric eventually discovered what was going on from the woman who had introduced them. She rang to break the bad news that Carla had moved on and was now dating Mick.

A cuckolded Clapton, who was by now convinced Carla was the love of his life, became gripped by an obsession with her that lasted the rest of the year. In his 2007 autobiography, he said his fixation with Miss Bruni had taken some 'grizzly' turns and when he guested with the Stones a couple of times, he knew she was somewhere in the background. The fact that Jagger had the nerve to play around with his girlfriend behind his back caused a rift. 'For a while, I found it hard to think of him without malice,' Clapton wrote in his memoirs. 'Later on, of course, I quietly felt both gratitude and compassion towards him, first for delivering me from certain doom, and second for apparently suffering such prolonged agony in her service,' he added, in a joint dig at his ex and his old pal Mick. Afterwards, Clapton's AA sponsor insisted he embark on a 'four-step' programme which involved Eric making an inventory, listing all his resentments towards Carla and Jagger. It forced him, he admits, to accept he was responsible for making his own bad choices in relationships and subconsciously ruining the genuinely good things that came along. Was he choosing women, he asked himself, who would walk away from him – as his mother had done – because he felt he did not deserve any better?

In the bleak weeks and months that followed, when madness and mania threatened her, Lory Del Santo's thoughts went back incessantly to that one evening. Time after time, she replayed the events in her mind: Conor had returned from a trip to the circus with his father and when she had put him to bed, he pretended to be asleep, before jumping out after Lory had gone to bed herself and snuggling under the blankets with her for the night. The following morning, Conor was dead. The four-year-old had risen as usual on 20 March 1991, in the fifty-third-floor New York apartment where he was staying with his mother and his mother's boyfriend, Italian businessman Silvio Sardi. Wearing his favourite red pyjamas and slippers, Conor had been playing on the floor of his bedroom with his nanny and Lory, who was about to step into the shower, had called to him to hurry up and get ready because his father was coming to collect them. Conor had shouted back, 'In a minute.' She could hear him jabbering excitedly about what he had seen at the circus the previous evening, how he had seen an elephant for the first time. As Lory ran the shower, she remembered thinking about Conor and the elephants.

Then, as little boys will do, he began running excitedly from room to room, for no other reason than he was young and full of beans. Now out of the shower, Lory went looking for him, but was distracted by the sound of the fax machine ringing. To this day, she tortures herself that if she had just ignored that fax, with its estimate for some repair work, Conor would still be alive. Instead, she stayed a few minutes, comparing the price with other quotes she'd been sent. She could hear Conor running around excitedly, playing a game of hide and seek with the nanny. Elsewhere in the duplex apartment, a 36-year-old janitor and odd-job man called Jose Pastarna, who had never worked there before, was busy spring-cleaning the living room. Conor ran into the room, with the nanny following, and the janitor stopped the nanny to tell her to be careful because he had opened the window to air the room. In the second it took for her to stop, Conor ran straight through the open window. He was used to climbing the low step up to the window, a 6ft by 4ft glass wall, and not realising it was open, he lost his balance and fell out. He landed on the roof of the adjacent New York Genealogical and Biographical Society, forty-nine floors below. Immediately afterwards, Lory recalled: 'Suddenly, I heard a blood-curdling scream and my blood turned to ice. It was a really terrible scream and it came from Conor's room, but it wasn't Conor. It was the nanny.'

His mother hurried out in her bathrobe. 'I rushed to the room and shouted, "Where's Conor?" Then I saw the window and understood at once,' Lory recalled. 'All the strength left me and I collapsed on the floor. When I recovered my senses, I realised what had happened – my baby was dead. I would never see that little blond angel again. The building's concierge phoned for an ambulance, but, of course, it was too late.'

Clapton was across town in his room at the Mayfair Regent, on 64th Street. That morning, he sprang out of bed early, to get ready to walk over to collect Conor and Lory for a trip to the Central Park Zoo. He'd booked a table at one of his favourite Italian restaurants, Bice in Midtown Manhattan, for after. But at 11 a.m. his phone rang. Lory was on the other end of the line, hysterical and screaming that Conor was dead. Confused and in the first stages of shock, the possibility that his son could have been killed seemed so ridiculous that his first reaction was to stop Lory in her tracks and say incredulously, 'Are you sure?' Somehow, she explained through her sobs that he had fallen out of the window. Clapton hung up and began making his way to the apartment. Walking up Park Avenue, he was in a daze of denial, but when he reached the apartment building, the Galleria, on West 57th Street, where Lory and Conor were staying, the sidewalk was lined with police and paramedics. Too scared to go in and face the awful reality of what had taken place, Eric walked on past the police tape and the people milling around outside, craning necks to get a look at what was going on.

Finally, he plucked up the courage to enter the building and take the elevator up to the flat. Inside, a kind of madness, brought on by shock, had come over Lory, who was rambling incoherently like a crazy person. By contrast, Eric later recalled that a kind of calm, almost serene detachment came over him as she wailed and bawled. He retreated within himself as a coping mechanism to deal with the unimaginable horror of what had just happened. He spoke to the police and the medics, who told him the grim details of the accident. The apartment's living room had floor-to-ceiling windows that stretched along one wall. They had been designed with a cantilever arrangement so they could be opened to be cleaned, but no guards had been installed.

With Lory beside herself, it was left to Eric to go to the mortuary at Lenox Hill Hospital alone to identify his son. Staff there treated him for shock and when he spoke to friends back home in England later that day, they were frightened that he was still incoherent. Pattie later wrote in her memoirs that Roger Forrester went to the mortuary ahead of him and identified the body, before asking that the light bulbs in the morgue be changed so the room was less starkly lit when Eric went in to see his dead son. In fact, Forrester was in his office in London when Eric rang him to tell him what had happened and raced straight to the airport to get a flight to New York. Eric remembers that the staff there had done their best to make the boy look as normal as possible. But, still, looking at his angelic face, he could only say to himself that this wasn't his son; it looked a bit like him, but Conor was gone. Later, he saw him again at the funeral parlour, where he said sorry to his boy for not being a better father.

Just twenty-four hours earlier, he had been buzzing with excitement about finally bonding properly with Conor. Thus far, the relationship had been, in Eric's own assessment, at best 'haphazard'. Now, he felt that Conor was at an age when they could begin to communicate and it was time to make moves to organise a life together. He cancelled all work for the year and, starting with a blank slate, set out to become the father he desperately wanted to be. Ironically, the night before the boy's death, he felt as if they had really turned a corner.

He was in New York because Conor's mother and her boyfriend Sardi were thinking of moving to Manhattan permanently and were looking to find somewhere to stay long term. For the moment, they were staying at the Galleria, a swish condo on the fringes of Midtown. Eric arranged for him and Conor to spend the evening at the Ringling Bros. Barnum & Bailey Circus, at the Nassau Coliseum on Long Island. Astonishingly, perhaps, it was the one and only time he had ever taken his son out by himself. Conor was breathless with excitement and was mesmerised by the elephants. For Clapton, it was his first realisation of what being a father actually involved. When they got back, he excitedly informed Lory he had resolved to take care of Conor all by himself on future home visits, telling her: 'Now I understand what it means to have a child and be a father.' Now the promise of good times for 'Skipper' and 'Arf' – Conor and Eric's respective pet names for each other – had been extinguished.

Later, Lory recalled of the belatedly burgeoning relationship between father and son: 'Eric would never play with Conor. He would just look at him as if he was a world apart from him. Eventually, I said I knew it was a matter of time and patience before he adjusted. The tragedy is that the day he realised what Conor meant to him was just the day before our son died.'

In the wake of the accident, Lory was near deranged with

grief. 'It seems as if my baby is still here,' she wailed soon afterwards. 'I speak to him as if he's still around, just as I did moments before he fell. I open his wardrobe, touch his clothes and take his toys out. Conor is dead and I want to be dead as well. Maybe for Eric it is different. He has his music and his concerts. His life still has purpose. But not mine.' Of the cleaner, Pastarna, she added: 'With my own hands, I would like to kill him. He behaved like an irresponsible fool. Then after he had done all this, he didn't say a word – not even to justify his actions or ask my forgiveness.'

They took the coffin back to Hurtwood, the house filled with the Latin wails of Lory's devastated family. For his part, the detachment Clapton felt continued; he was part and not part of what was happening around him. A large gathering of friends arrived for the funeral service at St Mary Magdalen church in Ripley, on a drab, cold March day. Phil Collins and George Harrison joined the mourners and Eric's drummer Steve Ferrone read the Bible passage 'Suffer little children'. Movingly, there was a teddy bear wreath, and Lory sent a little horse made of orange chrysanthemums. As his coffin was lowered into the ground in a plot close to the church wall, the boy's Italian grandmother tried to throw herself in and had to be held back by relatives. Pattie was also there to pay her respects. At the wake at Pat's house, next to the church, Pattie tried to talk to Lory, who was too grief-stricken to communicate.

There was anger from some of the congregation about the large number of press and TV crews. But Clapton recalled that he was unmoved by their presence. He remembered: 'When we buried him there was a wall of reporters and photographers right there in the church. And it was beyond me to react to that. It didn't impinge on my own grief in any way. I try to look at it in a positive way. For such a young man, Conor had this incredible impact. He was famous overnight.' The night after Conor had been laid to rest in a tiny ornate copper and bronze casket, Lory slept at Hurtwood, the couple staying up, praying into the night. When she and her family were gone, Eric was left alone at the house, where in the days that followed, he spent his time reading and re-reading the letters of condolence. In the wake of the tragedy, he was inundated by letters and cards, including from Prince Charles, Keith Richards and the Kennedys. He was also swamped with messages from women offering to have his children to heal his mental scars. One wrote: 'I have got a little girl who is four years old and we would love to move in with you and help you start your life again.' He described them as 'sweet, but also a little sick. It's hard to know what the motives are sometimes.'

Most poignantly, however, he also received a letter written to him by Conor in Milan a few days before his death, saying how much he loved and missed him and was looking forward to seeing him in New York. In his memoirs, Clapton described the early months after Conor's death as a 'waking nightmare'. As he struggled to come to terms with what had happened, he was unable to sleep for weeks on end. He was also eaten up by guilt. 'All I felt was numb,' he said later. 'Then gradually I realised I wasn't suffering enough. When that hit home, I just went off the edge of the world for a while.' Part of the issue was that his relationship with his son had been so semi-detached. 'It wasn't a day-to-day relationship,' he added. 'We were very distant for long periods of time and so when we got together it was very intense. We fought very hard . . . Trying to whip a three-year-old into shape is very difficult when you're not dealing with things on a daily basis. There was a lot of angst. But then it came full circle. He was teaching me how to grow up and I couldn't believe that. And I fell in love with him at that point. It was an unbelievable experience.'

The healing did not begin until two months after the tragedy, when he and Roger went on a sailing holiday around the Caribbean which started in Antigua and took in, among other islands, Nevis and Barbuda. Eric took a little gut-string guitar along and slowly the music began again. So did his tears, and he started writing a song in memory of his son. That was a vital part of the process of coming to terms with Conor's death. Eric recalled: 'I knew intuitively that if I played, it would medicate me. I was bereft and I went into a numb zone and what I did to keep myself afloat was play. I had a guitar in my hands all day until I went to sleep.'

If the path to sobriety is about nothing else, it must be rooted in honesty. Sometimes that honesty can be unflinching and hard to hear. That, after all, is the thing about honesty. A year after Conor's death, Clapton mused on the subject of finally being clean – now four years and counting – in a book called *Getting Sober . . . And Loving It*. He speculated about how his son's death had been the true test of whether he had it within him to stay on the wagon and that, yes, he had been able to take positives out of the tragedy. 'The death in sobriety of my son gave me something that I could give back,' he remarked. 'I could sit at the head of the table in fellowship meetings and say, "I haven't picked up a drink today and I didn't pick up a drink the day he died." I knew it was such a great message for those in doubt. And that was the first time it all gelled. It was a horrible thing to happen, but I can't say I wish it hadn't happened because that is life.' The book, a collection of personal accounts of getting clean, was published in association with SHARP, a recovery programme. Quietly, Clapton donated a whole wardrobe of his Armani cast-offs, most worn only once, to the SHARP charity's shop in west London, close to the Fulham Road. Bargain hunters found backstage passes and plectrums in the pockets of £2000 top-of-the-range 'black label' suits by the Italian designer, while the whole place was jammed full of rails of last season's exquisitely cut trousers and jackets, all Italian size forty-six, plus scores of ties and row upon row of size seven shoes, most of which had never been worn.

Producer Russ Titelman had spent the previous months honing down the tapes of the 24-night run at the Albert Hall, selecting the six best takes of each song. But a grieving Clapton couldn't listen to them. 'I hated everything I heard,' he recalled. 'For some reason, my soul went dead to music. Music couldn't reach me. I botched it. My part of the job didn't get done.'

Instead, he chose to attempt to deal with the loss by going on a massive spending spree. He commissioned work on a villa in the grounds of a hotel on Galleon Beach in English Harbour, on Antigua's south coast. He also bought a house in Chelsea, with a courtyard and small walled garden, and three days later was making an offer on a huge Georgian house and country estate near Oxford. The latter caused a furious bust-up with Forrester, who vetoed the purchase in a high-volume exchange of views at his office. This time, Roger won the day. Unthinkably, Eric almost sold Hurtwood too. Of course, it doesn't take a shrink to know that he needed to keep his mind off his grief, and Hurtwood was full of so many bad memories.

Meanwhile, Eric made the most of a drop in art prices due to the early 90s recession and invested in works by Degas, Matisse and the contemporary Italian artist and sculptor Sandro Chia. Like every other interest, collecting soon became an obsession. 'I found going to the auction houses was a bit like going to the races – there was that same buzz, and, by goodness, you could get addicted to that too,' he said at the time. Yet, there was the sense that it was less about acquisitiveness and more about a drive, a yearning for self-improvement. He desperately wanted to become an expert on fly-fishing, on the finer points of a Fernand Léger drawing, or the most sought after Patek Philippe moon phase watch.

Shortly after Conor's death, Lory discovered she was three months pregnant by Silvio Sardi. Their son, Devin, was born on 23 August 1991, two days after what would have been Conor's fifth birthday. Then, two years after Conor's death, she lost another son, born three months premature, who died of an infection at two weeks. She and Sardi, who had by then become her husband, had another son, Loren, in 1999. She says she and Clapton have not once spoken to each other about Conor's death since.

There is rather a bizarre postscript to the story of Eric Clapton and Lory Del Santo, one that goes to the very heart of the contradictions involved in human relations. It is a tale of love, hate, vengeance and retribution. Nine months after Conor's death, Lory checked into a lavish suite at the Sun Plaza Hotel in Hiroshima, Japan. There, she had arranged a secret tryst with Clapton's best friend, George Harrison. And on the room-service menu would be three days of passionate revenge sex.

Lory hooked up with George in December 1991, when Harrison and Clapton were on a tour of Japan together, and spent the time locked behind the door of the ex-Beatle's room. She says that both she and Harrison were after one thing: 'sweet revenge'. For George, he wanted to get even because he never forgave Clapton for stealing Pattie from him. Lory, meanwhile, wanted payback over the fact that Clapton had effectively 'frozen her out' after Conor's death, refusing to talk about their loss and leaving her to deal with her grief alone. 'George probably had revenge in his mind, but so did I,' Lory remembers. 'We were both hurt, angry with Eric. With Eric, I couldn't talk. He was always very distant, even worse after Conor. And I was not sleeping with Eric at that time.

'But what might have started as revenge became so special. I will never forget that time. It was amazing. We had so much to talk about. It was not all about sex. It was so private, so special. He asked a lot of questions about Eric. He needed to. And I needed to talk. George was so sweet and very caring.'

Between bouts of sex, she says, they discussed the devastating impact Clapton had had on both their lives. She admits: 'We were hurting. We had this loneliness. So both George and I got even [with Eric]. I realised, "Wow! George Harrison really likes me . . . And I like him a lot!" He was a very quiet person. He cared whether I ate, he let me talk. He cared about what I had to say. Time just flew by.' At one point, she says, Harrison, who was married to his second wife Olivia Arias at the time, arranged for the hotel's Olympic-sized swimming pool to be closed off so the pair could have it to themselves. 'In the pool, he was so sweet. He kept massaging my feet,' recalls Lory. After their three days of bitching and sex, she says they went their separate ways: 'George did everything to perfection. No gifts. He called me and he said, "I hope to see you." But I knew we would never see each other. I am sure he knew. He told me, "You are so sweet. I can't believe a man would never want to be with you forever. There, in Hiroshima, that was a perfect moment for us.' Unsurprisingly, perhaps, neither told Clapton about their liaison. 'It is not that George and I were hiding,' says Lory. 'But we spent a lot of time in his suite upstairs. We wanted to have a private time. The memory of those three days are still with me.'

Which is not to say that Eric did not know that Lory had joined Harrison on tour. In fact, Miss Del Santo's then boyfriend Silvio Sardi had sent Clapton a fax, warning him that they had broken up and she was coming out to visit him unannounced. In the missive, he told Clapton he was worried about her sanity. Unable to deal with her, Eric let Harrison take over Lory as his 'travelling companion'.

Ten months after Conor's death, Clapton would be made to relive the ordeal in a coroner's court in Guildford – convened because the boy's body had been returned to England. He was forced to hear the grim details that his son's chances of survival from the fall were nil and that a pathologist had concluded the force of the impact was equal to being hit by a car at 100mph. Somehow, he kept his composure, graciously absolving of any blame the janitor Jose Pastarna, whom, he told the court, may not even have known a child was in the apartment. Clapton also spoke movingly of his son from the witness box, saying that the last time he had seen Conor he was frisky, full of energy and full of life. He could be naughty, he observed, but would obey if he knew he was being given a serious command.

In the meantime, Yvonne Kelly had written to Clapton to offer him the chance to get to know his daughter, Ruth, properly and become a father to her. But the secret of her existence was about to be revealed. In February 1992, the *Sun* ran a front-page splash under the headline: 'Clapton's Secret Girl, 7'. When he heard that the story was about to leak out, Clapton rang Pattie to warn her. She still had no idea he had fathered the little girl. At the time, Ruth was living with her mother and Yvonne's husband Malcolm Kelly, a painter and decorator, in a rose-coloured timber cottage set in three acres close to the sea on Montserrat. And it was the moustachioed Malcolm who raised the child as his own daughter. According to islanders, during Clapton's stay there recording *Behind the Sun*, he had become pally with Durham-born Malcolm and the two men were often seen out and about in the capital, Plymouth.

He and Yvonne had moved to the Caribbean island after falling in love with the place while on honeymoon in 1978. But Ruth had been conceived during a rocky patch in the marriage and, at some point, Yvonne had flown back to England to meet up with Clapton before returning to her native Doncaster to have the baby at the town's maternity hospital. But it was Malcolm's name that appeared as the father on Ruth's birth certificate. And the secret of her true parentage had been kept even from Malcolm's parents, Matt and Sadie Kelly, who for seven years believed she was their natural granddaughter. They only found out when Ruth blurted out one day: 'My natural father is Eric Clapton. Didn't you know?' Unsurprisingly, it all came as something of an unwelcome blow to the couple, so much so that Sadie needed hospital treatment for shock. They said at the time that during a Christmas Day back in Yorkshire, Ruth had taken a phone call from Clapton and then came bounding in, full of it. The couple confronted their son, who admitted he had known the whole time that Ruth was Clapton's child and that although he rarely saw Ruth, Eric had been paying maintenance (Ruth had been enrolled at St Christopher's, the only private school on Montserrat, when she was four). Their son told them he believed Clapton was keen to see more of her, but was sensitive to the fact that Mr Kelly had accepted her as his own child. Understandably, the couple were devastated that they had found out the true situation from the lips of the child rather than from their son and daughter-in-law.

Not long after Ruth became part of his life, Clapton said: 'Ruth's mother invited me to become more involved. Until then, we weren't quite sure how we were going to approach it. I began spending more time with them. Yvonne knew that it would help, and it was true. I was able to hold a child again, and to be held by a child. Ruth has been a tremendous support. I had no idea how much power a child could have on an adult life, how much it can make you feel valid, unique and strong.' But, given his own upbringing without his natural father, he was speculating on the damage that could already have been done to her. 'I am convinced that she will be touched one day,' he added ominously. 'That sex and drugs will be part of the picture. She is coping, but there has to be some buried anger that she will need to medicate in some way.'

In early 1993, Yvonne moved back to Britain with the eight-year-old Ruth, after splitting from her husband, and settled in a modest first-floor flat in Doncaster. Every couple of weeks, Ruth and her mother would travel down to London to see Eric. Oddly, perhaps, Ruth would often be taken alone with her father to his recovery meetings. Soon, he was travelling up to Doncaster to see Ruth appear in children's plays in the local church hall.

That same year, Eric gave up his last vice of smoking, with the help of hypnotherapy. Well, perhaps not his very last vice. He was, indisputably, still in the grip of a heavy-duty addiction to beautiful women. San Lorenzo, the stylishly laid-back Italian restaurant in Beauchamp Place, Knightsbridge, became his office. And office romances were on the menu. He would habitually position himself at the same lower-floor table by the stairs. From this vantage point, he had a good ten-to-fifteen-second window from which to eye up the procession of lunching ladies, as they passed from the upstairs bar down to their tables. One who regularly caught his eye was another San Lorenzo devotee, Princess Diana. They had first been introduced backstage at a charity concert for Prince Charles's the Prince's Trust at Wembley Arena in June 1987. Clapton later cringed that he had rather presumptuously addressed her as 'Di'. For her part, the princess didn't bat an eyelid. According to a society friend of Clapton's, who was also on speaking terms with Diana, the attraction between them was 'absolutely obvious'. 'There was a "Carry On" film element to it,' says the friend. 'A lot of winking, and overtly steamy looks. A story went around that one time when she and Eric were both at San Lorenzo, Diana began sucking suggestively on a piece of ice as she gave him the eye. Everyone loved that.' Did things ever go any further? 'Well,' says the friend, 'they were both free agents and Eric's always liked a challenge.' (Diana and Charles had announced their separation in December 1992.) Also, as two of her most high-profile customers, Clapton and Diana could rely on the utmost discretion of San Lorenzo's ubiquitous owner, Mara Berni.

Perhaps whatever there was between them soured, because a decade after her death, Clapton would describe Diana as a 'manipulative and sick person'. 'It's that kind of thing – the burning martyr,' he added. 'What people will give up for the idea of being a burning martyr. It's not that Princess Diana was responsible for her own death, but I do think she contributed in some way to creating that public hunger. She was responsible for that side of it.'

What is certainly the case is that Eric could be found at the restaurant on an almost daily basis in the early nineties, with an ever-changing succession of beautiful women, including: actress Sharon Stone; supermodel Christy Turlington; Paula Hamilton, the Volkswagen advert model; Gae Exton, the former girlfriend of Christopher Reeve; actresses Patsy Kensit and Stephanie Beacham; and TV presenter Davina McCall. His success with women was not only down to his status as a millionaire rock god. Those who found themselves on the receiving end of the Clapton charm offensive discovered that he had a knack, either natural or carefully contrived, of getting on terms of intimacy very quickly. Some compared it to being smooth-talked by a rather flirty advertising salesman. For others, everything about him seemed genuine. The reality was, probably, that it was a bit of both. One thing that was beyond question was that the Clapton charisma was a potent weapon in the battle of the sexes. It was built to a large extent on his unalloyed vulnerability and the perception that, for all his twinkly eyed laddishness, he should not really be allowed out alone without a responsible adult. Even his notoriously terrible driving, crashing through red lights and leaving streams of fuming drivers in his wake, seemed endearing to the carousel of women he chauffeured out to lunch in his Mercedes or Ferrari. Often, an hour or so before she was due to be collected, the object of his affections would open the door to a courier bearing some exquisitely tailored Armani creation, a gift from Clapton for her to wear on their date.

All of this skirt-chasing, like his rash of house buying and art collecting, gave the impression that, while his sobriety had been preserved in the wake of Conor's death, he was replacing booze with other distractions without really dealing with his loss.

That sort of catharsis would only come through music.

## FIFTEEN

# Crossroads

Amid the mayhem backstage at the Grammys, Eric Clapton cut a serene figure. As TV crews, trailing yards of rubber-clad cabling, set up blinding arc lights and stills cameramen, their rented tuxedos wet with sweat, jostled for position. Eric gave them a beatific smile as he cradled his half-dozen awards as though he was doing nothing more out of the ordinary than transporting shopping bags from the car to the kitchen table – 24 February 1993 marked his zenith. A month earlier, Cream had been inducted into the Rock and Roll Hall of Fame in Los Angeles. And if Live Aid had sounded the starting gun on Clapton's transformation from strung-out has-been to budding national treasure in Philadelphia nearly eight years earlier, his all-conquering appearance at the Grammys that night completed the process. He won six Grammys: Best Male Pop Star, Best Male Rock Star, Record of the Year, Song of the Year – for 'Tears in Heaven' – Best Album for his *Unplugged* record, and Best Rock Song for his acoustic version of 'Layla'.

A tearful Clapton dedicated the awards to his son Conor and told the 15,000 audience at the Shrine Auditorium in Los Angeles: 'I have received a great honour, but I have lost the one thing I truly loved. I am very moved, very shaky and very emotional. I would like to thank a lot of people, but the one person I would like to thank is my son, for the love he gave me and the song he gave me. I really don't know what to say. I am totally overwhelmed. This has blown my mind.' Earlier that day, in an interview with *CBS News*, he'd said: 'I still don't truly accept Conor is dead. I still don't believe that I won't see him in a couple of weeks. I was as close to him as I have ever been to anybody. It's the closest relationship I've ever had because I invested so much hope in it. After he died, I just started to play. It calmed me down. It was a tranquilliser. It was safe anaesthetic. It was my way of coping. Losing him was unbelievably devastating. I don't know if I shall ever recover.' And speaking about 'Tears in Heaven', which he wrote about Conor's death, he added: 'All I would say is when I sing that song I am singing for him. I am singing for my angel.'

Yet, if Eric had got his own way, the album that garnered him such a clean sweep of the annual music awards may never have reached the ears of the millions who flocked to buy it. In January the previous year, he became the latest big name to agree to play an acoustic session for MTV's successful *Unplugged* series, which had previously included the likes of Crosby, Stills & Nash, Elton John, Sting, Don Henley and Aerosmith. But it was Clapton's performance that would become the one that defined the *Unplugged* phenomenon.

The session was recorded at Bray Studios, near Windsor, on 16 January 1992. Alongside Clapton was a familiar line-up of Steve Ferrone on drums, Nathan East playing bass, plus a new addition, Andy Fairweather Low, once of Amen Corner, on guitar, Ray Cooper on percussion, Chuck Leavell on keyboards and backing singers Katie Kissoon and Tessa Niles. The show, which premiered on MTV Europe on 27 March, featured folk and blues standards like the Jesse Fuller tune 'San Francisco Bay Blues', Bo Diddley's 'Before You Accuse Me', Robert Johnson's 'Walking Blues' and 'Nobody Knows You (When You're Down and Out)', which was made popular by Bessie Smith. They sat alongside an ambitiously re-worked, laid-back version of 'Layla', performed as a shuffle and an octave lower than the original.

There were newer numbers too, such as 'Old Love'. But the standout song was 'Tears In Heaven', which Clapton had written for Conor in Antigua. In it, he asked the question whether his loved ones, including his son and his grandfather, would remember him if they were to meet again in the afterlife. The song had actually made its official debut on the soundtrack of the 1991 film *Rush*, a crime thriller starring Jason Patric and Jennifer Jason Leigh. Whereas he had worked on *Edge of Darkness* and the Lethal Weapon films with the American composer Michael Kamen, for *Rush*, which was directed by Lili Zanuck, Clapton was hired to write the whole score with the help of Hollywood composer and orchestrator Randy Kerber. Zanuck insisted they put 'Tears in Heaven' in the film and when it was released as a single in January 1992, it became Clapton's only number one that he'd had a part in writing (his co-writer was Will Jennings, who would later go on to write another blockbuster weepy, 'My Heart Will Go On', sung by Celine Dion on the soundtrack to the 1997 movie *Titanic*).

There was also a new song, 'The Circus Left Town', later renamed 'Circus' when it appeared on his subsequent album, *Pilgrim*. The song recounted his last evening with Conor at the Long Island circus. In an interview to accompany the *Unplugged* session, Eric said of his decision to include songs about his dead son: 'I think my audience would be surprised if I didn't make some sort of reference to it. And I wouldn't want to insult them by not including them in my grief in a way. And so I do intend to make these things known and I will play them in concert and put them on record and it is for me a healing process and I think it's important that you share with people that love your music.'

Yet he had been dead set against releasing the *Unplugged* session as an album, deeming the performance not good enough and he argued it should get only a limited-edition release. And as far as he was concerned, the songs about Conor were part of a catharsis, written to stop him going mad and not initially meant for public consumption. Roger Forrester's wife Annette remembers her husband having to go into battle with an adamant Clapton in order to persuade him that they had a huge hit on their hands. Not for the first time, his manager was proved spot on. The album of the concert became the biggest selling of his career, reaching number one in the US, Canada, Holland, France and Australia, and number two in Britain, selling fourteen million copies in its first two years on the shelves, a massive ten million alone in the US, where it went diamond.

It said something about how distant his relationship with Conor's mother had become in the intervening period that the first time Lory heard 'Tears in Heaven' was in a shopping centre in Milan. She would spend the next ten years desperately trying to avoid listening to the song because of the bad memories it stirred. It would soon lead to negative connotations for Clapton too. During a tour of the US in the summer of

1993, he made the mistake of trying to open shows with 'Tears in Heaven', which only succeeded in leaving him frustrated and upset by the way the fans whooped and hollered throughout. Eventually, he would drop the song, and another he wrote for Conor, 'My Father's Eyes', from his set-list, though they both made a return in 2013.

Throughout his recovery from alcoholism, he had developed a strategy for dealing with such bumps in the road. One was simply to spend his way out of the doldrums, and back at his new house in Chelsea, he began buying pictures by Italian conceptual artist Carlo Maria Mariani, as well as more work by fellow Italian Sandro Chia. He also paid £40,000 for a piece by the German visual artist Gerhard Richter. He began expressing himself through the shorthand of therapy-speak, and phrases like 'emotionally intimate' started to trip off his tongue. He began counselling sessions with Chris Steele – the director of the alcohol and addiction unit at the Priory – who, with husband Richard, had become a close friend. He also saw a therapist who practised a method of counselling devised by American John Bradshaw, an expert in 'personal growth'. His method focused on delving into a patient's family background to heal their 'wounded inner child', as a way to get to the root of their problems.

But it was music that played the biggest part in retaining his equilibrium, and by way of combining his two passions, for music and for his recovery, in January 1993, he took to the stage for his inaugural alcohol-free New Year's Eve bash at Woking Leisure Centre, which was for family and friends and those trying to avoid booze.

One destructive pattern of behaviour he couldn't shake,

however, was his continued taste for women who, for one reason or another, were totally unsuitable for him. After a brief fling with actress Susannah Doyle, he began a relationship with artist and designer Francesca Amfitheatrof, another dark-haired Italian in her mid-twenties, to whom he quickly became 'addicted'. Within months, he was, to use his own words, 'on my knees', the relationship a damaging succession of tempestuous break-ups and make-ups which he took to boring his friends about at length. Bizarrely, he blamed getting involved with her on his weakened state after so recently quitting nicotine. Yet the stormy relationship limped on for a further three years, despite the fact that he once admitted he wanted to 'strangle' her every time they met.

Unsurprisingly, Forrester was keen to exploit the mass-market success of *Unplugged* with a follow-up album with similar crossover appeal. Clapton had different ideas. Having won over a new audience with the unapologetically middle-of-the-road *Unplugged*, he decreed his next album should consist of faithful covers of his favourite blues songs, down to playing them in the same key as the originals. Forrester would have been forgiven for pulling out what little hair he still had because, on paper, it looked like a classic case of celebrity conceit, an indulgence that pandered to Clapton's purist tendencies over the commercially driven agenda Forrester was given to follow.

By way of further distancing *From the Cradle*, which was released in September 1994, from the more slick production of his previous albums, Clapton also insisted that the record would be recorded live in the studio, with no overdubs. In the event, a Dobro overdub was added to 'How Long Blues' and a drum overdub on 'Motherless Child', the 'Barbecue' Bob Hicks song, first recorded in 1927, which includes the lines: 'If I mistreat you, girl, I sure don't mean no harm. Well, I'm a motherless child, I don't know right from wrong.' Another standout moment was his version of the Leroy Carr number 'Blues Before Sunrise', though Clapton's version was fairly faithful to John Lee Hooker's take on the song. Also included was 'It Hurts Me Too', the blues standard first recorded by Tampa Red in 1940, though Clapton lifted the guitar opening and solo from Elmore James's later version. If there were moments where the album began to resemble a blues theme park, it was only because Clapton insisted on remaining true to the essence of the likes of Freddie King's classic 'Someday After a While' and King's 1961 stomper 'I'm Tore Down'. But Eric, who went back to playing Gibsons – including a couple of ES335s – on several of the tracks, ensured this was no karaoke affair, thanks to his powerful, subtle playing and growling voice, even if there were moments, admittedly, when the whole thing was in danger of becoming a pastiche.

But the disagreement over the trajectory of his career only served to put a strain on his once close relationship with Forrester. Where in the past there was barely a cigarette paper between them on any important issue, now there was rancour and one-upmanship. Roger had been right about *Unplugged*, and Eric was delighted to be proved right about *From the Cradle*, which, in spite of his manager's warnings that it was a mistake, scored another big hit. The record went to number one in America, where it sold three million copies and went platinum. It also went platinum in Holland and Spain, and gold in the UK, France and Germany. The froideur between them was not helped by a miserable two-week cruise Eric took with Roger and his wife Annette around Antigua.

Sadly, the mood of positivity engendered by big sales of the record was not to last long. Two months after the release of the album, Rose, who had endured a long battle with emphysema, died of cancer. She was laid to rest in the same village graveyard as Conor, with Lory and Pattie as mourners. Eric had been spending more time with Rose and his mother, but his relationship with Pat was complicated by her growing dependency on prescription medication and her jealousy of her mother over Eric. If he made the mistake of visiting Rose first on his trips to Ripley there would be trouble, with both women vying over him.

Also at the funeral was Alice Ormsby-Gore. She had come back into Clapton's life after her worried family contacted him to say she was in hospital in Shrewsbury, after vanishing for a time in France on a junkie trip. He persuaded her to check into the Priory. But no good deed goes unpunished and within days the hospital called Eric to say that Alice's anger towards him over his treatment of her all those years earlier at Hurtwood needed to be dealt with if she was going to be able to progress with her rehab treatment. It was decided she should be allowed to confront Clapton in a session overseen by a counsellor. This being the new, caring and clean Clapton, he agreed. Alice repaid the favour by ranting at him non-stop for an hour. In his memoirs, he described the realisation of the damage he had caused her as 'terrifying'. He could barely believe the things she told him he had done, which she'd hung on to for more than two decades to 'fuel her need for oblivion'. After completing her course, she went to a halfway house in Bournemouth. Four months later, in April 1995, Alice would be dead too. She had left the halfway house and found a bedsit to move into, but had injected a massive dose of heroin on top of booze. Her body was not discovered for several days. Locals in the rundown district where she was living had become used to seeing her shuffling around the streets, deranged and shabby.

As for Pattie, following their divorce, she and her ex-husband had kept enough of a cordial relationship that she'd asked Eric to buy her a house in the country, and one was bought for £345,000 in the spring of 1995, in West Sussex. In fact, unbeknown to Eric, his name was inserted on the deeds but with an agreement that Pattie could live there rent-free.

But while things had worked themselves out agreeably with his ex-wife, his dysfunctional and erratic relationship with Francesca Amfitheatrof shuddered to its inevitable conclusion. In the meantime, however, he was still squiring a succession of beautiful women to his favourite table at San Lorenzo, while in New York, he had dates with the beguilingly beautiful Hollywood star Uma Thurman. Finally, Amfitheatrof called time on the affair and moved back in with her ex-boyfriend.

But his relief did not last long. The split almost immediately coincided with yet more bad luck. In May 1996, his wisteria-covered Chelsea home was destroyed by fire, caused by an electrical fault that had started in the roof space and spread downwards. Eric had arrived back after an evening out to find it ablaze. He rushed in to rescue his guitars, then watched helplessly as it burnt from the safety of the private courtyard of the house in a quiet mews. The fire acted as a form of catharsis.

Eric judged that a new start was in order and the damaged house was cleared and everything was sold so he could begin again with a blank page. With typical capriciousness, he put his collection of twentieth-century art into storage and sold it the following year at Christie's in London for £500,000, having grown bored with it. Instead, he painted the bare walls of his now repaired townhouse pristine white.

The transformation extended from his taste in art to what he wore. With his carefully chosen paintings gone from his walls, in came garish graffiti art. His wardrobes of Armani were sent to the charity shop and replaced by skater clothes by Japanese label Visvim (albeit for the sort of skater who could afford £200 for a grey T-shirt and £500 for a pair of high-top baseball boots). He even began designing clothes with a couple of skaters called Simon and William, who had a shop called Fly on the King's Road. If it all smacked worryingly of a mid-life crisis at the age of fifty-one, it was because it was. At the same time, he began dating the talented American singer/songwriter Sheryl Crow. However, their relationship reportedly fell by the wayside because she smoked cannabis and Clapton was worried he might be tempted to try it again and ruin his recovery.

Subconsciously, he was also preparing for a parting of the ways with Roger Forrester. The seed of their ultimate falling-out had been planted a couple of years earlier, in 1994, when Clapton, who had started participating in group therapy sessions at the Priory, was complaining to the hospital's director, Chris Steele, about how many drug addicts there were in Antigua and how he was thinking of selling up there. Chris and her husband Richard advised him to take their programme to Antigua instead and build a treatment centre. Quickly, a plan was devised for Clapton to join forces with the then US owners of the Priory, who were keen to open several similar centres around the world. It was a novel idea, given that Clapton's initial attraction to Antigua had little to do with the natural wonders of its 365 palm-fringed beaches and warm, glistening waters – though they were undoubtedly a welcome bonus – and was focused instead on the more synthesised pleasures of booze and narcotics. 'As a drinker and a druggie it was heaven for me because you could get any drug you wanted and every other person you met was an alcoholic,' Clapton explained. 'I used to come here and drink and do a lot of drugs too. I didn't see the alcohol and drugs as a problem: they were advantages back then. When I was doing all that stuff, this was the perfect place to be. But when I stopped doing it, I thought maybe I had to relinquish it all, because I couldn't come here anymore, because it was not really safe to be sober here. That's when I first noticed the problems for the other addicts. I knew there was another way.'

Buoyed up by his plans for the island, at the same time, Clapton began building a new home for himself there, on a bluff overlooking the sea near the resort of Falmouth. Certainly, he was under no illusion that the plan for the Crossroads Centre, as it would be called, was entirely altruistic. His reasoning was that if he was to remain clean, he had to help others get clean too. But with building already well underway, the head of the Priory in America agreed to sell his stake in the Crossroads project to another healthcare business which did not want to build a rehab facility in Antigua. It meant scrapping the plan or buying the stake from the new owners. Forrester was understandably nervous about how much of his own fortune Clapton was now having to sink into the project, already $4 million and counting. Nor were matters helped by the fact that foundations had been badly laid and the half-erected building was already falling apart. Roger counselled restraint, but Eric was having none of it. In fact, the setback only made him more determined than ever to push ahead with the scheme. He recruited Anne Vance, who was a consultant for the European Association for the Treatment of Addiction and had formerly worked for the Betty Ford Clinic in California. They agreed that neither was interested in getting involved in a project that made a profit from someone else's illness. Instead, they came up with the plan to charge better-off patients from around the world in order to fund free beds for those living not just on Antigua but the other Caribbean islands as well.

It was a significant nail in the coffin of his relationship with his manager. Another source of tension was Clapton's resolve that, after years as a gibbering wreck, he wanted to start making decisions for himself, often without seeing the need to seek Forrester's approval first. A case in point was over his decision, after a personal phone call from Luciano Pavarotti, to appear at the opera singer's annual charity concert in aid of War Child in Modena in June 1996.

Now they were also disagreeing about music as well. Clapton began working with Simon Climie, the singer-turned-producer whom he had met at Olympic Studios in Barnes, west London. London-born Climie had a brief heart-throb period as a pop star in the duo Climie Fisher, who had a big hit with 'Love Changes (Everything)' in 1988. He went on to write and produce for the likes of Rod Stewart, George Michael, Aretha Franklin, English girl band Eternal, Michael McDonald and Italian singer Zucchero. Climie came from a new and different school of producers from the ones Clapton was familiar with and used Pro Tools, the complex digital audio software that allowed records to be recorded and edited on a laptop. Their first collaboration was low-key. In 1997, they recorded as the techno-edged TDF – short for Totally Dysfunctional Family – to make music for one of Giorgio Armani's fashion shows. And, in a throwback to the attempts at anonymity during his Derek days, Eric was credited simply as 'x-sample'. They also did an album called *Retail Therapy*, which was aimed at the club scene and which, they agreed, should also be released anonymously. Not for the first time, it was an attempt by Clapton to have his music listened to without the baggage of his fame and reputation.

Now, with the help of Climie, Clapton set about making an album with the possibly dubious ambition that it would be 'the saddest record of all time'. The fact that only two songs, 'My Father's Eyes' and 'Circus', had been written before recording commenced and the whole process took the best part of a year, racking up huge studio costs, only further exacerbated the strain on Clapton's relationship with his manager, who was bristling about how much money it was costing. Worse still, what little he heard of the sessions, Forrester did not appear to think much of. For his part, Eric was neither seeking nor taking Roger's advice anymore. The album, called *Pilgrim*, which was eventually released in March 1998, was something of a diversion for Clapton after the predominance of covers on his previous two albums and was his first collection of new material since *Journeyman* nine years earlier. In all, he either wrote or co-wrote twelve of the album's fourteen tracks, the exceptions being the St Louis Jimmy song 'Goin' Down Slow' and the Bob Dylan-penned 'Born in Time'. The album, which stretched to an epic 75-minutes plus, opened with the lyrically clever 'My Father's Eyes', which was written in Antigua after Conor's death and which dealt with religion and Clapton's feelings of inadequacy as a parent and his lack of a natural father.

*Pilgrim* was certainly not without its highlights, like the purposely cold 'One Chance', but, for the most part, the record sounded like Clapton had been spending rather too much time with his new skater friends. The surfeit of drum programming and electronica may have made it sound more modern than his previous throwback records, but the downside was that the new technology invested it with a clinical edge at odds with Clapton's mellow, nuanced voice and emotive, if understated, guitar work. Perhaps in an attempt to placate Forrester, the record also, touchingly, included a ballad, 'You Were There', which he wrote about the vital role Roger had played in his life. Vocally, Clapton was channelling the high soulfulness of Curtis Mayfield, particularly on the title track and another song, 'Inside of Me', but whatever fire he wrought from the material was too often extinguished by Climie's detached production. Even so, *Pilgrim* went platinum in America, selling a million copies and getting to number four, while it went gold in the UK, getting to sixth place on the album chart. But by previous standards, sales were disappointing and the turnover of his manager's company, Roger Forrester Management Ltd, shrank from £1.4 million, the previous year, to £500,000.

'My Father's Eyes', which won Clapton a Grammy the following year for Best Male Pop Vocal Performance, was also put out as a single. Its release inspired Canadian journalist Michael Woloschuk to attempt to discover the true identity of Clapton's natural father. In March 1998, Woloschuk published an article in the *Ottawa Citizen* which named Eric's real father as Edward Fryer, an itinerant Canadian musician and former serviceman who had died in 1985. Born Edward Walter Fryer, on 21 March 1920 in Montreal, he had left home at fourteen, losing contact with his family. In the meantime, he'd learnt to play the piano and earned a living singing and playing in the bars and nightclubs of the city before enlisting in the 14th Canadian Hussars on 17 July 1940. Already married, Fryer was deployed to England in 1942 and, while stationed there, he continued to top up his army pay by entertaining drinkers in local pubs. However, artillery noise damaged his hearing and he was injured in an accident with an armoured car, which meant that for the rest of his life he suffered from phlebitis and dragged his left leg. When he was twenty-four, Ted, as he was known to his fellow soldiers, met fifteen-year-old Patricia Clapton in a Surrey dance hall where he was playing piano and she fell pregnant.

When Fryer and his fellow soldiers were ordered home in 1945, he failed to arrive at the ship taking them back and was listed as AWOL. On 4 September 1946, he was given a dishonourable discharge and went off radar, spending years as a wandering musician, moving from town to town and woman to woman, making a living by singing staples like 'My Way' and 'Raindrops Keep Falling On My Head' and playing piano in hotel bars. Coincidentally, he would spend some of his time on the road playing the juke joints and dives of Mississippi, home of the Delta blues that would become so important in the life of his illegitimate son. Married at least four times, he had already got through a handful of wives by the time he married Yvonne Colson in 1965. Their daughter, Eva Jane, was born in 1968, but he walked out on Yvonne when Eva was three. Yvonne does not mince words about him, describing Fryer as a 'selfish rotten son of a bitch, putting it bluntly'. Eva Jane, twenty-three years Clapton's junior, was living in a trailer park in Winter Haven, Florida, when the truth about Eric's father came out.

Prior to that marriage, Fryer had had a relationship with a singer called Cecilia, by whom he had a daughter, Sandra, and a son, Ted, both born in Sault Sainte Marie, Ontario, where, for a while, Fryer and Cecilia ran a teen dance club.

Later, Fryer spent years sailing America's east coast. He was also a talented artist and began selling his paintings to help pay for his travelling. A non-drinker, he spent his later years living on a boat, *Jupiter IV*, an old Newfoundland fishing schooner, on which he kept an electric organ, with his common-law wife Sylvia Nickason, who was born in Leeds, but emigrated to Canada when she was eleven. The couple would dock the thirty-foot boat in Port Darlington, on the shores of Lake Ontario, in the summer, then sail down the east coast of America to Florida in the winter months, where Sylvia would get work as a waitress. After Fryer's death from cancer, on 15 May 1985, at the Sunnybrook veterans' hospital, Miss Nickason says she had his body cremated, then danced on the deck of the boat, holding the urn containing his ashes, before scattering them on Lake Ontario.

Clapton's initial reaction to the revelations in the *Ottawa Citizen* was one of anger that he'd had to find out through a newspaper. But, later, he would concede that it had allowed him to put some perspective on his own life and made him question why he had brushed the issue of who his real father was under the carpet for so long. 'There were so many similarities: this thing with women and playing music,' he said later. 'Any time it got tough, he just took off. I was told by my family that he was dead. But I wasn't convinced. Denial is a sort of armour that is so powerful. I put something in place at a very early age – which I think is still there – that any time anyone mentioned my father, I would just immediately go, "No, it doesn't matter to me. I'm fine with that." But I know there is a whole lot of other stuff underneath that may not get addressed.'

Inevitably, once the identity of his father had been unmasked, the skeletons in the closet of this family of strangers began to fall out. A picture of Fryer emerged as a drifter: a selfish, lonely and troubled man who once tried to commit suicide by driving a rented car into the Niagara Gorge. Meanwhile, newspapers tracked down family members and discovered that Clapton's half-brother, Ted, then thirty-nine, was a guitar-playing heroin addict who had dropped out and was thought to be sleeping on a park bench somewhere in Canada. The last time Ted's wife, Conchita, had seen him was when he excused himself from a restaurant dinner table with the words: 'Honey, I'll be right back.' He walked out and had not been seen since.

Ted was finally tracked down by a Canadian journalist, living the life of a junkie and hiding from the police, in Hastings

Street, in Vancouver's drug-infested downtown area, where he was wanted for petty theft. When the reporter approached him to tell him he was Eric Clapton's brother, Ted replied: 'Yeah, and happy April Fools to you too.' It transpired that Ted's story had haunting similarities with that of the famous brother he had never met. As a young guitarist playing in local bars, he had emulated Clapton's statue-like pose on stage in a punk band called Poisoned, which had once opened for the Psychedelic Furs. And, just like Eric, his father had abandoned him at a young age and he had sought solace from his feelings of rejection in heroin. He subsequently checked into rehab. Both Eva and Ted made contact with Clapton, but several years later, he had not met either of them. 'A lot of people were hovering, making themselves available, and so I backed off,' he said in 2004. Later still, he would cast doubt on whether Fryer was actually his father, after being shown pictures of him and concluding they did not look alike. His doubts were reinforced by the fact that his mother remained non-committal about whether Fryer was the right man, and Eric was reluctant to press her on the point because he felt he was treading on thin ice. He was also put off by the thought of the complications of taking on a new family in the shape of Fryer's various offspring.

By the late spring of 2015, Ted Fryer was styling himself as Eddie. When I tracked him down in Vancouver, he was in a pretty desperate state. Clapton's half-brother was bedding down for the night at the rundown homeless hostel that had been his only shelter in the past few weeks. For Eddie, the prospect of spending the night in the refuge was only slightly less dangerous than sleeping on the street. When I visited him there what confronted me was a scene of sub-Dickensian squalor.

Outside the door, people were sleeping rough covered in coats and blankets. Once inside a steel security door, the first floor sleeping accommodation consisted of a smelly narrow corridor at which tatty black sheets had been hastily strung up to act as makeshift doors to the tiny rooms. The fifty-five mainly drug addicts, who lived there free of charge, were expected to share, but after being asked to bunk down with a homeless man and his dog, Eddie had chosen instead to spend the previous night on the floor of the corridor.

Violence and robbery were commonplace, but it was still preferable to another shelter in the Canadian city's notorious downtown eastside where 52-year-old Eddie, who still bore a livid bruise over his eye, had recently been attacked with a metal pipe and robbed of his jacket by another inmate while he slept.

The physical likeness between the brothers was undeniable and Eddie had hooded eyes and sharp nose. There, however, the similarities ended. While Clapton had long since triumphed over his addictions, Eddie had singularly failed to overcome his demons. He told me he had been diagnosed with 'end-stage' liver cirrhosis and the outlook was bleak. Doctors had informed him he had just three to six months to live if he carried on his reckless lifestyle. His only hope of a cure was a liver transplant, but he has been refused one until he stopped taking drugs.

The years of abuse had clearly taken their toll. Despite being eighteen years his brother's junior, the Eddie I met could have passed for an old man. He was spending his days shuffling, painfully slowly and hunched over a walking stick, around the streets of one of Canada's poorest neighbourhoods – a result of swollen legs caused by his illness. Yet despite his failing health, he was stoically – and proudly – refusing to beg Eric for help.

'I've told Eric I don't want anything from him,' he said. 'He knows about my life, but I don't want him to feel I'm pressurising him. He has had his own tragedy in his life and he doesn't owe me anything. The subject of me going to his rehab facility has never been on the table. I haven't asked and he hasn't offered. I'm a fighter, I always have been and I've come close to death many times before. I'm still here and I don't intend to give up. Every day for me is a blessing because I'm alive.'

An intelligent and compassionate man despite his addiction, which he was attempting to wean himself off with the heroin substitute Methadone, Eddie spoke lucidly and candidly about his famous brother.

'A few years ago, I had really got my life together and went to America to form a band and we made a demo which I sent to Eric,' he remembered. 'Eric wrote back to me that it really scared him to receive it because he said it was the most important CD he'd ever got and he really wanted to like it. He said he had put it on his mantelpiece at home and left it there because he was too worried to play it. But a while later I got another contact from Eric. He said he'd played it and his exact words were, "I was blown away by it." But he also said discovering about his siblings had triggered a lot of heart-break for him and he told me, "Please, be patient". I thought that was a bit strange because I had not asked him to do anything for me. I just wanted him to hear me play.'

Unlike Eric, Eddie knew his father – if only at a distance. When Eddie was six his parents' marriage broke up and he was raised by his mother and a wealthy stepfather. Astonishingly, Eddie told me that later – just like Eric – he was led to believe by his mother that his father had died when, in fact, he was alive and well and living in Florida. Like Clapton, he blamed the lack of a father for his drug-taking.

Some of the other half-siblings, like Eva Jane, had been ignored by Clapton. 'Eric was not interested in talking to me,' she told me nearly two decades after discovering the family connection. But Eddie revealed that he and Clapton did quietly begin corresponding by letter after he wrote to the star in 2000 to send him the CD. 'When I found out about Eric, I just felt that it was meant to be,' Eddie said. 'The first riff I ever learnt on the guitar was from *Sunshine of Your Love*. There was just so much we had in common. My style of guitar playing is even similar to his.'

It was the realisation he had a famous and talented brother, said Eddie, that made him vow to turn over a new leaf and for a while he overcame his drug problems. He became engaged to his girlfriend Farah Tejani and moved out of the ghetto, finding a lakeside mobile home 400 miles away from Vancouver in the picturesque village of Nakusp, where he got a job on a building site, getting up at 4am to practise the guitar before work.

'I didn't want to make contact with Eric until I had been able to turn my life around,' Eddie added. 'We started writing to each other via Eric's assistant Vivien Gibson. I told Eric that I had got out of my problems and was working hard at my music.' The two kept in semi-regular contact, but Eddie says he was upset when he read what he took to be derogatory remarks Clapton made about their father.

'I wrote to tell Eric not to believe everything he heard about my father,' Eddie added. 'His ex-wives said a lot of bad things about him, but he certainly was a ladies' man – so was Eric and so am I. We all three have that in common. Eric has had problems with drugs like me and our father was a drinker at one time, and he became addicted to painkillers.'

As he got his life back on track, Eddie formed a band called Eddie Fryer and the Lost Tribe and in 2009 they opened the show at the Nakusp international Music Festival, alongside – ironically – the Yardbirds. He also played on the same bill as Stevie Wonder. But gradually his old demons came back to haunt him. Years of drug taking, the effects of dust inhalation on building sites and hepatitis C led to internal bleeding and local doctors told Eddie's fiancée Farah they were going to turn off his life support machine. Eventually, they relented and had him airlifted to hospital in Vancouver.

But being among his old haunts again after five years away led him back into temptation and he and Farah split up. Farah takes up the story: 'Eddie started to busk for money and he would always begin with a song by Eric, his favourites were *Wonderful Tonight* and *My Father's Eyes*. Eddie had a blue check shirt and at the back where the sun would beat on it, the shirt would be lighter blue, but in the front it would be darker. That's how long he was outside. People loved him because he has a great voice and played beautifully. When he performs he shines. But he's very humble. He would never tell people when he was busking the story of his brother. He never wanted to ride on the tailcoats of Eric.'

But as he sank back into heroin addiction, Eddie sold his expensive guitars and lost his belongings because he could not afford to pay the bill where he had put them in storage. Without Eddie's knowledge, Farah began writing to Eric to keep him informed of his half-brother's progress.

She says: 'When Eddie nearly died I contacted Eric. I sent emails through his assistant Vivien to tell him that I didn't want anything from him, but I just wanted to tell him his brother was in a health clinic and he was on Methadone. I also told him where Eddie could be reached. After three days I got a reply from Eric that just said, "Thank you. Would you please keep me informed?" Then when Eddie got sick again, I wrote again and said that his situation was delicate and Eric replied – this time a little bit later – and again said, "Please do keep me informed." It sounded like a standard automated reply, but it wasn't. I believe in my heart that it was from Eric.'

'It's just a really sad story. Eddie's going from shelter to shelter and to see someone so sophisticated and talented like that really hurts me. He's been given three to six months to live. There was one time when he was very fearful of death and I saw a tear in his eyes. But other than that he is such a fighter. He's so determined to get clean, but the problem is the area where he is living and the people. He gets a small disability allowance, but it's gone in a couple of days because people persuade him to give them loans or buy them things. He is too kind.'

When we spoke Eddie insisted he would love finally to meet Eric, but admitted it had been a few years since he has written to his brother. 'I stopped writing because I was sick and I didn't know what my life expectancy would be,' he said.

'I didn't want to conceal my problem from Eric, but I wanted to deal with my issues and then get together when I was better. I didn't want to lay my problems on his doorstep.'

But despite his desperate situation, he still harboured a dream that one day they would finally meet and he'll join his brother on stage. 'I learnt Eric's whole live set, note for note, so I would be ready if he called,' Eddie said. 'One day, I'm sure it's going to happen.'

In October 1998, four years after the plan was first mooted, the Crossroads Centre opened in Willoughby Bay, Antigua. It was designed to be an unashamedly luxurious affair, with views from the swimming pool of the sparkling turquoise ocean beyond, in a bid to attract well-off Americans and Europeans who would pay $9,000 a month (by 2014, the cost had risen to $27,500). But of the thirty-six beds the centre had when it opened, twelve were reserved for locals, whose treatment was given free. Shortly after its doors opened, Clapton said: 'The most important thing in my life is that I stay sober and that in doing so I set an example, just by being there, and that I hand that on to somebody. I've always thought that the greatest thing about being sober is that I am able to be responsible, to help somebody. This is as important as leaving any kind of musical legacy. I know I touch people with music and I know that, in some cases, it may have been to the point of saving somebody's life, maybe. But there's nothing quite like what happens between one alcoholic and another – that's somehow a deeper thing.

'One of the things I had to acknowledge, second time around, when I went back into treatment, was that being a musician was not going to save my life. In fact, it could destroy me because if it meant that in order to write a song I needed to drink, then perhaps being a musician was not such a great idea.' His sobriety had become the single most vital thing in his life, pushing his lifelong obsession with music into second place. 'Music is great fun and I love doing it. I love making music and sharing it, but it's not as important,' he remarked.

However, his determination to see the project through had come at the price of his near quarter of a century partnership with Forrester. They had been so close that when Eric first checked into rehab, he was asked to write down the name of his significant other. Without thinking, he wrote down his manager's name. Even in his drink-addled state he knew that wasn't right. But the final straw, according to Clapton, was his vision for the Crossroads Centre. 'My manager saw me getting more and more involved in this and began to feel more alienated,' Eric said at the time. 'As a result, our relationship was probably destroyed by this. In the end, we split company because our philosophies had grown so different. It was very tough for him to hear me say this was more important to me than my career, because he'd obviously been very involved in making my career work. So for him that was quite a slap in the face.'

For his part, Forrester would have been forgiven for thinking that his client's zeal for launching a rehab facility could have clouded his judgement about just how big a chunk of his fortune would be eaten up by the project. Not that Eric was not fully aware, even when Crossroads was up and running, that it retained the potential to be a bottomless pit and a drain on his resources. There was serious talk within his camp that the project could see him go broke if it went belly-up. But Clapton was candid that the exercise also had its personal benefits. For starters, it made him less likely to fall back into old ways. And it didn't take an expert in addiction to work out that the high-profile benefactor of a world-renowned rehab centre had more riding on him staying clean than your average alcoholic or junkie. If he was to fall off the wagon, it would be a hammer blow to the credibility of the project. Plus, unsurprisingly, helping others made him feel good about himself. And if he felt good about himself, Clapton reasoned, he was less likely to drink or use. Speaking about the Crossroads Centre soon after it opened, he observed: 'I need to be able to go to bed and sleep. I need to be able to eat and have some respect for myself. And I would not have been able to have that if I'd walked away from this. I would have held on to all of my money, but I wouldn't have felt right about myself. I'm prepared to go down in flames with this, because my heart is in it. If we at Crossroads get one person sober, it'll have been worth every penny, because you can't put a value on human life.'

In desperation, Forrester wrote to him, laying out in detail the success Clapton had enjoyed with him as his manager – the numbers of records he'd sold and the money he'd made. He also gave it to him straight that he thought the way he was going about things was wrong, that he was making mistakes in everything from his approach to making albums to the seating arrangements at his shows. The writing was on the wall as far as their once intensely close relationship went. Clapton went to his manager's office to sack him wearing a string of Tibetan dZi beads, which, legend has it, are supposed to have been dropped from heaven, hoping they'd bring good luck. Forrester, who was clearly not expecting to be fired, was shocked and pale. In his 2007 memoirs, Clapton said he had not seen Forrester since that day. Forrester says they did meet again in 2012, when Eric made a trip to see his old friend and the two men shared a non-alcoholic drink in Roger's local pub in Frimley Green.

Clapton celebrated the split by buying a house in Venice, California, and he was there in March 1999 when his half-sisters Cheryl and Heather contacted him to say that his mother, Pat, who had moved back to Canada following the death of Rose and had been ill for some time, was dying. He flew from LA to Toronto and asked a counsellor to sit in, as the subject of her imminent death was discussed with her. But Pat, stubborn to the last, was having none of it and refused to believe she was not about to get better. A few days later, she slipped into a coma and Eric and her family were with her when she died.

At the end of her life, mother and son had not so much staged a reconciliation as reached an understanding. For Eric, the sense of betrayal and abandonment remained. Tellingly, perhaps, his dedication in his 2007 autobiography was made to all the most important women in his life: his grandmother, Rose, his wife, Melia, and his children, Ruth, Julie, Ella and Sophie. His mother did not receive a mention.

The timing of Pat's illness coincided with Eric being linked to a series of famous and beautiful women, including Naomi Campbell and Sharon Stone. Yet, while he was the envy of men, with his seemingly infallible ability as a babe magnet, he began to find, worryingly, that sex was beyond him. 'It took a couple of years while she [his mother] was dying and I went through a very funny period during that time,' he remembers. 'My ability to be around members of the opposite sex was absolutely ruined. I kept trying to start things with people, but I couldn't have sex, couldn't do anything. I don't know why. It was affected by what was taking place with my mother. I was absolutely dysfunctional and I wasn't able to contribute anything. At the same time, I desperately wanted to make a connection, so I'd start things with people then not be able to go to the next level. I knew something truly traumatic was coming up and I was numb,' he adds.

It is, it goes without saying, a subject that a psychiatrist would have a field day with. But it didn't take Jung to know that his attitude to women and sex was inextricably tied up with his dysfunctional relationship with his mother. Her abandonment of him as a child, not once but twice, had set the template. Throughout his life, he set his sights on women he felt were unavailable to him. Then, when he had won them, he forced them to reject him by his drunkenness, drug-taking, boorishness and abuse. For him, women were a self-fulfilling – and self-defeating – prophesy. If a woman rejected him, it was, in his mind at least, because he was not good enough. But if she loved him, he rejected her because the act of loving him proved conclusively that *she* wasn't good enough, if she could settle for someone as messed up and wretched as him. He was well aware that most of the girlfriends he had chosen since Pattie shared with his mother the fact that they were 'unavailable' and sometimes 'unstable'.

Likewise, sex had become just another fix. 'I used to identify my self-esteem with sex,' he told an interviewer in the late nineties. 'If I could get a girl to have sex with me, it meant that

I was OK with myself. It had nothing to do with respect or affection or love – it was just a fix. And, like a fix, it gives me a hangover. I got to the point where I thought, "Well, if that's all it is, it is just not good enough."'

Little did he know he was about to meet the new Mrs Clapton.

# SIXTEEN

# Melia

Not long before meeting Melia McEnery, Clapton, with all the confused logic that comes of too many sessions on the couches of £400-an-hour psychoanalysts, was ruminating on the possibility that he might – at very long last – be ready to think about settling down. 'Yes, I value my solitude and privacy and boundaries,' he opined. 'But I now feel better able to make those known to someone. In the past, my problem was that I wouldn't know how to tell someone I needed to go out or be on my own. My way of interpreting that was to say, "I can't be with someone." And of course that's not true. I can. I've learnt more about respecting my own needs. So, I probably could do it quite easily if I found someone who'd done the same amount of work in this area as I feel I've done.' If it all sounded a bit over-thought, then it most likely was. And, in truth, someone who had done 'work' on themselves was probably the last thing he needed.

What he got, instead, was a good Catholic girl whose eminently sensible, studiously uncomplicated view of relationships, it turned out, was exactly what Eric had been crying out for. Disconcertingly, however, at the age of twenty-three, Melia was thirty-one years his junior.

The couple met on 12 June 1999, when a party was thrown by Giorgio Armani at Quixote Studios in West Hollywood, to preview a selection of guitars from Clapton's collection, prior to an auction of a hundred of his most iconic instruments at Christie's in New York in aid of the Crossroads Centre. True to form, Eric arrived at the bash with not one but two American dates. Before long, however, his eye had been taken by Melia and a friend of hers called Satsuki, who were both employed by Armani to show the celebrity guests to their seats and generally look good. Cheekily, Melia, who like the rest of her colleagues working at the event was under strict instructions not to pester the celebrity guests, bowled up to Clapton to ask him to pose for a picture with her. Rather crushingly for his ego, she told him the picture was not for her, but for her uncle, who was a big fan. Nonetheless, Eric, having lost none of his guile when it came to women, said he would only consent to have his snap taken if she and her friend agreed to have dinner with him the following day. In the event, he couldn't wait that long and picked them both up from the Emporio Armani shop, where they worked, to treat them to lunch. Somewhat bizarrely, the three of them then 'dated' for about a month, though given Clapton's, ahem, 'problem', nothing sexual happened.

Eric was not at the guitar sale, held on 24 June, because he was rehearsing in LA, but he watched proceedings from a closed-circuit TV feed into the studio. He had promised himself he would buy back one guitar, a stunning sunburst 1930 Gibson L-4 arch-top acoustic, with an estimated value of $6,000 to $8,000. But when the auctioneer, Cathy Elkies, let slip Clapton was planning to make a bid, it only served to push the price up and bidding finally stopped at $57,500, with Eric having long pulled out. The list of guitars included 'Brownie', the 1956 Tobacco Sunburst Stratocaster on which he played 'Layla'. Ms Elkies remembers that when it was brought out, the 800 people, mainly men, in the auction room stood up en masse and did a spontaneous group bow of respect to the instrument. Brownie, which came with a case stencilled with 'Derek and the Dominos', had an estimate of $80,000 to $100,000 put on it. It actually sold for $497,000. Another sunburst Strat, a 1954 model, which had been used on his 1985 tours, went for $211,500, and a 1974 Rodeo Man Martin acoustic sold for $173,000. By close of play, the event, which was the brainchild of Clapton's film producer friend Lili Zanuck, had raised $4.4 million for the Crossroads Centre.

The following week, Eric and his two new girlfriends travelled to New York, where he was to play at a Crossroads benefit gig at Madison Square Garden, on a bill that included Bob Dylan, Sheryl Crow and Mary J. Blige. After the show, Eric reluctantly left Melia behind to return to England, but he could not stop thinking about her. By the time he'd headed back to LA, Melia was away visiting her family in Columbus, Ohio, so, as a consolation prize, he dated Satsuki until she got back to town. By now, he was ready to break up the threesome; he gave Satsuki the push and invited Melia back to Britain with him.

So what did Melia have that all the other women he had dated since Pattie didn't? For one thing, she wasn't famous, and for another, she possessed a quiet but obvious self-possession. Clapton says of their first meeting: 'She occupied her space with absolute authority. It was clear she was capable of being an adequate partner for anyone.' Plus, Melia was everything most of his famous former dates weren't – a down-to-earth Mid-Western girl, winsomely pretty without being beautiful, and from an extremely close-knit family with a love of children and a longing for them.

The third of six children born to Walter and Laurie McEnery, she was born in Hawaii, but grew up in the small town of Worthington, near Columbus, Ohio. Her father ran a construction business, where Laurie also worked, and, like the rest of her siblings, Melia, who is of Korean/Irish extraction, was educated at a local Roman Catholic school and attended the nearby Saint Michael RC church. Home, during her childhood, was an eight-bedroom timbered house on the sort of well-tended street that exists everywhere in America. In short, her upbringing was one of good-old-fashioned, small-town homeliness: God, Mom and apple pie, in that order.

At the time, Melia, who trained as a graphic designer, had been living in LA with her 27-year-old boyfriend of six years, Chris Losinske, her sweetheart from back home in Ohio, who was working as a £150-a-week assistant in a coffee shop, though they had been through a recent break-up. Soon, however, Clapton was taking her on dates to swanky restaurants, or to dinner at the homes of the likes of Hollywood director Rob Reiner. Those who know him well insist Eric was instantly 'hooked' on Melia. One says: 'He spoke about her differently than he did his other girlfriends. Right from the start, he had that look – the one that says this is really, really serious.' It was hardly coincidental, of course, that within just a few months of his mother's death, he was head-over-heels in a real relationship, one based on friendship, love and mutual trust – even if he did have to wait till the age of fifty-four to find it. He has said of that time: 'The three of us dated for a little while and what was interesting was it was like a little parable being presented to me. My wife was the safe, secure, friendly, available one. Her friend was fast, unavailable, dangerous, and I immediately veered towards that and caught myself just in time. It was synchronistic because if my mother had still been alive and I'd been in that dilemma, I would have got caught up in it and I would have gone for the fast one because it would have fitted in with all the craziness. But because I felt like I was starting a new phase, I thought I should give something else a try. I'd never stayed with somebody who was just there for me before.' The only problem was the age gap and, to begin with, Clapton was understandably bothered about what people were whispering about them. It also goes without saying that matters were not helped by the fact that he was four years older than his new girlfriend's father, Walt.

But Eric was soon telling anyone who'd listen that the age issue was irrelevant, so long as the relationship was 'grounded in mutual respect and honesty'. All of which raised more than a few wry smiles among those who had known him long enough to remember the days, not so long ago, when Pattie had had to tolerate being demeaned by his flagrant flings with so many women he could barely remember their names.

This newish conversation to candour at all costs also extended to the promotion of his records. But his honesty often had his record company PRs and marketing men tearing their hair out. When he released *Clapton Chronicles – The Best of Eric Clapton* in October 1999, he was asked by one music journalist if the album, which contained some of his more forgettable forays in pop, such as 'It's in the Way That You Use It' and 'Change the World', really was his best work. Clapton replied: 'No, of course not. Don't be ridiculous. It's a way of marketing a couple of new songs I've written for film soundtracks by packaging them with some older songs. It's not meant to be a serious study of my legacy.'

Increasingly, he was keen to make records he enjoyed doing, rather than those which would necessarily be big sellers. The following year, he began work on a collaboration with B.B. King, to be entitled *Riding with the King*. It was a project they had been discussing off and on since they'd first met in 1967 at the Café au Go Go in New York, though the two men had recorded together once before, a version of 'Rock Me Baby', on King's 1997 duets album *Deuces Wild*.

Clapton called in Simon Climie to co-produce the album with him and hired a Texan guitar player, Doyle Bramhall II, whose father Doyle had been a collaborator with Stevie Ray Vaughan. Also on board was Andy Fairweather Low, and Jimmie Vaughan gave a cameo performance. The record, while featuring a smattering of newer material, none written by Clapton, was a slick and skilful trawl through King's back catalogue and an array of blues standards, including 'Ten Long Years', 'Help the Poor', Big Bill Broonzy's 'Key to the Highway' and 'Worried Life Blues'. It was something of an unexpected success when it was finally released in June 2000, selling more than a million copies in the US alone in the first two months on the shelves and going double platinum. It also won a Grammy for Best Traditional Blues Album. But while Clapton chose the tracks and oversaw production, this was, to all intents and purposes, a B.B. King album, with Clapton as guest star. And Eric was happy to defer to the great man, taking a sideman's role to singing and many of the guitar solos. None of which, it should be said, was to the detriment of the record. On the sleeve notes, Clapton waxed lyrical about how making the album had been a dream come true. 'B.B. is my hero, always has been,' he wrote. Significantly, among his thank-yous to the various people who had made the album possible, he included Melia, who in the autumn of 2000 had told him she was pregnant with their first child.

Her announcement, made while they were holidaying in Antigua, was happily greeted by Clapton, but it was also the cause of some consternation on his part. The subject of starting a family had been raised between them, but he had not been overly enthusiastic. And while he quickly grew to like the idea, matters were complicated by the fact that a world tour was already scheduled and would feature a band which included Steve Gadd on drums, Nathan East on bass and Billy Preston on piano. As the birth date drew closer, Melia went back to Columbus and Eric arranged for a house to be found there, where they could stay after the baby was born. Meanwhile, his tour manager, Peter Jackson, was tasked with organising it so that Clapton would be able to commute to his shows in the US on a private plane from Columbus, thus allowing him to spend as much time as possible with Melia in the run-up to the birth.

At the same time, long-term plans for where they would live as a family were being discussed. Originally, the idea had been to settle in California and the couple looked at properties in the big-money enclave of Santa Barbara, north of Los Angeles. But soon Hurtwood Edge was once again making her siren call to him and they returned home to Surrey. It was there, over the New Year, that Melia's parents met their prospective new son-in-law for the first time, when they flew to England to visit Clapton and Melia. She had broken the news to her family that she was pregnant with Eric's baby the previous week, during the Christmas holidays in Ohio.

As they waited for the arrival, Clapton set to work making another album, *Reptile*, which was recorded at the back end of 2000 and was dedicated to his uncle Adrian, who had died that spring. Eric was wracked by guilt that he had not been able to intervene to help Adrian, whom he had always regarded as an elder brother, deal with his drinking problem. What made the tribute more poignant was that the two men had gradually drifted apart over the years. At the time that the record came out, in March 2001, a nine-year-old Eric smiling quizzically on the cover, Clapton said of Adrian: 'My inability to love him in his lifetime was a source of great pain for me, and his passing gave me the release to express that.' And in the album's liner notes, he explained the title, writing: 'Where I come from, the word "reptile" is a term of endearment . . . it is used sparingly and with the greatest respect, it's not an insult, it's a sign of recognition.' The record, he added, was made to honour 'the greatest reptile of them all, my uncle Adrian'. Pictured inside was a 'rogues gallery' of fifty of the most significant 'reptiles' he said he had met on his travels. Movingly, one of the faces staring out was Conor's.

Once again, Simon Climie was brought on board as co-producer, and Clapton put together a band for the album featuring Billy Preston and Curtis Mayfield's former band, the Impressions. The influential Mayfield had died in December

1999, almost a decade after he was paralysed from the neck down following a freak accident in Brooklyn, New York, when a stage lighting rig collapsed on him during an outdoor concert, robbing him of his ability to play the guitar.

Unsurprisingly, this was Clapton in reflective and often maudlin mood. But given the wealth of genuine emotion that had inspired the making of the record, it was a shame that the opening track, the Latin-inspired 'Reptile', sounded so wretchedly like lift music. It was followed by 'Got You on My Mind', which followed the *Unplugged* model for sing-along versions of blues standards in a style veering dangerously towards a Cockney knees-up down the Old Bull and Bush. Then, there was the J. J. Cale-penned 'Travelin' Light', which saw Clapton doing a passable impression of the Oklahoman crooner. The lyrics include the sexagenarian Cale's immortal – and possibly optimistic – chat-up line: 'We can go to paradise. Maybe once, maybe twice.' And while Clapton's playing was assured and subtle on the Ray Charles number 'Come Back Baby', a lacklustre – and oddly faithful – cover of the Stevie Wonder song 'I Ain't Gonna Stand For It' begged the question why it was on the album in the first place. And, too often, Clapton's self-penned songs, of which there were no less than seven, were wishy-washy, a bit dreary and samey. Meanwhile, the instrumental 'Son & Sylvia', written for Adrian and his wife, was undoubtedly tastefully played, but sounded unfortunately like the theme tune to a 1970s American drama series.

Melia gave birth to their daughter, Julie Rose, in the late evening of 15 June 2001, at Riverdale Methodist Hospital in Columbus. Weighing in at 7lb 1oz, Julie, whom Eric named after the girl in the Kinks' song 'Waterloo Sunset', was not a well baby for the first few months and, unable to feed properly, she suffered seriously with colic and spent much of her early weeks screaming. But Clapton, who had once been so vehemently opposed to having children he hoped Pattie's IVF treatment would fail, embraced fatherhood with all the zeal of the late convert. He and Melia became devotees of *The Baby Whisperer*, the bestselling book by British childcare specialist Tracy Hogg.

At the end of June, while doing three shows at Madison Square Garden, he went into a Manhattan jewellers on the spur of the moment and bought a ring by Italian designer Buccellati. Then he went to see Melia's father and formally requested her hand in marriage. And within thirty minutes of being given the OK by Walt, Eric was going down on one knee to ask her if she would be his bride. All of which was a welcome departure from his first 'on your bike' proposal to Pattie, twenty-two years earlier.

Melia, unlike his other girlfriends, cleverly embraced his solitary hobby of fishing and proved herself a natural. Hardly surprisingly, perhaps, Eric dropped his 'no women on the road' edict and actively encouraged her and Julie to join him when his tour reached Japan in October. It was while Eric was in Tokyo, on 29 November, that word reached him from their mutual friend, publisher Brian Roylance, that George Harrison had died in Los Angeles of lung cancer, having fought the disease for four years. Clapton had not seen him since December 1999, when he went over to Friar Park to comfort George and Olivia after Harrison was attacked and stabbed in a raid on his home by an intruder called Michael Abram.

On New Year's Day 2002, Clapton and Melia married in front of a handful of friends at the fifteenth-century St Mary Magdalen church in Ripley. In order to keep the press off the scent, invited guests – who included Melia's parents, Eric's aunt Sylvia, plus Andy Fairweather Low and his wife Barbara – had been told they were there for the christening of six-month-old Julie by the local reverend, Chris Elson. But at the point where he would normally have given a closing prayer, Rev Elson began instead: 'Dearly beloved, we are gathered here together to join the hand of this man and this woman in holy matrimony.' After the service, Clapton silently led Melia outside to visit Conor's grave.

Following a dinner at Hurtwood in 2002, Eric, Olivia Harrison and Brian Roylance began planning a charity tribute concert in George's memory. Clapton lined up a band which included Andy Fairweather Low, Henry Spinetti, bassist Dave Bronze and Gary Brooker for the show at the Albert Hall on 29 November, the first anniversary of the ex-Beatle's death. The first part of the show was given over to Ravi Shankar, whose Indian orchestra gave a performance of a special composition called 'Arpan'. Then, musical director Clapton led a troupe of musicians, including Tom Petty and Jeff Lynne, for a two-hour performance of Harrison's best-known songs. Later, the band was joined by Sir Paul McCartney and Ringo Starr, as well as George's son Dhani, and McCartney and Clapton sang a duet of 'Something', the song Harrison had written for Pattie.

Two months later, Melia gave birth to Clapton's second daughter, Ella Mae, on 14 January 2003. A few weeks earlier, on Christmas Day, Julie had been rushed to the intensive care unit of the Chelsea and Westminster, after being diagnosed with viral pneumonia. Thankfully, she recovered quickly, but perhaps because of the scare, Eric was now saying publicly he wanted to 'start from scratch' as a father. And that would involve, he insisted, spending more time at home with his young family and less time on the road. By way of proving the point, in March, he played a gig for his eldest daughter Ruth's fellow sixth formers at the private Birkdale School in Sheffield, to raise funds for the school orchestra.

But if he thought easing up on touring would make recording easier, he was wrong. As preparations began for a new album, he found – like many a writer before him – that he was being plagued by the tyranny of the blank page. He had been spending time at Simon Climie's house, working on ideas, but the simple fact was that his domestic happiness was not conducive to songwriting. Eric took himself off to France alone, with the intention of coming up with the words for a new batch of songs. The plan was to come up with half a dozen; he came back with just one. The problem was that, without the angst that had pretty much summed up his previous near sixty years, he found the inspiration cupboard was worryingly bare. And once recording began in earnest, it was soon clear that the dearth of new material was becoming a problem. Clapton came up with a solution. Instead of getting anxious about it, they would use the empty recording time to play a Robert Johnson song, for something to do. Less than two weeks later, they had recorded a complete tribute album by default. *Me and Mr Johnson* was the record Clapton had always promised himself he would make one day. In style, the fourteen songs were reminiscent of *From the Cradle*, with Clapton in fine vocal form and with his guitar often taking a secondary role. Again, however, sales were on a downward trajectory, but the album went gold in America, where it sold 500,000 copies, and silver in the UK.

Meanwhile, Japanese musician and designer Hiroshi Fujiwara and Stephen Schible, the producer of *Lost in Translation*, were brought in to make a documentary, *Sessions for Robert J*, about the making of the album. For the film, Clapton and his band performed at 508 Park Avenue, the building in Dallas where Johnson recorded in 1937.

*Me and Mr Johnson* was released in March 2004, two months after Clapton was awarded a CBE in the New Year's Honours List (a decade earlier, he'd received an OBE for his 'contribution to British life'). Now plans were already well under way for the first Crossroads Guitar Festival, to be held over two days at the Cotton Bowl Stadium in Dallas in early June. Among the players performing to raise money for Clapton's Antigua rehab facility were Buddy Guy, B.B. King, Carlos Santana, Robert Cray, John Mayer, J. J. Cale, Joe Walsh and Jimmie Vaughan. Clapton had come up with the idea for the concert some years earlier, after appearing in front of Bill Clinton at the White House in 1998 to commemorate the thirtieth anniversary of the Special Olympics.

Later that same month, he held his second guitar auction to benefit the Crossroads Centre. This time, 'Blackie' – described by Christie's in prosaic terms as 'circa 1956 and 1957, a composite Fender Stratocaster' – was included, and went for £959,500 at the sale in New York. It set a world record for Blackie, which had been more or less in retirement since 1985. Also included was the cherry-red Gibson ES335 Eric had owned since the mid-60s, his first serious guitar. The Gibson, which had an estimate of $60,000 to $80,000, actually sold for £847,500. Meanwhile, the beautiful 1939 Martin 000-42 Clapton had played much of his *Unplugged* gig on went for $791,500, a record for an acoustic guitar. The total raised, which included instruments donated by the illustrious Guitar Festival line-up, reached $7,438,624. Poignantly, the day before the auction, Eric made a final pilgrimage to see some of the 88 lots and say goodbye.

Perhaps to make himself feel better, he bought himself a nice consolation prize – a £400,000 Ferrari Enzo, one of only 399 built. And back home, he took up shooting pheasant, which, like almost anything else he embarks on, soon became an obsession. He invested in expensive shotguns and went to shooting parties on grand estates, bringing home what he killed to eat. His taste for menacing game with his shooting cronies had been sparked by pigeons cooing in the eaves of Hurtwood. While some might have found the sound soothing, Eric said it kept his kids awake and bought a gun to blast the blighters. Soon, Melia was joining him, training both barrels of her own Purdey on unsuspecting fowl. Typically, Clapton has no truck with those who are squeamish about so-called 'country pursuits'. Those who are, he says dismissively, have watched 'too many Disney movies'. Having also developed a taste for country attire, he became a part-owner of sporting outfitters Cordings.

His aversion to extraneous noise also meant touring, once almost an addiction, had become fraught with difficulties. He became increasingly bothered by noisy hotel rooms and spent nights being kept awake by the rumble of elevators, or people making a racket in the next room. The situation was only made worse by the fact that jetlag suddenly became almost impossible to shake. Grouchily, he would insist on changing rooms – and hotels – several times, but was still lucky if he managed three hours' sleep a night. Meanwhile, he became susceptible to illnesses caused from temperature changes, which made him develop a phobia of air conditioning. On tour, he often took to staying holed up in his hotel room alone, rather than venture out. With Melia pregnant with their third child, Clapton was saying that he was thinking of giving up touring because he'd grown tired of the road. He told *Rolling Stone*: 'This is definitely the last time. It's hard. It just doesn't work for me anymore.' Rather eccentrically, when he was travelling around the world doing shows, he began stuffing his dirty clothes in a duffle bag and taking them down to a local launderette, where he would separate them out into whites and coloureds and sit there waiting with the other punters as his clothes went through the wash and spin cycle.

His pared-down approach to life in his fifties also stretched to his travelling wardrobe. Gone were the racks of suits, and custom-made diamante guitar straps. Now he went on the road with one holdall containing two pairs of jeans and three sweaters. But travelling tired him out and whereas once he'd prepared for gigs by downing two bottles of Courvoisier and half a ton of weapons-grade toot, now he needed to have an hour's nap in the afternoon in order to raise the stamina for doing a show in the evening. Increasingly, too, he was desperate for the tour to finish and, towards the end of every leg, he would count the days until he could get back to his young family. Even so, the end of a tour invariably brought on a steep comedown and depression.

Away from work, he became set in his ways. In Ohio, where they bought a house near Melia's parents, he watched England playing cricket on cable TV and yearned for home. Meanwhile, at Hurtwood, he insisted on having forty winks each afternoon on the sofa in the front room. Encroaching old age also gave him licence to spout his opinions on everything from marriage to sex. 'It sounds so fucking strange for me to say this! I've come to the idea that sex really is just for procreation,' he said at the time. 'But I'm finding out in my recovery that I've always used sex as some kind of tool. As a way of holding someone hostage, to make an impression, fixing myself, fixing them. It's never been for what it really is, which is an expression of love and as a means of continuing our existence on earth. But I've found I'm happier if I'm doing it in a monogamous relationship and there's no deceit and there's no lies and it's a pure expression of affection.'

Yet again, however, this loved-up feeling of bliss would serve as an antidote to creativity. Towards the end of 2004, he began his second attempt at making the album of what he was, ominously, calling 'family songs'. But once more, he found it almost impossible to write anything. So, by way of putting off recording, he got in touch with Ginger Baker and Jack Bruce to float the idea of a reunion of Cream. Given that he had always been the one who was cool about reforming, it was noteworthy that it was Clapton now who was going 'cap in hand' to Jack and Ginger, to sound them out about getting back together. And, in November, news finally leaked out that Cream would reform for a series of shows the following May. The venue of the gigs would, fittingly, be the Royal Albert Hall, where the band's last gig had taken place exactly thirty-six years earlier (although they had actually played together since then, performing versions of 'White Room', 'Crossroads' and 'Sunshine of Your Love' at the Rock 'n' Roll Hall of Fame in Los Angeles in 1993).

However, the members of the band's rhythm section were not in the best possible shape for the fray. The Jack Bruce I met in Suffolk that summer was not a well man, haunted-looking and rake-thin. The previous year, Jack had come close to death, after being diagnosed with liver cancer, and needed a transplant. Meanwhile, Ginger had developed a degenerative spine condition that meant playing was often agony.

But both men could have done with the money. Baker had set up a short-lived recording studio in Lagos, Nigeria, in the early 1970s, making music with Fela Kuti, the Nigerian multi-instrumentalist and composer, and developing an expensive taste for polo. Stories did the rounds in Lagos that Ginger was effectively run out of town by some dangerous local characters. He then had stints in Italy and America, and eventually found his way to South Africa. By 2013, he was back where he'd started – broke, after blowing all the money he made from the Cream reunion gigs on yet more polo ponies.

As final plans were being laid, Clapton explained why he had finally relented and decided to reform the band: 'It's something I've been thinking about for a couple of years now,' he said. 'We're all getting on a bit and I wanted to do it before it was too late and while we still have the energy. It will be a great thing just to see if we've got it in us to get back to where we were.' The trio rehearsed for a month in advance of the four gigs at the beginning of May 2005. In the meantime, Eric and Melia had added to their growing family with the redheaded

Sophie, who was born on 1 February, and the following month, Clapton celebrated his sixtieth birthday with a giant party at the Banqueting House in Whitehall, Eric dewy-eyed as Melia gave a speech in his honour.

As far as Cream was concerned, to begin with, the old bad feelings were briefly rekindled. But following a minor spat involving the three of them, a period of unexpected harmony followed. Twenty-four hours before the first gig, Eric came down with the flu and was on antibiotics. The fans, who had paid up to £600 a ticket, didn't seem to care and gave them a three-minute standing ovation before they'd even played a note. The gigs were a resounding success. Jack Bruce may have had to spend portions of the show resting on a stool, and Ginger's bad back meant that his quarter-of-an-hour drum solo on 'Toad' was, mercifully, reduced to a slightly more manageable eight minutes, but nearly four decades apart had not dulled their fire. The critics were almost unanimously positive. Andy Gill, in the *Independent*, wrote that the band was 'If anything, better than its younger version. We shouldn't be surprised: all three have developed immeasurably as musicians since the demise of Cream.'

Meanwhile, Robin McKie, in the *Observer*, raved: 'Jack, Ginger and Eric may have looked a little frail, but from the moment they launched into an exuberant "I'm so Glad", it was clear they had emerged from a hiatus of thirty-seven years with their musical powers intact. This was to be a blissful night for any Cream fan. Ditching their old twenty-minute solo indulgences, the band played a tight, restrained nineteen-number set with a sharpness and drive that belied the passage of those decades.' Only Tim de Lisle, in the *Mail on Sunday*, was prepared to pour cold water on them saying, 'But there was something missing. The only emotion flowing around the hall was nostalgia . . . In the end the audience divided along age lines. For those over fifty, it was a triumph. For the rest of us, it was a great event rather than a great show.'

The concerts went so well that they were immediately offered a fortune to play Madison Square Garden in New York five months later, in October. Even so, the other two still needed to persuade Ginger, who was against the idea, before he eventually agreed. Clapton was left wishing they hadn't bothered. Where the London shows were well rehearsed and largely tightly executed, the three Manhattan gigs suffered from a severe lack of practice, with the trio only rehearsing for two hours the day before the first show. Later, Eric would blame the lack of preparations on their collective egos and, illogically, not wanting to waste money on accommodation costs just for the sake of having enough time to practise properly. The result, in his own words, was that they were 'a pale shadow' of the London gigs and that the sound in the huge venue was 'tinny'. 'Our mindset had gone back to the 60s and once again we were flying high on our egos,' Clapton noted. And some of the old animosity was back too.

Two years later, he said of Cream that he believed he 'would probably not be passing this way again'. Which was not strictly accurate. Time and, possibly, the prospect of yet another big payday made him look more favourably on a repeat performance. And a postscript is that, in 2014, advanced plans were in place for another reformation of Cream, before old hostilities reared their ugly heads. That spring, Bruce told *Rolling Stone*: 'Everybody had agreed about doing it, but then I think Ginger upset Eric. He said something or did something, so it's not happening.' Clearly, the old bad blood had not subsided. The bass player added: 'It's like I don't have anything to do with them actually very much. Ginger, from what I've heard, is a bitter old man. And I'm quite a cheerful old chap.'

Meanwhile, when he was asked about the shelved plans, Clapton replied tartly: 'I was pretty convinced that we had gone as far as we could without someone getting killed. At this time in my life, I don't want blood on my hands! I don't want to be part of some kind of tragic confrontation. There's no relationship between the three of us whatsoever – or between me and them, anyway. I don't talk to them from one year to the next.' A few months later in October 2014 Jack Bruce was dead after eventually succumbing to liver disease and Clapton and Baker were there to pay their respects at his funeral in North London.

With money in the bank from the Cream gigs, Eric went on a spending spree. He hired a yacht called *Va Bene*, a 157-foot beauty, built in 1992, that had once belonged to Formula 1 kingpin Bernie Ecclestone. Having heard that the current American owner was keen to sell, Clapton bought it with the help of a loan against earnings from a world tour planned for the following year. Even so, he still had to sell some of his rare Patek Philippe wristwatches in order to be able to afford the vessel. In 2014, *Va Bene*, which can accommodate twelve guests and thirteen staff and underwent a substantial refit in 2008, was available to rent for between $179,000 and $199,000 a week (£105,000 to £117,000). Around the same time, Clapton also bought a house in the South of France and, a year later, purchased another larger property in Melia's home town of Columbus, for when they visited her folks. He also began spending his money on vintage road bicycles – not to ride, just to look at – as well as collecting western belt buckles and garishly painted hot-rod cars.

The Cream get-together had only served as a temporary diversion from making the studio album Clapton had been putting off for the best part of five years. However, in August 2005, he finally released *Back Home*, which, in part at least, chronicled his new life as a husband and father. One track, 'So Tired', jokily told of the tribulations of staying up at night feeding babies, while the finger-picked title track was a paean to his belated domestic tranquillity. Another, 'Run Home to Me', was written about him sitting with Melia and his young family on a stony beach in Bognor, in the middle of winter.

Eric was candid that making the record had been a struggle. And it was the lyrics that were hardest to come by (in apparent desperation, he even began running them past his then toddler daughter Julie for approval). 'Writing about a relationship that is productive and successful and loving without being boring or self-indulgent is difficult,' he said when *Back Home* was released. 'It's much easier writing in anger or sadness about something that's gone and lost. I kept stopping because I didn't think it would work.' And therein lay the problem: fire, rage and self-pity had been replaced with mawkish contentment. Nowhere was this illustrated more depressingly than in his favourite song, 'Run Home to Me', which, he told journalists through misty eyes, always reduced him and Melia to tears on hearing it. It may have been a pleasant enough ditty which clearly meant a lot to the two of them, but instead of allowing it to remain something private, he released it and foisted it on the rest of us, in all its empty, trite sentimentality. Unsurprisingly, many reviewers were not kind. One went as far as to blasphemously rework the 'Clapton is God' quote, declaring bluntly after hearing the album: 'God is Dead.' Even worse, sales were disappointing. The album just scraped into the top twenty in Britain and got to number thirteen in America.

But if the glorious equilibrium of his home life was, ironically, part of the problem, there were obvious upsides. He grew to love playing the guitar at Julie's nursery playgroup, or messing about on the beach at Porto Cervo in Sardinia, which had become a new favourite destination on their yacht, and where he would happily get stuck into building sandcastles with the girls, a bucket and spade in hand. Meanwhile, the house in Antigua, with its various guest cottages, had come to resemble something akin to a sprawling luxury hotel. And whereas once he had slumped drunk in the cellar all night, now, on Christmas Eve, he secretly donned a Santa Claus outfit and wandered across the lawn, close enough for the children to see him from the window.

The downside was that he increasingly hated being apart from his brood, and began worrying about his children losing their father young. Even so, he steadfastly refused to exercise and rejected a hearing aid, despite being partially deaf. All in all, he positively basked in being a curmudgeon, as well as a conspiracy theorist who believed everything from politics to the World Cup was fixed. On tour, he was plagued by bad digestion, but whether he was in the US, Japan, Indonesia or Australia, he wouldn't miss speaking to the kids before their bedtime, and relied on iChat and iSight to stay in touch with them, which was quite a turnaround for the one-time technophobe. Bliss was driving home at last, through rhododendron bushes, to get to Hurtwood, where he and the girls could go for walks in the hills or feed Gordon, their pet pig.

Nevertheless, the will to play music was still strong enough for Clapton to fly to Los Angeles to begin working on an album with J. J. Cale. In many respects, Cale, who died in 2013, was the artist Clapton might have been – if the double-edged lure of money and fame had not won out. While he was adored by his fans, the Oklahoma-raised Cale could happily wander around the streets of his adopted home town of Escondido, thirty miles north of San Diego, where he lived in a modest house, looking like a grizzled ranch hand in his jeans, sweatshirt and cap. He rarely performed live and didn't put his picture on his albums for the first fifteen years in the business. Both men had already been pivotal in the other's career. When, in October 1970, Clapton released his debut solo single, the Cale-penned 'After Midnight', Cale himself was so broke he'd had to return from Los Angeles to Tulsa. The royalties he earned allowed him to go back to the West Coast and carry on in the music business.

Because J. J. had largely written the songs for this new joint album in advance, it took only a month to record, with Eric bunking down at Cale's place for a week prior to going into the studio. And, once again, as with his collaboration with B.B. King, Eric was happy to take a back seat on the record, which was released in November 2006. It was a critical, if not a commercial, success. It only reached number fifty in the UK album chart and twenty-three in the US, but it did win a Grammy for Best Contemporary Blues Album.

Afterwards, Clapton went on tour again, with a new band, featuring drummer Steve Jordan and hotshot Floridian guitar player Derek Trucks. But as he hit the road in February and March 2007 on a US tour, playing in the likes of Salt Lake City, Sacramento and Oklahoma City, Eric was saying he now dreaded going to airports, particularly in America, and was predicting that it would likely be the last time he'd visit a lot of these places.

Increasingly, collaborations were the order of the day. In February 2008, he shared the bill for three nights with Steve Winwood at Madison Square Garden, and in May the following year, a double album and CD of the event was released. A few months later, he and Winwood embarked on a fourteen-date tour of America, climaxing at the Hollywood Bowl in Los Angeles. And in the spring of 2011, he appeared at the Rose Theater, at the Lincoln Center in New York, with Grammy Award-winning jazz trumpeter Wynton Marsalis, to play a set of vintage blues and an ambitious New Orleans re-working of 'Layla'.

The hugely talented Marsalis had appeared the previous year on his latest studio album, 2010's *Clapton*, which was released at the end of September. It got to a very respectable number seven in the UK album charts – his highest chart position since *Reptile* in 2001. And it went one better in the US, reaching number six in the Billboard 200 and selling 47,000 in its first week alone. After the disappointment of the songwriting on *Back Home* five years earlier, it came as something of a relief that he co-wrote just one new track, 'Run Back to Your Side', with longtime collaborator – and the album's co-producer – Doyle Bramhall II. The rest was a bunch of mainly cosy covers, like the Hoagy Carmichael number 'Rockin' Chair' and the old Fats Waller song 'When Somebody Thinks You're Wonderful', plus a rather listless version of the done-to-death Irving Berlin tune 'How Deep Is the Ocean'. High points were Clapton's restrained playing on Little Walter's slow blues 'Can't Hold Out Much Longer'.

But anyone looking for searing guitar work would come away unsatisfied. Despite giving the record a four-star review, David Fricke, in *Rolling Stone*, conceded: 'If you need the old prowess, stick to the live half of Cream's *Wheels of Fire*.' Yet, Randy Lewis, in the *Chicago Tribune*, enthused: 'Clapton soars with the elemental styles he has lived and breathed for most of his career.' But despite such positivity, overall the album had rather worrying echoes of the lucrative but creatively redundant *Great American Songbook* route taken by fellow Brit Rod Stewart.

Increasingly, music had been relegated in his list of priorities. His sobriety, more than his music, or even his family, had become the number-one main concern. It was, he said at the time, the 'single most important proposition in my life'. And one advantage of his continued sterling work for his fellow recovering addicts was that it gave him the opportunity to play with some of his favourite musicians. Following the success of the inaugural Crossroads Guitar Festival, two more were staged in the summers of 2007 and 2010, both at Toyota Park in Bridgeview, Illinois, and featured line-ups which included Jeff Beck, Sonny Landreth, Buddy Guy, Vince Gill, Jonny Lang and Ronnie Wood. Meanwhile, in March 2011, Eric raised a further £1.3 million for the Crossroads Centre with an auction of a further 130 of his guitars and amplifiers, speakers and suits, at

Bonhams in New York. Pick of the bunch was a 1948 hollow-bodied Gibson L-5P, arch-top semi–acoustic, which sold for £51,000 – three times its estimate. A mahogany guitar inlaid with pearl and made by Tony Zemaitis, reached £47,000, and Clapton's 1957 Fender Twin amp, described as the 'holy grail' by *Guitar Aficionado* magazine, sold for £23,250.

And while his charitable endeavours were still raising fortunes, on the personal front too, Clapton, while not in the huge earning league of some of his fellow rock stars, was still turning a healthy profit, which was only added to by his trained eye for an investment. In 2012, as he got close to fifty years in the business, his company, Marshbrook, posted a doubling of income from the previous year, to £7.2 million. And in November that year, he sold a very rare 1987 platinum moon phase Patek Philippe watch, rated by experts as one of the ten most significant wristwatches in the world, at Christie's in Geneva, for £2.3 million. But even that paled into insignificance compared to the previous month in London, when he sold an abstract painting by German artist Gerhard Richter at rival auction house Sotheby's for $34.2 million (£21.3 million), setting a new record for the price paid at auction for the work of a living artist.

Making a killing must have put him in a generous mood because that November, Eric put his grievances with Mick Jagger over Carla Bruni to one side and appeared with the Stones on stage at London's O2 Arena, to play the Muddy Waters tune 'Champagne and Reefer', as part of the band's fiftieth anniversary celebrations. And he was in collaborative mode again on his twenty-first studio album, the appallingly titled *Old Sock*, in March 2013. It included a duet with Paul

McCartney on 'All of Me', the song made famous by Billie Holiday. Elsewhere, there were two new songs, 'Every Little Thing' and 'Gotta Get Over' – on which Chaka Khan featured – though neither was written by Clapton. The rest were covers of his favourite songs, from his childhood and beyond. Touchingly, Clapton also added a re-working of the Gary Moore song 'Still Got the Blues', featuring Steve Winwood, as a tribute to Moore, the prodigiously talented Northern Irish guitarist who died aged fifty-eight in 2011. In fact, the two men had only met on a couple of occasions, but Moore – who was a huge fan of Clapton – would have been thrilled at the accolade. Indeed, Moore was such a fan of Cream that he reformed the band, with himself in the Clapton role, for the 1993 album *Around the Next Dream*, under the banner BBM (Bruce-Baker-Moore).

*Old Sock* was the first album to be released on Clapton's Bushbranch label and it signalled the end of his thirty-year involvement with Warner Bros, with Polydor taking over the distribution in Europe and indie label Surfdog Records in the USA and Canada. The label may have changed, but the record continued the trend of getting an absolute kicking from some music critics. Giving it a one-star rating, Paul Mardles, in the *Observer*, wrote: '[Clapton's] first album in three years is so dull, its versions of tracks by everyone from Peter Tosh to Gershwin, Taj Mahal to J. J. Cale, seldom amounts to anything more thrilling than might be heard in the back room of a pub.' Meanwhile, Andy Gill, in the *Independent*, pronounced it a 'low-powered affair – the kind of thing old rockers slip into after too long spent relaxing on some Caribbean island'.

A month after its release, Keith Richards became the latest

big-name guitar player to sign up to the Crossroads Guitar Festival bandwagon, when he joined Clapton on stage at Madison Square Garden in New York to perform 'Key to the Highway' and 'Sweet Little Rock 'n' Roller'. But while Keef, Mick and co. remained seemingly indefatigable, as Clapton announced his 2014 world tour, he was saying it might be his last. In programme notes for a series of seven gigs in Japan in February, he wrote: 'I may not be able to come back. I've been coming here for forty years, since before some of you were born. It's the best place I've ever played. Thank you for having me.' A few months earlier, he was saying adamantly that it was his plan to stop touring at seventy, though he would continue to do one-off gigs. And as if in preparation for giving up the rigours of life on the road, the tour, which ended in Poland in June, included only two dates on home shores, in Glasgow and Leeds. The Glasgow show was somewhat ill-starred, however, with Clapton walking off stage at the Hydro Arena midway through 'Cocaine', before returning for an encore, by which time some fans had left. Many of those who'd paid £67 for tickets took to social media to complain. For his part, Eric blamed the break in the show on problems with the PA, amid newspaper reports that he'd muttered something into the microphone before marching off stage.

At the same time, he released a new album, entitled *The Breeze*, which was a tribute to his late friend J. J. Cale and featured contributions from Mark Knopfler, Willie Nelson, John Mayer, Tom Petty and Derek Trucks. In October Clapton announced he would be performing a series of concerts at the Royal Albert Hall the following May by way of belated 70th birthday celebrations. The gigs would also mark fifty years since he had first appeared at the London venue with the Yardbirds.

His 70th birthday itself was celebrated with a big fancy dress party in Surrey at which the host arrived dressed as Kermit the Frog – although it was a blink-and-you-miss-it turn. After talking the applause of his invited guests, he retired to change out of the costume and into civvies.

The belated birthday gigs at the Albert Hall were preceded at the beginning of May by two shows at Madison Square Garden in New York during which John Mayer stepped up to support Clapton during a stomping version of *Pretending*. Jimmie Vaughan joined Eric on stage for *Before You Accuse Me* and collaborators Derek Trucks and Doyle Bramhall II traded solos on *Let It Rain*. Later that month, Clapton kicked off a seven-night stint at the Royal Albert Hall. To make the most of the hype surrounding the shows, Reprise released a 51-track 'best of' album celebrating his three decades on the label, entitled *Forever Man*. Meanwhile, work began on a DVD and CD, called *Slowhand at 70 – Live at the Albert Hall*.

But he was reiterating his assertion that, for him, touring would soon be off the agenda. 'The road has become unbearable,' he sighed. 'It's unapproachable because it takes so long to get anywhere, and it's hostile out there. Everywhere. Getting in and out of airports, travelling in cars. I like my life too much to have it ruined by other people's aggression.' Elsewhere, he gave the impression that the small miseries of human life had left him feeling cranky and a bit cantankerous. Following his birthday celebrations, he had a major falling out with his eldest daughter Ruth as family sources revealed to me that he had taken exception to her giving away private details of Clapton family life with her regular postings on social media. Apparently, a particular bone of contention was that Ruth had let the cat out of the bag about her father's Muppet-themed get-up at the bash.

Later that summer, Ruth went on to Twitter to ask fellow users not to link her name to Tweets about her father, adding: 'we no longer have a relationship and it is just causing me hurt' – though she later deleted it.

Those close to the 30-year-old Ruth were divulging that after one row, she had informed her father she no longer wanted to be part of his life. The situation was all the more painful, I was told, because the rift has meant that Clapton had not seen his only grandchild, Ruth's two-year-old son Isaac, for several months. The rift coincided, rather embarrassingly for Clapton, with news that his old friend Rob Fraboni – who had been Eric's best man at his wedding to Pattie – and his former tour manager Larry McNeny had banded together in the hope of raising money to help Eric's homeless half-brother Eddie after reading about his plight.

For his part, Eric was already predicting the day when he would hang up his guitar for good. 'Physically, it might be that I can't, if it just hurts too much. I've had posture problems from playing heavy electric guitars on stage,' he added. 'One side of my body scrunches up, that gives me lower back problems from time to time. At the moment, I've got tendonitis, which means that if I make a barre chord, I get pain all the way up my arms into my neck and shoulders. So, there'll come a time when I'll think, "Is it worth it? You don't sound very good. You're missing things, your timing is gone." I watch myself to see if I'm deteriorating. I'm not really, at the moment, but I'm not where I was, there's no doubt about it. I don't want to have someone come up to me and say, "You know what? You shouldn't be doing this anymore." I'd rather come to that conclusion myself.'

# EPILOGUE

## Messenger

Towards the end of his life, Muddy Waters would sit in familiar bullfrog repose and counsel Eric Clapton, gently cajoling and encouraging him in the way a master reserves for his favourite student. The real message was unspoken: the importance of maintaining the blues legacy was sacrosanct, and soon Waters, as the elder statesman and keeper of the flame, would need to pass on the baton. Clapton, whom he called his 'adopted son', was the only musician equipped to carry it henceforth.

Often, the burden of being the chosen one, tasked with the role of unofficial guardian of a form of music he assimilated rather than was born to, has weighed heavily on Clapton's shoulders. Much is due to the fact that the blues is fundamentally a solitary business. It was the reason he was attracted to the music of poor black folk from a world away in the southern states of America in the first place. It was one man against the world, and Clapton's virtuoso talent for the blues only served to make him even more of a loner than he was already. 'Anyone that's any good at something to the point that that is what you are, they're loners because nobody else can understand that or share it with you,' he once said.

After more than fifty years in the business, his sense of being the perennial outsider remains. He has railed on occasion at what he's seen as the lack of respect shown to him by young white musicians in his homeland. Britain's music scene was polarised and too bound up in fashion, he concluded. 'Instead of feeling like I belong, I feel like an outcast,' he has observed. 'I feel disrespect from the white community.' He has a point. But, then, many among the narrow-minded music cognoscenti have never forgiven Clapton for not being black enough, poor enough or dead enough. If he had gone the way of Jimi Hendrix, Janis Joplin, Buddy Holly or Hank Williams, who all died in their twenties, he would, in all likelihood, have been deified in the same way. God knows, he tried hard enough to join them during his grim heroin seclusion at Hurtwood with Alice Ormsby-Gore, or, later, when he sat up nights with a loaded shotgun, a bag of coke and a bottle of brandy for company. For one reason or another, he survived and, as he knows only too well, a dead icon trumps a living one every time out of the box.

So why did he live when others, equally talented and equally bent on self-destruction, fell by the wayside? 'The truth is, as far as I can see, I'm not meant to have died,' he offers by explanation. 'I obviously have a reason for being here and it's important for me to stay in touch with what that reason is.'

Yet, for all his annoyance that he has not always been afforded the respect he deserves in his own country, for all his lavish holiday estates around the world and his ocean-going yacht, his homing instincts have always drawn him back to England and – in particular – Hurtwood Edge. There have been times in the past when he has considered moving to

Switzerland, for tax reasons and to avoid the attentions of the tabloids, but he says: 'I am English. I don't fit anywhere else. There's something about the English, the working-class complaining ethic, this working-class attitude. I don't approve of it, but it runs through my veins. And we did invent something, the English gentleman, which is really something to be proud of, I think. We've all got that sense of it, even if we're not born well. We all know when we're offending somebody and back off. No one else has that. There are no French gentlemen. There are no American gentlemen. But the great thing about English people is that they moan and groan a lot, but they'll get on with it.'

Likewise, with time and maturity, he has been able to come to accept – and no longer rail against – the fact that, musically, his best days belong to another era. And while the early jibe that he was the 'master of blues cliché' stung him, undoubtedly, part of his enduring popularity has rested on the fact that he has been wise and single-minded enough never to let fussiness encroach on his style. When it comes to playing, the goal for Clapton, as he's grown older, has always been the uncomplicated over the glossy. 'That's why I like to go without playing for a while,' he observes. 'If you're actually physically incapacitated a bit, it can make it sound nice and rough. Or you go for the more obvious things. And if you play a lot, you tend to avoid the obvious, and that's when sophistication creeps in. The last thing I want to be is sophisticated.'

Astonishingly, given his contribution to popular music, and the guitar in particular, he has questioned whether he will be remembered. He used to tell a story about watching a TV show some years ago which listed the one hundred most important records ever made. 'It was a long programme and it went all the way through the hundred, and I wasn't there,' he remembered. 'And I've had to accept that I don't really have a significant role in the history of music. If I can live with that, I can get a great deal of contentment in my life. If I was to fight against it – "Where's my record? Don't these people know who I am?" – I would be in a state of anxiety pretty well all the time. Everyone's dust in the end.'

Did he really believe that? Later, as he approached his seventieth birthday, in March 2015, his thoughts inevitably turned again to his legacy. Speaking about being custodian of the blues, the role to which he was assigned by Muddy Waters all those years earlier, Clapton pondered: 'If anything, that's what I'd like as my epitaph: He was a great messenger. A very gifted interpreter.' At the same time, the yearning for that killer solo – the one to beat them all – was still there. 'One of the reasons I believe in reincarnation', he once mused, 'is that I still haven't got the sound I want. I sometimes hear it in my head, but I never get it out of my amplifier.'

# Acknowledgements

I would like to thank everyone who so generously gave up their time to help me with the research of this book – their assistance was invaluable.

My thanks also go to my agent Dorie Simmonds, and to Simon Thorogood at Headline for his support and advice.

# Picture Credits

P1: © Mirrorpix (top); © John Olson/The LIFE Picture Collection/ Getty Images (bottom) / P2: © Tom McGuinness (top); © Clifford Ling/Associated New/REX (middle); © Michael Ochs Archives/ Stringer/Getty Images (bottom) / P3: © Jeremy Fletcher/Redferns/ Getty Images (top) / P4: © Paul Popper/Popperfoto/Getty Images; © Dezo Hoffmann/Rex (bottom) / P5: © Herb Schmitz/REX (top); © GAB Archive/Redferns/Getty Images (bottom) / P6: © REX (top); © David Cairns/Express/Getty Images (middle); © Bettman/CORBIS (bottom) / P7: © Mirrorpix (top); © Michael Ochs Archives/Stringer/ Getty Images (middle); © Michael Putland/Getty Images (bottom) / P8: © Michael Ward/Getty Images (top); © Keystone-France/ Gamma-Keystone via Getty Images (bottom) / P9: © AP/Press Association Images (top); © Graham Wiltshire/Redferns/Getty Images (middle); © Graham Wiltshire/Redferns/Getty Images (bottom) / P10: © Paul Natkin/WireImage/Getty Images (top); © George Widman/AP/Press Association Images (middle left); © Startraks Photo/REX (middle right); © Crawshaw Victor/Mirrorpix (bottom) / P11: © Richard Young/REX (top); © Richard Young/REX (middle); © Richard Young/REX (bottom) / P12: © Robert Knight Archive/ Redferns/Getty Images (top); © STR/AFP/Getty Images (bottom) / P13: © KMazur/WireImage/Getty Images (top left); © Nils Jorgensen/ REX (top right); © Dave M. Bennett/Getty Images (middle); © PA/PA

Archive/Press Association Images (bottom left); © Richard Young/REX (bottom right) / P14: © Stuart Clarke/REX (top); © material reprinted with the express permission of: *Ottawa Citizen*, a division of Postmedia Network Inc. (top inset); © REX/Action Press (middle); © Graham Wiltshire/Hulton Archive/Getty Images (bottom) / P15: © Dave Bennett/Getty Images / P16: © Evan Agostini/AP/Press Association Images.

# Source Notes

Books: Some of the more significant books that have featured in my research include: *Eric Clapton The Autobiography* (Century), *Wonderful Tonight*, by Pattie Boyd (Handheld Books), *Survivor: The Authorized Biography of Eric Clapton*, by Ray Coleman (Futura), *Clapton: Edge of Darkness*, by Christopher Sandford (Victor Gollancz), *Stevie Ray Vaughan: Caught in the Crossfire*, by Joe Nick Patoski and Bill Crawford (Little, Brown), *Nothing But The Blues: The Music and the Musicians*, by Lawrence Cohn (Abbeville Press), *Searching for Robert Johnson*, by Peter Guralnick (Secker & Warburg), *Miss O'Dell*, by Chris O'Dell (Simon & Schuster), *Dandelion: A Memoir of a Free Spirit*, by Catherine James (Smashwords), *Mick Jagger*, by Philip Norman (Harper Collins).

Interviews: This book has been shaped to a large extent by my encounters over a more than 20-year period with significant figures in Eric Clapton's life, including, among others, Jack Bruce, Lory Del Santo and George Harrison. I also have greatly appreciated my conversations with Roger Forrester, a natural wit with a phenomenal memory, who was, without doubt, the most significant person in Eric's life for a quarter of a century and may be have been responsible for keeping him alive. Roger's wife Annette has also been a great help and offered me valuable insight into some of the most important periods of Clapton's story.

My interviews with Chris O'Dell, who at various times shared house space with George Harrison and Pattie Boyd, as well as Eric himself, also provided fascinating insight into the complicated dynamic at work in Clapton's friendship with George. She also had an almost unrivalled position as spectator in the dissolving marriages of both George and Pattie and Eric and Pattie.

From her vantage point, Catherine James offered me an invaluable firsthand depiction of Eric's first encounter with heroin, which would come so close to destroying him, as well as his close, yet intensely competitive relationship with Mick Jagger.

From a musical perspective, Top Topham, like Clapton a one-time member of the Yardbirds, a fellow blues aficionado and ex-schoolmate, gives a vivid description of the musicians, the people and places that shaped the teenage Clapton's beginnings in music and his growing devotion to the blues art form.

Printed media: I have made use of a library of newspaper and magazine cuttings stretching back to the mid-1960s.

Television: Some of the many television programmes that have helped in my research include, *Eric Clapton and His Rolling Hotel* (BBC, 1980), *The South Bank Show* (ITV, 1987), *Carl Perkins and Friends* (Channel 4, 1986), *Larry King Live* (CNN, 1998), *Classic Albums, Cream: Disraeli Gears* (Isis Productions, 2006).

Paul Scott.

# Index